Pregnancy, Birth, and Parenthood

≽⊱ ≽⊱ ≽⊱

Adaptations of Mothers, Fathers, and Infants

Frances Kaplan Grossman
Lois S. Eichler
Susan A. Winickoff

⚘ ⚘ ⚘

with
Margery Kistin Anzalone
Miriam H. Gofseyeff
Susan P. Sargent

Pregnancy, Birth, and Parenthood,

Jossey-Bass Publishers

San Francisco • Washington • London • 1980

PREGNANCY, BIRTH, AND PARENTHOOD
Adaptations of Mothers, Fathers, and Infants
    by Frances Kaplan Grossman, Lois S. Eichler,
and Susan A. Winickoff
with Margery Kistin Anzalone, Miriam H. Gofseyeff,
and Susan P. Sargent

Copyright © 1980 by: Jossey-Bass Inc., Publishers
                        433 California Street
                        San Francisco, California 94104

&

                        Jossey-Bass Limited
                        28 Banner Street
                        London EC1Y 8QE

Library of Congress Cataloging in Publication Data

Grossman, Frances Kaplan, 1939-
   Pregnancy, birth, and parenthood.

   Bibliography: p. 278
   Includes index.
   1. Pregnancy—Psychological aspects—Longitudinal
studies. 2. Childbirth—Psychological aspects—
Longitudinal studies. 3. Mothers—Longitudinal studies.
4. Fathers—Longitudinal studies. 5. Parent and
child—Longitudinal studies. 6. Adjustment (Psychology)
—Longitudinal studies. I. Eichler, Lois S., joint
author. II. Winickoff, Susan A., joint author.
III. Title. [DNLM: 1. Pregnancy. 2. Labor.
3. Parent-Child relations. 4. Adaptation,
Psychological. WQ200 G878p]
RG560.G76   155.9'3   80-16518
ISBN 0-87589-465-8

Manufactured in the United States of America

JACKET DESIGN BY WILLI BAUM

FIRST EDITION

Code 8024

The Jossey-Bass
Social and Behavioral Science Series

Preface

࿇࿇ ࿇࿇ ࿇࿇

In 1973, five clinical psychologists began meeting with a commitment to developing a project that would further our understanding of pregnancy, birth, and early parenting. As four of us were mothers or mothers-to-be, we did not fit the traditional conception of the disinterested, unbiased scientist-researcher. Rather, we were strongly committed to the view expressed by Levine (1974) that "every investigation in the social sciences takes place within a social context that to a greater or lesser degree influences not only the outcome of the study but also the design, the nature of measurement, and the form in which the research is reported" (p. 663). Thus, it seemed to us entirely appropriate that we would have a clear personal involvement in our topic and that we openly acknowledge that commitment. We cared deeply and personally about the life events we were studying and brought to our research interests both the biases and the acute awareness of the complexities of the subject that come from personal involvement in an experience.

Several of the authors began their training in psychology in programs with strong behavioral leanings, with the concomitant emphasis on laboratory research and the scientific method. Over the years we had become somewhat frustrated with the limited view of human behavior that this approach allows, yet we were convinced of the need for rigor in empirical research. In other words, we wanted to find a way to study at least some aspects of the essence of important human experience in a scientifically valid and replicable manner. Each in her own setting, we discovered psychoanalytic theory and enjoyed its freedom from experimental strictures in the explanation of human behavior, but we felt that the psychoanalytic approach did not sufficiently value experimental validity.

We, like other social scientists and concerned observers in the 1960s, became increasingly aware of the effects of major social and economic forces on human events and behavior, influences insufficiently emphasized by psychodynamic formulations. The ideas and writings of Seymour B. Sarason, his emphasis on understanding the social and historical context of behavior, as well as his strong respect for the limitations of professional and scientific thought, have strongly influenced us.

Finally, as women who were becoming more conscious of ourselves and our social context, we found that the existing body of psychological research and theory did not adequately describe our experience but in fact distorted or misrepresented a good deal of it. As mothers or mothers-to-be, we felt that the experiences of pregnancy and parenthood were among those most mythologized and most in need of a more adequate understanding.

From these concerns and interests arose this longitudinal study. The following chapters describe aspects of the experience of mothers, fathers, and infants during a critical developmental period in the family. The chapters are organized according to the time periods at which participants in the study were seen. Each chapter includes a review of the relevant literature, a description of those factors which we found to be predictive of the range of adaptation of mother, father, and baby at each time period, and some qualitative description of important aspects of the experiences of pregnancy, labor and delivery, and the first year of parenthood. Some of the research methodology is included in the chapters; readers who would like a more detailed look at measures, statistical tables, and research procedures will find this information in the appendices.

This book is intended primarily for social scientists interested in pregnancy, birth, the development of the family, and adult psychological development. It will also be of interest and use to health and mental health practitioners who deal with pregnancy, birth, and parenting, to educators who teach about these areas, and to professionals who plan intervention programs.

At the project's inception, Frances Kaplan Grossman was involved in teaching and research in the Department of Psychology at Boston University. Lois S. Eichler was primarily involved in clinical work at Cambridge Hospital and on the faculty of the Harvard Medical School. Susan A. Winickoff, Margery Kistin Anzalone, and Miriam H. Gofseyeff were all instrumental in founding the project while working to complete their doctoral dissertations with Grossman at Boston University. Susan P. Sargent entered the group later to work on her dissertation.* Grossman, Eichler, and Winickoff worked on the project from the beginning and wrote this book. Anzalone and Gofseyeff worked on the project for four years, during which time the research was planned and most of the data collected. Sargent joined the group in the project's third year and remained through the first year of writing.

Numerous individuals and several institutions have aided us substantially in our work on this project. The North Charles Foundation and Boston University's Graduate School each pro-

---

*Winickoff finished "Obstetrical Complications and Psychological Defense Style" in 1976. Anzalone's dissertation, "Postpartum Depression and Premenstrual Tension, Life Stress, and Marital Adjustment," and Gofseyeff's "Pregnancy and Maternal Adaptation in Women with Different Childbearing Motivations" were both completed in 1976. Sargent completed "Prepartum Maternal Attitudes, Neonatal Characteristics, and Postpartum Adaptation of Mother and Infant" in 1977.

vided a small amount of money to facilitate the beginning stages of the research. The Department of Psychology at Boston University was generous in its provision of secretarial staff, supplies, and computer time, and we especially want to thank William MacKavey, chairman of the department, for that assistance.

A number of graduate students in the Clinical Community Psychology Program at Boston University contributed their efforts for one or more years. These included Pamela Howard Varrin, Rheta Keylor, Ursula Stone, Hedy Ungerer, Susan Wise, Nickolina Fidele, Peggy Carr-Keany, Richard Michael, Frances Arnold, and Susan Gong. Of these, Pamela Varrin and Rheta Keylor completed dissertations on the two-year follow-up of this study, and Richard Michael is presently working on a thesis on these data. A number of other individuals made substantial contributions. Edith Jacoby did an incalculable amount of work and made more family data collection visits than anyone else. Ruth Balser worked with the project while completing her dissertation at New York University. Robert Reifsnyder, Jill Grant, Alice Guilmartin, and Chris McGoey all offered important services in a variety of ways. We also thank the obstetricians who believed in the importance of the project and allowed us to speak with their patients: Emanuel Friedman, Joseph S. Wallace, Sumner H. Gochberg, Max J. Bulian, Waldo L. Fielding, and Philip P. McGovern.

A number of staff members of the Department of Psychology at Boston University labored long and hard in typing and preparing various drafts of the manuscript. Karen Abrami, Marilyn Fartely, Emily Stein, Nobi Yonekura, Carol Doran, and Dianne Mangeri all provided services above and beyond the call of duty, and we thank them.

Without the support and cooperation of the participating families, the study could never have been done. We use clinical examples from these families throughout the text, but we have changed names and identifying data to protect their anonymity. We hope they found some personal gain from having participated. Both as scientists and as individuals, we enjoyed getting to know them and having an opportunity to observe an important stage in their development.

An essential source of support came from our husbands, who cheered us on, took care of the children, and appreciated our successes. Lastly, we thank our children for giving us our first and perhaps most important lessons in pregnancy and parenting.

July 1980   FRANCES KAPLAN GROSSMAN
Boston, Massachusetts

LOIS S. EICHLER
Cambridge, Massachusetts

SUSAN A. WINICKOFF
Cambridge, Massachusetts

Contents

The Authors

⚜ ⚜ ⚜

FRANCES KAPLAN GROSSMAN is an associate professor in the Department of Psychology at Boston University. She received her A.B. degree in psychology from Oberlin College (1961) and her Ph.D. degree in clinical psychology from Yale University (1965). Before coming to Boston University, she taught at Yale from 1965 to 1969. Grossman is the author of *Brothers and Sisters of Retarded Children* (1972).

LOIS S. EICHLER is on the staff of the Department of Psychiatry at the Massachusetts Institute of Technology. She received her B.A. degree in psychology from Mount Holyoke College (1967) and her Ph.D degree in clinical psychology from Boston University (1972). Her predominant clinical and research interests concern the developmental issues of women.

SUSAN A. WINICKOFF is a member of the Department of Psychiatry at the Mount Auburn Hospital in Cambridge, Massachusetts, where she does consultation and liaison work with obstetrical and gynecological patients. She received her B.S. degree in nursing from Columbia University (1965), her M.A. degree in psychiatric/mental health nursing from New York University (1967), and her Ph.D. degree in clinical psychology from Boston University (1977).

Margery Kistin Anzalone is currently a consulting psychologist to the Concord Academy and in private practice. Anzalone received her A.B. degree in English from the University of Massachusetts, Boston (1969) and her Ph.D. degree in clinical psychology from Boston University (1977).

Miriam H. Gofseyeff is a member of the Department of Child Psychiatry at the Harvard Community Health Plan. She received her B.A. degree in psychology from City College of New York (1967) and her Ph.D. degree in clinical psychology from Boston University (1977).

Susan P. Sargent specializes in work with children and families at the Cutler Counseling Center in Norwood, Massachusetts. She received her B.A. degree in psychology from McGill University (1969) and her Ph.D. degree from Boston University (1977).

Pregnancy, Birth, and Parenthood

≥≤ ≥≤ ≥≤

Adaptations of Mothers, Fathers, and Infants

1

Conceptual Framework and Methodology

As our world becomes increasingly complex and changes at an ever accelerating rate, many life events that were once managed in a manner that was guided by cultural tradition now create substantial uncertainties and require personal solutions. The beginning and end of life, the experiences of illness, marriage, and divorce—all these human situations are increasingly being examined more openly by members of our society as well as by social scientists. Out of an increased concern for the totality of the lives of all individuals and a growing awareness of the difficulties which our culture and its rate of change create for virtually all of its members, social scientists are beginning to look at various methods and styles of adaptation to major life events. Such studies may enable researchers to develop models that will be useful in teaching people how to cope with stressful life changes and in treating people who have difficulties coping.

The nuclear family remains the primary context in which young are born and reared in our culture, despite recent at-

1

tempts to develop alternatives, though many factors converge to render this institution far less stable than in former times. Once parents raised children in geographical and emotional proximity to an extended family that had a shared cultural heritage and values; today's parents often find themselves removed from these supports and isolated from the sense of continuity and tradition which used to provide a clear framework for childrearing and family life.

Concomitant with the disappearance of the extended family is an enormous change in people's views concerning roles for various family members. The women's movement of the past decade is the most recent of many social forces that has presented a serious challenge to the concept that a woman's main role is mother and keeper of the home and that a man's primary function is to work outside the home. An increasing number of people now believe that everyone, regardless of sex or past custom, is entitled to pursue his or her own goals and avenues of fulfillment. This feeling, in turn, seems to contribute to the increased strains on the nuclear family and to the rapidly rising divorce rate. Today, at least one in every ten households is headed by a single parent and approximately 23 percent of children born since 1970 will live for some period of time in what used to be called a "broken home" (Bane, 1976).

Regardless of how one may evaluate the moral rectitude of these developments, their impact on today's families cannot be denied. Also undeniable is the tenacity of the nuclear family as an institution to which most members of our culture, irrespective of their individual aspirations, seem to turn as a model to guide them in their undertaking of the task of parenting. In spite of a decreasing birth rate in this country, and an entertainment of life-style alternatives, childbearing still is a part of most adults' lives. People might want fewer children than parents did in the past, but the vast majority still do want to bear and raise children and to have the experience of being parents. Because of the different stresses and strains on families in today's world, mastery of parenting is often difficult to attain. And yet, most adults continue to attempt to achieve such mastery and gratification within the context of family life with children.

Social scientists can perhaps facilitate this attempt by deepening our understanding of the family as an institution. By examining the reality of parenthood as one central aspect of adult development and by demythologizing it, we can both contribute to an intellectual appreciation of the process as well as offer constructive suggestions concerning educational and supportive programs which might aid in the establishment and maintenance of healthy, adaptive families.

Mothers, Fathers, and Babies

As indicated earlier, we are not unmindful of the central importance of the impact of the broad social, economic, and cultural context on parenting, as so well—and grimly—described by Keniston and the Carnegie Council on Children (1977). Nor are we unaware that the majority of births in this country today are not to traditional married couples (Keniston and Carnegie Council on Children, 1977; Rapoport, Rapoport, and Strelitz, 1977). Our study, however, focuses on married couples who are having children because this model continues to be the cultural ideal, which strongly influences all parents. Studies of parents in less conventional contexts include Fox (1979) and Wise (1979).

Our study begins during the first trimester of pregnancy because the process of parenting begins at least as early as the conception of a new life. Conception is the beginning not only of the growing fetus but also of the family in a new form, with an additional member and with changed relationships. For couples having their first child, this is especially true; for already established families, new demands and needs arise that must be dealt with in order to insure the successful incorporation of the new offspring into a changed family system. Each prospective parent brings to this task a personal history as well as a host of individual personality characteristics which equip him or her well or poorly for the undertaking. How well individuals are so equipped and how flexible their personalities are have enormous consequences for the success of their parenting. The family is indeed a system whose members exert profound and complex effects on one other.

It is undeniably true that childbearing and rearing represent major new tasks for women and men in their adult development. Having a first child is a critical transition for most couples, effecting shifts in their social roles and in day-to-day responsibilities, and changes in each partner's self-concept and sense of place in the continuum of human experience. The process of becoming parents seems best understood as a time of normal developmental crisis with accompanying upheaval in physiology, roles, values, and relationships (Bibring, 1959; LeMasters, 1957). Questions are raised; change is demanded; feelings of disequilibrium and anxiety are present until new resolutions are achieved. A pregnancy is a critical turning point in the life of a woman and her family. Because of the degree of change involved, the outcome may reflect substantial psychological maturation, but there is also the potential for significant psychopathological regression.

Mothers. Much of the previous theoretical work on women's psychological health and its relation to motherhood comes from the psychoanalytic tradition (Benedek, 1960; Bibring, 1959; Deutsch, 1945). Psychoanalytic theorists tend to view adaptation to pregnancy and motherhood as a largely intrapsychic task, the completion of which is a necessary component of full maturity and healthy ego development. They emphasize a woman's historical relationship with her own mother and feel that having had a good relationship with a nurturant, loving mother allows a woman to accept her own femininity and enables her in turn to become a loving and nurturant mother.

Several empirical studies done during the 1960s support the position that the overall healthiness of a woman's personality is related to her good emotional adjustment to childbearing (Grimm and Venet, 1966; Shereshefsky and Yarrow, 1973). There is some, although less, support for the specific postulated relationships between aspects of feminine identification and adaptation to pregnancy and motherhood. Numerous studies have documented evidence for a relation between anxiety in pregnancy and a variety of complications for the mother and her newborn during labor and delivery (reviewed by McDonald, 1968). Thus it appears that pregnant women need to have good psychological health and possibly some particular readiness for the distinctively female aspects of pregnancy, birth, and mothering in order to cope optimally with these experiences.

A pregnancy is, most basically, a biological event; therefore another major dimension in determining the outcome of a specific pregnancy is the woman's physiological status. As her body is responding to the demands of pregnancy, physiological factors such as age, parity, nutritional adequacy, cigarette smoking, and alcohol consumption, as well as the presence of medical conditions such as heart disease or diabetes, have all been demonstrated to increase the risk to the mother, the infant, or both (Dalby, 1978; Friedman and Greenhill, 1974). There have also been efforts to link a history of certain types of premenstrual and menstrual difficulties with the "postpartum blues" syndrome (Hamburg, Moos, and Yalom, 1968), although no direct relation between hormonal factors and emotional adjustment postpartum has yet been demonstrated.

Fathers. Until fairly recently the father was considered somewhat a bystander as a pregnancy unfolded and a child was born; he was there, to be sure, but primarily to provide financial and emotional support for his wife. Recently, however, new ways of seeing men and women and their roles suggest that the man's experience of becoming a father is of great interest and concern as a major life event in his adult development. Although little formal research has been done about men's adaptation to this early phase in the formation of the family, it seems likely that some of the same factors that influence women also influence men. Thus, for example, one would expect that a man's general psychological health, his capacity to manage and not be overwhelmed by anxiety, his comfort with his masculinity, and his sense of having been well-nurtured as an infant and child would be important factors in his adaptation to becoming a father.

Couples. The marriage is an integeral part of the context in which a pregnancy occurs. The married couple as a dyad undergoes a maturational crisis as the two partners become parents. Both partners have to negotiate shifts in roles, patterns, and intensities of needs. Couples who already have one or more children have to plan for the place the new baby will occupy in the family. Their previously adequate patterns of dependency and communication may be rendered obsolete by the new crisis. Each partner has changed and successful negotiation of the new situation will be required for adequate adaptation. At the same time, the couple or family has the opportunity for a broadened and deepened relationship as they share the moments of joy, expectation, and even anxiety.

There is evidence in the literature that aspects of the interpersonal relationship between husband and wife may well be the most important context within which the woman's pregnancy unfolds and into which a new baby is born (see, for example, Dyer, 1963; Wenner and Cohen, 1968). The quality of the marital relationship, as well as features of its style, and the readiness of the couple to welcome a new member—all play a vital role in influencing the nature of the experience for both the man and woman, and ultimately in influencing the infant.

How well family members adjust to a pregnancy and a new baby is also affected by the kinds of stresses with which they have been living. Clearly, the serious illness or death of a close family member or the presence of great financial hardship will change the emotional atmosphere into which a new child is born. There is also evidence that stress relates to the obstetrical outcome of pregnancy. An accumulation of stresses such as moving, serious illness, or job loss during the six-month period prior to delivery increases the probability of some sort of complication during labor and delivery (Gorsuch and Key, 1974). Shereshefsky and Yarrow (1973) found the number of external stresses in a woman's life to be inversely related to her successful adaptation to pregnancy and to her postpartum adaptation. Clearly, the sociocultural environment, its supports and stresses, will influence how a family experiences a pregnancy.

Babies. The moment of conception is the beginning of the relationship between mother and child. Although expectations and fantasies are present beforehand, it is during the months of pregnancy that the two lives exist as part of a closely interacting system. It is clear that the developing fetus is not completely protected from noxious influences in the uterine environment: it is affected by what the mother ingests, inhales, or is otherwise exposed to. Less clear, but a subject of considerable interest, is the effect of maternal emotional states on the developing child. Convincing descriptions exist that extreme maternal emotions such as fear, anxiety, or grief can cause dramatic increases in fetal activity and that after birth these babies are more irritable than the norm (reviewed by Williams, 1977). Scientists are only beginning to systematically study these difficult questions, but it does appear that mother and infant interact in a profound way during the full nine months of pregnancy.

When babies arrive, they enter situations that may be more or less stable, more or less complex, more or less happy. And once babies appear, they bring their own particular needs and styles to the situation. A baby's individual temperament interacts with both parents' personalities, determining both the quality and the specific characteristics of the adaptation the family achieves (Pedersen, 1975).

Adaptation to pregnancy and parenting, then, is a process influenced by many different factors—including the psychology of the man and the woman, the woman's physiology, sociocultural dimensions such as the quality of the marriage, life stresses, and sources of support, and finally the characteristics of the new child.

Research Goals and Methods

This book is the result of a longitudinal study which focused on the experience of pregnancy and the first year postpartum. The specific goals of this research were: (1) to increase theoretical understanding of the process of childbearing, including the contributions and complex interactions of mother, father, and infant as the family system develops; (2) to identify those factors early in pregnancy that are predictive of adaptational problems in pregnancy, delivery, the postpartum period, and the first year of the child's life—factors which could then become the focus for programs of preventive intervention; and (3) to compare the experience of first-time parents with that of parents who already have one or more children.

More specifically, the present study focused on certain psychological and physiological factors that are important to the experience and adaptive success of couples as they have a first child or as they enlarge their families. The dimensions studied include the woman's psychological health and her physiological and reproductive history, the man's psychological health, their situation as a couple—including their marriage, stresses, and social supports—and finally, the baby's health and temperament.

Our goals required us to look at complex interactions among various dimensions of the participants' lives: the psychological, physiological, social-cultural, and marital, to name several. We also wanted to study not only mothers, fathers, and babies but also their relationships with one another. For this reason, both marital partners were studied extensively throughout the project, and the infant was included from the very early postpartum period. Families were seen a total of five times over an eighteen-month period, always in their own homes except for a hospital visit after delivery. The first visit was almost always before the beginning of the fourth month of pregnancy. The next visit was during the eighth month of the pregnancy. After the baby was born, the mother was interviewed in the hospital and the newborn was assessed. Finally, mother, father, and baby were seen at home two months after delivery and then again one year postpartum. Most often two members of the research team went on a given visit, one who was familiar with the family and one who was not, a method we hoped would both maximize the comfort for the family and yet reduce the bias in the observations.

The actual measures administered at these various sessions included semistructured interview data, projective tests, standardized and "home made" paper-and-pencil tests, and observations. (Appendix A contains detailed descriptions of the measures, interscorer reliabilities, and the scores the families received.) During the pregnancy, we studied each partner's psychological health, including measures of characterological and pregnancy-related issues, sociocultural supports and stresses, and marital adaptation and style. In addition, we rated women's physiological status in terms of medical risk factors. After the infants were born, we assessed their temperaments, and later their physiological functioning, general adaptation, and motor and cognitive development. In the postpartum period, we looked at the general psychological adaptation of both parents and at their relationships with each other and with their infant.

The measures were selected to contribute to a research design that preserves the wholeness of the individual and reflects the uniqueness of individual differences and complexity as appreciated by the clinician, while yielding clear-cut reliability and standardization. Since few measures exist that satisfy both of these requirements, we used combinations of measures and methods that together provided a full, yet also convincing, picture of these families as they experienced pregnancy and childbirth, and as they and their new infants navigated the vicissitudes of family life. Appendix B presents the statistical conventions we adhered to and methods we used. (Some of the findings are presented in tables in the text. Others can be obtained by writing to Frances K. Grossman, Department of Psychology, Boston University, 64 Cummington St., Boston, Mass. 02215.)

The sample for the study initially consisted of eighty-four married couples and nine additional women whose husbands chose not to participate. These volunteers were recruited from women who were, early in their pregnancy, seeking prenatal care from several private obstetricians or from the clinics of two major teaching hospitals in the Boston area. We suspect, as others have found (for example, Westley and Epstein, 1969) that people who volunteered to participate in our study tended to be psychologically healthier and more willing to open themselves to scrutiny than those who declined. (For more details about our sample, see Appendix C.) Despite our persistent efforts to involve couples from a variety of socioeconomic classes, the final sample was predominated by middle- and upper-middle-class families, with some lower-middle-class families represented. Almost all the families were Caucasian. The men were on the average almost thirty years old and the women twenty-eight, and they had been married approximately five years. For almost all couples, this was a first marriage. In forty-three instances, the women were pregnant with their first child; the other fifty already had from one to four children. When we first saw them, fifty-four women were employed outside the home on a full- or part-time basis and were earning between $2,000 and $25,000 annually. Among them were teachers, businesswomen, social workers, physicians, psychologists, nurses, and research technicians. In terms of religious affiliation, approximately one third of the participants stated that they were Catholic and one third Jewish. Most of the others described themselves as Protestant, and a small number said they had no religious affiliation.

Is is most important to note that this sample population is, in large part, a group of middle- and upper-middle-class married couples in a sophisticated metropolitan area who were seeking prenatal care for the wife early in her pregnancy, and who were willing to expose their thoughts and feelings about this event to a research team.

Philosophy

The practices and events associated with childbearing and childrearing are deeply embedded in the customs, beliefs, and attitudes of a culture. The content and quality of these experiences for contemporary American married couples, the strengths required of the participants in meeting the demands of the situations, the pitfalls most likely to cause problems—all are greatly determined by the specifics of their situation, as Rapoport, Rapoport, and Strelitz (1977) argue so compellingly. The findings presented in this book do not describe absolute and eternal facts about pregnancy, birth, and early parenting. Rather, they tell something about how a group of people living in a particular culture at a particular point in history deal with an important set of events in their lives.

Because our study focused on adaptation, we expected that we would see good adaptation and not-so-good adaptation, good mothering and fathering and that which was not so good. In fact, the more we observed, the less the good-bad dimension seemed to capture the complexity of what was happening. Rather, we were impressed by the infinite variety of ways and styles of coping. Any given style, or set of styles, was somewhat more or less successful for solving or meeting a particular problem the individuals, couples, and families were facing; yet each style also had implications and ramifications for the host of other problems facing the family.

Each family developed its own styles of dealing with the myriad issues raised by the new infant's needs. Some styles seemed slightly or quite a lot better; that is, they were more growth-promoting, more fun for all the participants than others. Some styles seemed slightly or quite a lot worse. Indeed, our research design committed us to evaluating individuals' and couples' adaptation as adequate or inadequate, good or bad. But such judgments should not obscure the clinical reality, which is the extent to which the families' styles of adaptation were different, infinitely varied, and incredibly difficult to categorize. Yarrow and Goodwin (1965) make a plea for recognition of the complexity and variability in mother-infant interactions. Some of that complexity is captured in the clinical descriptions included in the chapters.

A final aspect of the basic view underlying and directing this study is our respect for the very deep commitment of these parents to be the best parents they could be, given the constraints of their personalities and life circumstances. The families in the study were, by and large, trying hard and persistently to define good and productive lives for themselves and their children and, at least up to the first birthday of their child, doing it quite successfully.

❧ 2 ❧ ❧

Women's Experience of Pregnancy

For a woman, the childbearing period is one of the most compelling and profound phases of her life. Pregnancy and childbirth may be viewed as a time of normal developmental crisis which is a turning point in the life of a woman and her family. In this chapter, we will first review the literature on the psychology and physiology of pregnancy, and the effect of sociocultural and marital variables on the outcome of the pregnancy. We will then explain our research methodology and our findings.

The Psychology of Pregnancy

Psychoanalytic theorists have recognized the importance of childbearing in the emotional lives of women and have understood motherhood and motherliness as being essential aspects of an emotionally mature woman. This orientation originated with Freud, whose view it was that the most important tasks for a young girl were the renunciation of her wish for a penis and the substitution of the more realistic and attainable wish for

self. As conceptualized by Bibring, the emotional challenge
pregnancy and birth seems enormous and the possibility for
chological aberration considerable.

Perhaps reflecting the changing psychoanalytic views of
gnancy, Therese Benedek, who extensively studied the repro-
tive psychobiology of women, started with a view of preg-
cy as a time of vegetative calm due to both high hormonal
els as well as the gratification of the woman's basic wish for
hild (Benedek, 1960). She moved from this position to one
ich acknowledges both the calm, narcissistically gratifying
ments of pregnancy as well as the anxieties, regressive ten-
cies, and psychological challenge inherent in the process
nedek, 1970b).

In sum, the psychoanalytic writers were the first to recog-
e the complexity of the psychological tasks of pregnancy and
therhood. Their focus, however, was primarily intrapsychic,
1 they viewed childbearing and childrearing as the exclusive
ks of women. Although they made a significant theoretical
tribution to the understanding of the psychological processes
olved in pregnancy and childbirth, it was left for later writers
postulate the importance of the marital and sociocultural
lieu in which a pregnancy is undertaken.

Several large-scale studies carried out in the past two dec-
es have sought to contribute to our empirical knowledge of
psychology of pregnancy. Grimm and Venet (1966) fol-
ved women from early pregnancy through the early post-
rtum period, in an attempt to identify relationships between
ings of emotional adjustment in early pregnancy and later
tcome, both physical and emotional. They found no emo-
nal predictors of later physical outcome but did find that
men who were more independent and less neurotic were
tter adjusted emotionally in the postpartum period.

In a very ambitious study of first pregnancies of middle-
ss couples, Shereshefsky and Yarrow (1973) found that the
riables most predictive of postpartum success were intra-
ychic rather than external ones. Specifically, ego strength,
rturance, and the capacity to easily visualize oneself as
mother were most predictive of general adaptation to preg-

a child. This maternal orientation, once acl
Freud the hallmark of a healthy feminine sex
did not examine the actual experiences of con
and delivery, possibly because of his appare
a positive orientation toward motherhood l
the rest followed naturally and spontaneously

Thus, it remained for later theorists
exclusively on the psychology of women to
of the specific psychology of pregnancy and c
Deutsch did in her landmark work, *The Psy*
(1945). Deutsch advanced a theory of mot
the premises that pregnancy is the natural
deepest, most powerful wish of women and
development for women is very closely relat
ment of the "motherly ego."

Although Deutsch spoke of the enorm
logical task of successfully navigating the mo
Grete Bibring who, a decade after Deutsch's
area, espoused a view of pregnancy and ear
a time of normal psychobiological crisis that
tures with the crises of puberty and menopaus
As such, all three of these crises revive conflic
opmental periods which now require new sol
these crises leads to a new level of psycholog
integration. If this new reorganization is n
however, the result is a generally less satisfac
tioning which can lead not only to problems fo
self but also to problems in the mother-child re

Although Bibring stated that pregnancy
istics with other psychobiological crises, she
as also being unique in many ways. She stated
logical task of pregnancy is to turn one's emo
toward oneself and then toward the fetus as
grows physically, the mother's emotional att
creases. During the pregnancy, the healthy wo
ly fused with the fetus. At delivery, she mus
psychologically as well as physically from the
forth love her child as a person at least partia

nancy. In addition, women with more medical symptoms during pregnancy were judged to be adapting less well in the postpartum period.

A study from the Washington School of Psychiatry (Wenner and others, 1969) found that a number of psychological factors influenced the course of pregnancy, including the motivation for the pregnancy, the woman's feminine identification, previous emotional difficulties, and her relationship to her own parents. Most interestingly, though, this study found that of all the variables affecting the course of pregnancy, the marital relationship was the most important.

In a recent study of 101 primiparous mothers in Sweden, Uddenberg (1974) found that difficulties adapting to the pregnancy itself were most related to the mother's environmental and social situation, while problems in the postpartum period were more related to deeper intrapsychic issues concerning the mother's feelings about motherhood and about her relationship to her own mother.

Besides these larger studies, there have been numerous smaller studies of specific aspects of the experience and outcome of pregnancy. Most of this work has been done within the last two decades, since earlier researchers, with the exception of the psychoanalytic theorists, saw pregnancy as primarily a physical undertaking and did not consider the emotional aspects of it as very important, either experientially or in terms of their effects on obstetrical outcome. In recent work, specific psychological variables have been investigated in the occurrence of particular pathological conditions of pregnancy such as hyperemesis gravidarum (Chertok, 1972; Tylden, 1968), habitual abortion, and toxemia (reviewed by McDonald, 1968). Taken as a whole, the studies of psychological variables and obstetrical problems point to some psychosomatic influence on reproductive functioning.

Anxiety is one of the psychological variables most productively studied in its role during pregnancy, at least in part because it is such a major feature of the experience. One controversy revolves around whether there is any clear pattern for most women in the ups and downs of anxiety. There have been many attempts to plot the course of anxiety throughout pregnancy and childbirth, but no clear consensus has emerged (reviewed by Sherman, 1971; see also Osborne, 1978). There have been more definitive findings concerning the psychophysiological concomitants of anxiety during pregnancy and childbirth. Several studies have found that pregnancy symptoms such as nausea, backache, dizziness, fatigue, and gastrointestinal discomforts are highly correlated with measures of anxiety (Brown, 1964; Grimm and Venet, 1966; Zemlick and Watson, 1953; Zuckerman and others, 1963). Brown found such high intercorrelations between anxiety, neuroticism, pregnancy worries, and bodily symptoms that he hypothesized that they are all manifestations of the same variable, anxiety. Similar findings were reported by Shereshefsky and Yarrow (1973).

Perhaps some of the difficulty in understanding the vicissitudes of anxiety in pregnancy derives from the relationship between anxiety and psychological defenses. Uddenberg, Nilsson, and Almgren (1971) found that primiparous women who did not experience nausea during pregnancy had moderate adaptational difficulties during pregnancy but more postpartum problems than women who had either moderate or severe nausea. In a later article (Uddenberg, Fagerstrom, and Hakanson-Zaunders, 1976), they argue that pregnancy and childbirth constitute a developmental stage that requires an adaptational process. This process must occur during pregnancy for adequate resolution, and it often involves considerable anxiety. A woman's denial of pregnancy or her excessive repression of related issues reduces anxiety but results in inadequate preparation for delivery and for motherhood. The majority of these findings suggest that certain pregnancy-related symptoms in a primiparous woman may indicate that she is expressing and working through some of the inevitable conflicts.

The Physiological Dimension

Another major dimension crucial to an understanding of the process of childbearing is the physiological one. Variables related to the medical and obstetrical history of women have been studied in regard to their relationship to the psychological course and outcome of pregnancy. Hamburg, Moos, and Yalom (1968) found low parity to be associated with postpartum depression, while Wenner and Cohen (1968) found high parity to be so associated, and Kaij and Nilsson (1972) found surprisingly little relationship between age, parity, and postpartum difficulties. Illnesses during pregnancy have been found to relate to psychological difficulties postpartum (R. Cohen, 1966; Gordon and Gordon, 1959).

The physiological variables that have received the most attention in psychological studies of pregnancy have been those associated with endocrine factors. Numerous early studies (Blumberg and Billig, 1942; Bower and Altschule, 1956) note the use of hormonal treatment in postpartum psychoses. More recently, Hamburg, Moos, and Yalom (1968) found postpartum depression to be significantly related to a history of greater menstrual difficulty, early menarche, and prolonged menstrual flow. The authors suggest that these findings might be influenced by individual differences in progesterone metabolism. Similarly, Melges (1968) found a strong relationship in her sample between a history of premenstrual tension and later postpartum depression. More recently, however, Nott and others (1976) found no relationship between hormonal levels, measured before and after delivery, and experienced mood of the parturient women.

In sum, the evidence for the impact of physiological variables on the *psychological* outcome of pregnancy and the early postpartum period is somewhat controversial. However, the need to include such variables in any predictive study is unquestionable.

The Sociocultural Dimension

Another area of fruitful investigation has been the relationship between stress, social supports, and the outcome of pregnancy. In these times of increased social isolation of the nuclear family and of increased complexity and, at times, disruptiveness in our life-styles, an increasing number of researchers have asked if these social patterns and stresses affect the experience and outcome of pregnancy. Indeed, pregnancy is now considered by most knowledgeable observers as a life stress itself (Holmes and Rahe, 1967) and one which is likely to be associated with other significant stresses, such as increased financial strain, a change in work status, and a change of residence, usually to larger and more expensive quarters.

Life stress has been found to relate to the psychological outcome of pregnancy: to postpartum emotional problems (Gordon and Gordon, 1967) and to adaptation to pregnancy and the postpartum period (Shereshefsky and Yarrow, 1973). Although socioeconomic status, another aspect of what we term the sociocultural dimension, has been found to relate to a variety of outcomes of pregnancy and birth, such as fetal and neonatal mortality, low birth weight, and the like (Illsley, 1967), little is known about how this variable relates to the experience of pregnancy and childbirth. Given Handel's (1970) view that social class has emerged from studies as the largest social influence on parenthood in the United States—compared with such factors as religion, ethnic group, urban-rural residence, and the like—it is probable that it is predictive of various aspects of the childrearing process.

Age, which is at times considered a physiological variable in pregnancy research (for example, Kaij and Nilsson, 1972), can also be thought of as a sociocultural factor, insofar as it establishes and defines the context of a pregnancy at a given point in a woman's life.

Finally, a number of researchers have raised questions about the role of social support in reducing the negative effect of stresses and crises on people's lives, particularly during periods of physical illness (for example, see Johnston, 1971). It seems intuitively likely that the number and kind of a woman's interpersonal supports and her perception of the support available to her would influence her experience of pregnancy and childbirth. Whether a woman has someone with whom to talk over the day-to-day details of her experience and particularly with whom to share the nuances of her fantasies, her fears, and some of the private details of her physical condition, will have a considerable effect on her emotional comfort during pregnancy. Our impression is that although the need for closeness and sharing with one's husband is important, there is a particular kind of confirmation and helpful communication that can come only from other women who are currently pregnant or who have been through the experience.

To summarize, the experience of recent stress as well as the socioeconomic status of a woman both have an effect on the physical and emotional experience and outcome of pregnancy. The availability of social support might also play a role, as might age. A comprehensive view of pregnancy adaptation must include some evaluation of these four factors as part of the sociocultural dimension.

The Marital Dimension

Another variable that has received attention in pregnancy research is the quality of the marriage. Some clinical and empirical evidence suggests that the quality of the marriage may be one of the most important dimensions influencing both partners' experience of and adaptation to pregnancy, childbirth, and early parenting.

For example, Melges (1968) found that an unhappy marriage was one of several characteristics producing postpartum depression. And as we mentioned earlier, Wenner and Cohen (1968) found that, contrary to their expectation that successful adaptation to pregnancy was most related to the woman's physical and emotional health, for their sample an uncomplicated pregnancy was more related to the success of the marital relationship. Deutscher (1970), in his clinical study of ten middle-class couples, found that the seven with good marital relationships before the birth of the baby had little postpartum difficulty, in contrast to the three couples in his study with inadequate communication, feelings of emotional distance and alienation, and discomfort about the decision to have a baby, all of whom experienced a degree of postpartum difficulty.

Using a psychoanalytic perspective, Benedek (1970a) and Jessner, Weigert, and Foy (1970) looked specifically at the role the husband needs to play during pregnancy in order to ade-

quately support his wife; Lewis and Weinraub (1976) studied
this problem from a family systems orientation. All emphasize
the importance of the father's providing reassurance to the
mother, reducing her anxiety about pregnancy, birth, and childrearing in order to allow her to carry out these activities comfortably and effectively. In Shereshefsky and Yarrow's (1973)
study, the overall marital adjustment of the couple was strongly
related to a variety of measures of maternal adaptation. Surprisingly, their measure of the husband's responsiveness to his wife
during her pregnancy was predictive of very few aspects of her
adaptation.

Meyerowitz (1970) reported that women in his study
who were dissatisfied with their pregnancies were also dissatisfied with their sexual role. In his data, wives accepted the pregnancy if they felt it brought them closer to their husbands and
tended to reject it if they felt it alienated them from their
husbands.

The First-Trimester Contact

In the context of this overview of previous studies, we
undertook the research reported here. We were interested in
deepening our understanding of the relative contributions which
various factors—psychological, physiological, sociocultural, and
marital—make to the way a couple copes with pregnancy and
early parenthood. Some aspects of the present study are partial
replications of previous findings. But we have also attempted to
integrate the findings of those studies into a more comprehensive view of the experience.

Our first meeting with the couples took place in their
homes; this meeting was usually very early in the pregnancy,
nearly always before quickening. We explained again the considerable amount of time and energy the families in the project
would be expected to contribute. After we answered their questions, and they had signed the informed consent form, we began
the formal interviews. We interviewed the women and men individually at length concerning their feelings and thoughts about
the pregnancy, as well as about a number of other aspects of

their lives. In that first meeting, we also asked them to complete a number of paper-and-pencil measures and a projective test.

In this chapter, we report our findings of the women's experiences of early and late pregnancy.

From the initial contact, our primary goal was to gather baseline data about these women. In addition, we wanted to be able to describe and evaluate their adaptation to the pregnancy thus far and to see which factors predicted better pregnancy adaptation. As predictor variables, the women's psychological health, the extent to which they were physiologically at risk for a problematic pregnancy, the extent of their sociocultural assets and liabilities, and characteristics of their marriage were of particular interest.

Psychological Health. The woman's life adaptation was measured by combining a large number of independent ratings, based on the taped interviews, of the degree to which she was coping successfully with the major tasks of adulthood. These tasks included work or activities, marriage, and relationships with her own parents; one indicator of coping ability was the relative absence of serious physical and psychological problems. In addition, we administered paper-and-pencil measures of both anxiety and depression. From the interview tapes, we rated the extent to which the woman perceived her mother as nurturant and identified with her. Paper-and-pencil measures of her conscious motivation for the pregnancy and the extent to which she described herself as having culturally designated masculine and feminine characteristics were obtained. Each woman was given a TAT-like test, which rated the woman's positive, negative, or ambivalent emotions in response to a series of pregnancy and infant-related pictures. Finally, we had a paper-and-pencil measure of the women's tendency to respond to test questions in a socially desirable way, out of a concern for the honesty of our participants and the validity of our measures.

Marital Dimension. The woman's adjustment to marriage was assessed by means of a paper-and-pencil scale designed to measure both her satisfisfaction as well as the amount of conflict she experienced in the marriage. We also rated the marriage on a continuum of traditional to egalitarian, on the basis of the husband's and wife's separate descriptions of the usual division of household tasks. Finally, there was a paper-and-pencil measure of the woman's sexual activity level and degree of satisfaction with her sex life.

Physiological Dimension. A paper-and-pencil measure was used to assess the extent to which the woman was at high medical risk for a problematic pregnancy, including such factors as obesity, previous obstetrical complications, fertility problems, chronic illness, and the like. In addition, we had a paper-and-pencil measure of the woman's usual, that is, prepregnancy, level of premenstrual tension.

Sociocultural Dimension. The measure of socioeconomic status was based on the husband's education and occupation, the wife's education, and her occupation if employed. A paper-and-pencil measure reflected the interpersonal support available to the women, and another reflected the number and impact of the life changes they had experienced as a couple in the year prior to the pregnancy.

Adaptation to Pregnancy

The experience of first learning that one is pregnant is a powerful one and often serves as a culmination of many of the personal and contextual themes in a woman's life. For many women, there is an awareness right from the beginning of the pregnancy that their lives are about to be changed in major and irrevocable ways. The beginning of a pregnancy is the time when women quite literally begin to share themselves and their bodies with another being, a relationship that will continue for the many years of motherhood. This event naturally produces profound changes in the ways a woman views herself, her body, her relationship with the child's father, and her future with her as yet unknown offspring.

Whether the pregnancy is a consciously planned one or accidental and how much ambivalence the couple feels are factors that have substantial consequences for the woman's response to and experience of the next nine months. Issues of increased dependency and neediness arise and an intensification of anxiety occurs due to the number and magnitude of changes pregnancy entails for women. The dimensions of a woman's management of her dependency needs, her motivation for the pregnancy, her anxiety, her physical symptoms, and her response to those physical symptoms were measured from our interview and constituted our measure of her adaptation to pregnancy.

Overall, our data indicated that the level of positive adaptation to the pregnancy was quite high for both first-time and experienced mothers. A large majority of the women felt that this was very much the right time in their lives to be having a child. When the pregnancies were confirmed, most reported that they had felt delighted, excited, or very happy.

At the time we first saw our couples, most had just recently had their pregnancies confirmed. For some of the women, the pregnancy was not yet a reality which they fully appreciated. Many had not yet experienced any physical changes and had difficulty grasping the fact of what was happening. Others, at this same very early point in their pregnancies, evinced a much greater understanding and emotional reaction to their situation. Some of these women experienced pregnancy positively, with much enthusiasm and anticipation, whereas others felt more ambivalent.

Our clinical impression was that those women who had other children seemed to experience less awe and wonder at the fact of pregnancy than did first-time mothers, for whom there was often a sense of surprise about their having conceived. For some first-time mothers, the pregnancy was the attainment of a goal that they had had for many years but which they had been unable to realize until now, for personal or professional reasons.

For some of our women, a major factor in the experience of the current pregnancy was having had some sort of pregnancy-related trauma in the past. In many cases, their feelings about these events deeply colored the early months of pregnancy. An illegal abortion eight years earlier had provoked such guilt and regret in one woman that she had feared every since that she would be unable to conceive when she wanted to. Her pregnancy, then, was not only a great relief to her but also a strong stimulus to relive the disturbing events of so many years ago.

Women with a history of miscarriage showed a strong sense of restraining their excitement about the pregnancy until the end of the first trimester, or until after the point of the pregnancy when they had previously miscarried. A woman who had had a stillborn child the year before declined to participate in the study because the pregnancy meant the risk of another such devastating loss and the feelings were too private and painful to be scrutinized. For this small group of women, their past experiences and their present fears and anxieties were a very prominent aspect of their feelings about the current pregnancy.

In general, and not surprisingly, women whom we judged to be more psychologically healthy—as reflected both in good life adaptation and low levels of anxiety and depression—and who were more positive about wanting the pregnancy were better adapted to the pregnancy at this early stage. These aspects of emotional well-being predicted strongly for first-time mothers; only depression predicted experienced mothers' adaptation to the pregnancy, with more depressed women being judged as doing less well with the pregnancy at this early time.

It seems that for women pregnant for the first time, the pregnancy becomes absolutely central to their lives, and their reactions to it are more global: they are the pregnancy and the pregnancy is them. Clearly for women who have experienced pregnancy before, this is no longer the case. The pregnancy in itself is not as important as an experience, and these multiparous women are also occupied caring for their other child or children.

Interestingly, for the sample overall and more strongly for first-time mothers, the greater their usual premenstrual tension, the less well they adapted to early pregnancy. None of the sociocultural nor marital variables predicted the women's adaptation to the pregnancy at this early point.

Considering the men's scores as they related to the women's adaptation, women who were more anxious early in pregnancy tended to have husbands who were also more anxious, and couples tended to share a similar level of satisfaction with their marriage. Men's scores did not predict their wive's pregnancy adaptation at this first contact.

Thus at this early point in pregnancy, and particularly for first-time mothers, general psychological health seems to be the most important predictor of adaptation. The reason that a history of premenstrual tension predicts difficulties in early pregnancy adaptation is not entirely clear, because of the inextricable intertwining of psychological and physiological factors in this phenomenon. We speculate, however, that a history of premenstrual tension is related to conflict concerning feminine identity and body functioning. Thus women who experience conflict about the occurrence of menstruation are also more likely to experience conflict about pregnancy, which is the unparalleled feminine bodily experience.

Excerpts from some of the interviews with women in our sample serve best to illustrate the quality of their experience at this early visit.

Katherine, anticipating her third child, exemplifies the sense of enthusiasm and readiness of many of the women in the study, despite the fact that this third pregnancy was not a planned one. However, she was somewhat high in anxiety. By the time the researchers interviewed Katherine, she seemed to have done a great deal of constructive psychological "work" about the unplanned nature of the pregnancy and was coping with it extremely well. This interview illustrates a number of concerns of the women at this early stage.

Interviewer: How have you been doing?
Katherine: Fine! Last month, I was nauseous and tired, but now I feel good.
Interviewer: Did you plan to have the baby?
Katherine: No.
Interviewer: How did it happen?
Katherine: We jokingly say it was an immaculate conception. I was using a diaphragm, but, since I'm regular, I didn't use it the first few days after my period, and the doctor said that can happen.
Interviewer: How did you feel when it happened?
Katherine: I was basically happy, and then scared—mainly shocked. I felt "Me! How could it happen?" The

	other two were so carefully planned. Of course, unconsciously, maybe I wanted it.
Interviewer:	Do you think you did?
Katherine:	Well, I know I always wanted three children. I was planning to go back to work part-time next year when Amy's in nursery school and work for two years and then have a third. My husband is very content with two children and he said, "Let's wait. Work a couple of years and then let's see what happens." So I think it was more difficult for him to acclimate himself to it [the pregnancy] than for me.

After this explanation, she reached her final affective conclusion about the pregnancy, stating exuberantly, "Now, I'm very happy. It couldn't be planned better, but it wasn't planned." This exuberance continued in her other comments.

Interviewer:	What's your feeling about the spacing of your children?
Katherine:	I think it's a perfect time. Amy will be in nursery school and will be over three and will be able to understand a lot. When I had her, Steven was under two and was still very demanding. I think this is better.

Part of the reason Katherine was feeling so good about the pregnancy, we suspect, was her capacity to deal comfortably with her increased dependency at this time, as well as her husband's responsiveness to these needs.

Interviewer:	When you're feeling bad, physically or psychologically, does your husband generally know about it?
Katherine:	Yes.
Interviewer:	How does he know?
Katherine:	He can just tell by my mood, and I tell him a lot.
Interviewer:	What does he do about it?
Katherine:	He's very sympathetic, very understanding.

Interviewer:	What has this pregnancy been like for him? Not the fact of the baby but the pregnancy?
Katherine:	I think, the shift this has made for us is just what this is going to do economically. He's very concerned whether we can afford another child in these times, and that's weighed most on him. It's made us think about a lot of things, like if each child needs a separate bedroom. We only have three bedrooms. And how will this affect our family life? Right now, everything's so smooth, and we wonder if it will upset the equilibrium.
Interviewer:	Did you ever consider aborting?
Katherine:	For about a few hours we did. My husband was more firm about that; he didn't want me to have an abortion. We sort of felt that this baby was meant to be. One thing is that I don't feel any responsibility for it, any guilt. I think that six months from now, if I hadn't been able to get a job and then I got pregnant, I think I'd feel that somehow I had some control over it. I'm glad it happened this way because I feel that I was as naive as my husband.

Clearly, Katherine was struggling with the issue of the unplanned pregnancy. She seemed to still feel somewhat shocked and disrupted in her control over her own life and that of her family. And yet, she persevered to arrive at a positive position about the situation. Her comments revealed her ambivalence and fears about returning to work; the pregnancy has "gotten her off the hook," for the time being, about finding a job, an undertaking about which she seemed to have more reservations than she was able to admit. She seemed to be trying to understand every aspect of this situation, from her responsibility in causing it to the effects it will have on sleeping arrangements. Perhaps, by focusing on many of the ramifications she was trying to reexert her control over the situation, lest she be overwhelmed by some other surprise. And indeed, she seemed to be rather successful in this attempt.

Interviewer: Do you ask special things of your husband now?

Katherine: Oh yeah. I use it. I'll say, "Oh, I'm so tired, could you help Amy out of the car."

Interviewer: Do you think of what it will be like to have the new baby?

Katherine: Not really, I can't picture it yet. It's not a reality yet.

Interviewer: Do you have any visual images of it yet?

Katherine: I hope, what I see is this nice, quiet, undemanding baby who's cooing and laughing a lot and being entertained by Amy and Steven. Just more busy, more commotion, but happy.

Interviewer: Do you think about labor and delivery yet?

Katherine: Yes. I don't look forward to it. It hurts a lot.

After describing some of the thoughts she and Mel had been having about practical issues such as names and sleeping arrangements, Katherine acknowledged: "I think it's easier to talk about those things. For us it was such a shock that we were going to have another baby, but those things are easy and fun to talk about."

Interviewer: How do you think the children will react?

Katherine: Very well. When Amy was born, it was hard on Steven, and I worried a lot about that. This time I don't foresee any problems. They seem happy about it as much as they can understand.

Interviewer: Can you think of anything else that would be useful for us to know?

Katherine: Just that, this is the same as the other times in that I can't really believe that it's real yet. In another month, I'll probably be out to here but right now, it's still not very real to me.

Other women felt more oppressed by the early somatic discomforts and felt generally overwhelmed and ambivalent about the experience. This following excerpt is from the interview with Jane, who at the time was thirty and had been married for seven years. She and her husband, a dentist, had one child. Her pregnancy seemed to make her feel tied down and overburdened with responsibilities; she had a strong, fatalistic feeling that there was no way to meet her own needs for the foreseeable future, with a second child on the way.

After stating that this second child was planned and wanted, Jane showed her sense of helplessness and depression:

Interviewer: Do you have any special reasons for looking forward to this baby?

Jane: Just that we want two children and we've had a lot of pleasure from Mark.

Interviewer: Any special qualms?

Jane: Qualms in that I have no freedom at all with Mark. He's very demanding. I probably made him that way, and I'll probably do it again. I'm just getting some freedom for myself now, and then I'll have to start all over again—that bothers me.

Her negative feelings about the undertaking of pregnancy is matched by her physical response:

Interviewer: How are your feeling physically?

Jane: Lousy, I feel nauseous all the time and I can't stand food. I have some medication which helps, but I still feel crummy.

In spite of feeling so bad, emotionally as well as physically, Jane seemed relatively unable to ask for obviously needed help which might alleviate her suffering. She prefered to withdraw rather than seek support.

Interviewer: When you feel bad, physically, does your husband know? Can he tell or do you have to tell him?

Jane: A combination. Sometimes I'll feel bad and he doesn't notice. He's learned since last time, when I had to tell him more. Now he just figures that I feel lousy and just takes that for granted.

Interviewer: Do you find it difficult to ask for help at times
                 when you do feel bad?
Jane: I can ask for the things that must get done, but
                 other things that I feel should get done—I feel
                 that that's asking too much, but it still bothers
                 me that it's not being done and I can't do it.
Interviewer: Do you feel the need for extra assistance, not
                 only around the house but emotionally as well?
Jane: The only emotional support would be instead of
                 getting angry at me when I'm depressed to just
                 leave me alone. I don't really communicate that
                 much. I prefer to just be off by myself some-
                 times.

Her difficulty in asking for assistance and support, which seemed to be exacerbated by her husband's relative insensitivity to her needs, left her in a particularly vulnerable position. According to Wenner and Cohen's (1968) discussion of the healthy management of dependency during pregnancy, Jane and Ralph were engaged in a pattern of relationship which was not likely to provide her with adequate support during this stressful time. That is, they were neither mutually interdependent nor had they agreed that one was to be dependent and the other more actively giving.

Because of superstition, Jane tried not to anticipate what the baby would be like. In fact, the only fantasy she allowed herself about the postpartum period was that she'd be sharing the burden then:

Interviewer: Do you think of what the baby will be like?
Jane: I try not to. Superstition, I guess.
Interviewer: So you never catch yourself having a daydream
                 or picturing how it will be?
Jane: Just that after it's born, I'll feel better and
                 we'll all be sharing the good parts and the bad
                 instead of just me suffering all the time.

Jane felt a sense of conflict between her own needs and those of others in areas other than mothering. She talked of how she experienced this conflict even before having children:

Interviewer: Did you enjoy teaching before you had Mark?
                  Did you enjoy being with the children?

Jane: I did as far as working with them went, but
                  I didn't from a selfish point of view. I was teach-
                  ing them art, and I never had enough time left
                  over to do my own painting.

Even at this very early stage, she was concerned about labor and delivery and worried that she might have to have a caesarean section, in spite of the fact that there seemed to be no indication to that effect at this point.

Clearly, Jane had a problem in meeting her own needs while finding a comfortable balance between those and the needs of her family, particularly her son. She seemed to accept this condition of deprivation as a necessary part of pregnancy and of motherhood. While this attitude might be at least partially realistic, it also seemed to impede her from taking an active, problem-solving approach towards the difficulty. Her fatalism seemed to make her painful fate more probable.

In sum, at this early point in the pregnancy, we found, as we expected, that women who were generally healthier and more comfortable with their lives were also feeling better about the pregnancy. We also note the presence of a theme that will reappear many times in later stages of the undertaking, that for first-time mothers, pregnancy seems to be a much more consuming and emotionally compelling experience than for experienced mothers.

Eighth Month

We saw the couples next in the eighth month of pregnancy. At that meeting, we interviewed the husband and wife together for about a half an hour, and then we gave each a packet of paper-and-pencil forms to complete.

We had several measures of how well the women were doing with their pregnancies at that point. An adaptation to pregnancy score, rated from the interview, reflected our sense of the extent to which the woman had accepted the physical and psychological changes the pregnancy had brought, felt she had grown and not stagnated during that period, and seemed emotionally prepared for motherhood. We measured marital adaptation, by judging from the taped interviews the extent to which the couple reflected a sense of shared, enjoyed experience, a sense of comfort—as opposed to unresolved struggle—in the relationship, and a sense of having been brought closer by the pregnancy. A third measure from the interview assessed their emotional and practical preparedness as a couple for the impending birth.

In addition, we repeated the anxiety scale and the conscious motivation scale, and asked the couple to fill out the life change measure reflecting the past six months of their lives. Finally, the women filled out a symptom checklist describing the frequency with which they had experienced thirty physical and emotional symptoms during each of the three trimesters of the pregnancy.

At this second meeting, we found a very different picture from the one which greeted us in the first trimester. In the eighth month, most of our couples presented a picture of excitement, fatigue, and anxiety. The majority of the couples expressed the feeling that the pregnancy seemed to be lasting a long time, that the limitations it imposed were increasing as their tolerance for those limitations was decreasing. Almost all were looking forward eagerly to the delivery, not only because they would finally meet their long awaited offspring, but also because the pregnancy would then be over. When asked if they would miss being pregnant after the delivery, the overwhelming majority of women answered with a resounding no.

Most of the ego resources of the women, and to a lesser extent of the men, were being turned at this time towards the final preparations, both practical and emotional, for the birth. These preparations often coincided with other changes in the family, such as moving to larger quarters, changing jobs for the men or leaving jobs for the women, and dealing with the feelings of other children—a formidable number of stresses during this already stressful time.

In spite of the many factors shared by most of the couples at this time, there were many differences in how various individuals were coping, differences related to many of the dimensions we measured during the first contact.

As mentioned earlier, our assessment of a woman's psychological health at eight months consisted of measuring her level of anxiety, the degree of physical and emotional symptomatology she experienced throughout the pregnancy, her current motivation for the pregnancy, and our rating of overall adaptation based on the joint interview. Looking first at anxiety, we found that, for the group as a whole, anxiety levels were not significantly changed from the rating obtained during the first-trimester contact. In other words, women were approximately as anxious in the last trimester as they had been early in pregnancy. Since we do not know either their prepegnancy nor their middle-trimester anxiety levels, we cannot comment on the viscissitudes of anxiety during pregnancy. For the total sample, the only dimensions from our early contact that predicted to anxiety at eight months were the original levels of anxiety and depression as well as the woman's marital satisfaction. Those women who initially reported themselves to be more anxious and depressed, as well as those who initially expressed less satisfaction with their marriage, were also more anxious in the last trimester. For first-time mothers only, those women who had reported greater sexual activity and satisfaction were more anxious at eight months than those who had been less sexually active.

Another measure of psychological health at eight months was the reported number and severity of various pregnancy-related symptoms, physical and emotional. Several of our predictor dimensions were related to this variable for our sample. Of our psychological predictors, we found that better general life adaptation, initially lower anxiety and depression levels, and a better adaptation to the early pregnancy all were related to fewer and less severe symtpoms throughout the pregnancy. To be sure, many of the symptoms listed in our checklist were psychological in nature, and therefore not independent of these other psychological dimensions, but many were also physical in nature. Their greater frequency and severity in women of less robust emotional health is an interesting finding and one which

lends support to the many studies positing a relationship between emotional and physical symptomatology during pregnancy (reviewed by McDonald, 1968).

Dimensions of the women's marriages also were predictive of physical and emotional symptoms during the pregnancy: A higher level of marital satisfaction was predictive of
fewer pregnancy symptoms for the group as a whole, but more
so for the experienced than for the first-time mothers. For the
first-time mothers, the more egalitarian the marital style, the
fewer the symptoms the women experienced during pregnancy.
Possibly, the issue of who performs which household tasks—in
anticipation of who will do which tasks for the baby—is a very
active one in couples having their first baby, and it seems that
a more egalitarian marital style promotes the woman's sense of
comfort, at least during the pregnancy iteslf. For couples having
their second or third child, this issue seems to be less important
in and of itself. Whatever style they have developed seems to
have become part of the more general dimension of marital
satisfaction, accounting for the stronger relationship between
that variable and general physical and psychological ease of the
pregnancy.

Of our sociocultural predictor variables, social class was
related to symptomatology during pregnancy for the group as
a whole. This is an expected finding in that women of lower
socioeconomic status often receive less adequate prenatal care,
suffer from increased stress in their daily lives and, as Scott
(1973) suggests, particularly in their marriages—factors which
perhaps help account for the greater number and severity of
pregnancy-related symptoms.

Finally, from our physiological dimension, we found that
those women reporting a history of more severe premenstrual
tension also described a greater number of pregnancy symptoms.
As we saw at our first contact, women with a history of more
severe premenstrual tension were doing less well early in pregnancy and continued to do less well at this eight-month contact.

Turning next to the rating, from the interview, of general
adaptation to the pregnancy at eight months, we found a surprising lack of relationships with earlier predictor variables. For the

group as a whole, only socioeconomic status predicted how generally comfortable a woman felt about the pregnancy in the last trimester, with women of higher socioeconomic status being better adapted than those of lower socioeconomic status. In addition, this relationship applied more strongly to first-time than to experienced mothers, for whom no predictor variable related to later pregnancy adaptation.

A possible explanation for why so few earlier variables predicted to pregnancy adaptation at eight months stems from the research methodology, which involved a joint interview with the wife and husband. We felt at the time that the couples were silent about a number of potentially problematic issues as they attempted to present a united and harmonious front towards each other and towards the researchers. Hence, our measure did not reflect some underlying but important issues in their adaptation. (The issue of motivation for the pregnancy, which is so important in a woman's adaptation to pregnancy, is discussed at length in Chapter Three.)

The Marriage at Eight Months

As mentioned above, we had two scores of marital integration from the eighth-month visit, both rated from the joint interviews with the couples. The first marital integration reflected the general comfort and mutual supportiveness—as opposed to struggle—within the marriage after the many months of the pregnancy. The second score—couple preparedness—reflected how practically prepared the couple seemed to be for the rapidly approaching delivery and the arrival of a new family member. The research team, following the numerous studies that have demonstrated the paramount importance of marital support to the outcome of pregnancy, believed that the optimal marital adjustment late in pregnancy is one in which both partners have experienced an increased closeness and mutual supportiveness during the pregnancy; have a sense, as individuals and as a couple, of having grown emotionally during the pregnancy; and have made room in the family for a new member. For many couples, these are difficult goals to achieve given the stresses inherent in the process of pregnancy. We felt that since the marital adjustment is so crucial to later well-being, it was important to try to understand what factors in the individuals' personalities as well as in their sociocultural context during pregnancy maximize the chances for attaining a well-functioning family system.

Looking first at marital integration at eight months, we found strikingly few significant relationships with earlier measures. For the group as a whole, only occupational levels of the women were predictive of this dimension in that women who were employed in lower-level occupations were having more difficulty with their marriages in the last trimester. Clearly, occupational level is closely related to general socioeconomic status, and the predictive power of occupation suggests that the increased practical and financial strains on people of lower social class take their toll, at least partially, on the marital adjustment to pregnancy.

In addition, there were two differences on this dimension for the first-time mothers as compared to experienced mothers. For primiparous mothers, the *more* recent the life stress and the fewer the previous medical difficulties in the woman's history, the better the marital integration at eight months. The former finding is indeed a surprising one in that it is difficult to understand how more, rather than less, stress is helpful to a marriage, unless one speculates that sharing a stressful situation helps the couple focus on each other and bond together in order to cope. Although a woman's previous medical difficulties, constitute a stress on the pregnancy, this stress may be seen as more of an internal rather than an external one. Thus, unlike the couple's shared external stress, it negatively affects the woman's psychological adaptation, perhaps rendering her more preoccupied with her own bodily state and therefore less available to focus her energies on her marriage.

For the multiparous women, the only measure that was related to marital integration at eight months was the style of the marriage. Couples with more egalitarian styles in their relationship felt closer and more integrated at eight months than couples with a more traditional relationship.

Looking next at the aspect of practical preparedness of the couples for the impending birth, we found several previously measured variables related to this dimension. Women with more children, those of a higher occupational level, those who had previously rated themselves as happier with their marriage, and those with more recent life stresses were more prepared at this point for their babies. Women who had rated themselves as having more stereotypically masculine traits were less prepared at this point. These findings were stronger for first-time than for experienced mothers, for whom no previously measured dimension was related to practical preparedness.

To conclude, treating the dimensions of the marriages at this point as outcome measures, we found few, if any, important correlations. In fact, the lack of correlations in this dimension seems rather interesting in that one might expect factors of the woman's psychological health and social class to be more influential in marital integration at this time. It is at least possible that the paucity of findings is partially due to the methodology used in that, as noted before, couples were interviewed together and might have been attempting to present themselves as feeling more positive than they really were. At a time so near to the birth of their child, our couples might have been unwilling, or unable, to acknowledge any difficulties in their marriages, sensing the extreme importance of a good relationship to the successful outcome of their undertaking.

Let us return to the two women we introduced earlier in the chapter and consider how they were doing at eight months. Katherine, who was doing fine, scored high on life adaptation, higher than average on anxiety, and lower than average on conscious motivation. She was very satisfied with her marriage, was of upper-middle socioeconomic status, had substantial interpersonal supports in her life, and was in the low medical risk category.

By the eighth month, Katherine and Mel had settled into the pregnancy, but did not seem to be consumed by it, as some of our less adaptive couples were by this point. Like many other couples, the husband seemed far more preoccupied with practical planning and details, and the wife seemed to be the one most

focused on the actual baby and its impending arrival. As before,
they both were coping quite well with the experience.

Interviewer:	How's it been going?
Katherine:	[Laughs.] Just fine. How's it been going, honey?
Mel:	Fine, we've just been concentrating on the two kids and getting the room ready.
Katherine:	It was a hard winter. Mel was sick, that's unusual, and we were scared he'd have to be in the hospital. It was really the hardest winter since we've been married, but not because of the pregnancy.
Interviewer:	Any symptoms?
Katherine:	No, just one cramp. [Laughs.] And he got it too!
Interviewer:	How does it compare to the previous ones?
Katherine:	I felt good then too; it's about the same.
Interviewer:	How about your moods?
Katherine:	[Laughs.] O.K. I've been up and down. Sometimes I explode, especially when I get tired. I guess it's a little worse when I'm pregnant.
Interviewer:	Mel, what's it been like for you with Katherine being pregnant?
Mel:	I'm just busy helping take care of the kids and running around, building the room for the baby. It hasn't been much of anything. The other two times we went to Lamaze courses, so we were very busy getting ready. But this time we're not doing anything except physical preparations of the house, so it's not much.
Interviewer:	Have you noticed any changes in yourself?
Mel:	Me? [Laughs.] No.
Interviewer:	Katherine, have you noticed any changes in him?
Katherine:	Sometimes we feel deprived. Because this summer, if it weren't for the baby and everything, we would have taken a vacation. It's very hard until your baby's here, for us at least. We're concerned with the baby being healthy, and we're curious about how it will be, the five of us together. We can't do things we usually do in spring

	like bike rides and tennis, so we have been feeling deprived.
Interviewer:	What do you think the baby's like?
Katherine:	It's nice. I think so—feels calm and I have good feelings about him.
Interviewer:	How has the pregnancy affected your relationship?
Katherine and Mel:	[Laugh.] No sex.
Interviewer:	Who's doing is that?
Katherine:	It's mine [guiltily] . We'll get back to it; we have in the past. There are good effects, too. I feel really good about it a lot of the time. I dread the labor and worry about it. But we are just looking forward to having the baby and the kids are excited. I just feel that if we can get through the first month, it will be fine.
Interviewer:	What sort of things do you think about when you think of the baby?
Mel:	I think about two kinds of things. I think of diapers, and baby bottles, and baby food, and all of these things we haven't even thought about in so long. We went to a restaurant the other night, and we thought about where we were going to put this third kid, just physically. How are we going to arrange it? But most of the time, we just sit and enjoy our kids and think how nice it will be to have a third one since we enjoy our other two so much. So we have two different kinds of feelings: the physical, drudgery aspect and, on the other hand, the enjoyment of it.
Katherine:	For me, what I keep thinking is that I just want to get beyond the first couple of months, which I didn't enjoy with the other kids.
Mel:	Well, Steven was uncomfortable in the beginning, but it was easier with Amy, we knew what to do.
Katherine:	We're not very confident about knowing what to do with a baby.

Mel: I'm confident!

Interviewer: Any dreams about the baby?

Katherine: I do. I dream about giving birth or that it's a boy or a girl. Happy dreams. The other night I had a dream about my school days. I was walking, carrying my books, and all of a sudden the books turned into a pile of laundry. I'm sure that's related to the baby. You know, carrying piles of diapers. [Laughs happily.]

Interviewer: What has it felt like being pregnant?

Katherine: I haven't had the euphoria that I had with the first one, when everyone treats you special, and you feel so good. Because now, I'm mainly with mothers and they do it all and it's not so special to be pregnant. I feel heavy and fat.

Interviewer: How will you feel when you're no longer pregnant?

Katherine: I'll probably still feel heavy and fat! [Laughs.]

Interviewer: Will you miss being pregnant at all?

Katherine: With my other two, I didn't miss being pregnant, but I did miss it when I stopped nursing. I felt very sad then. There are times when I just lie there and love the feel of the baby inside me, but I don't relish being pregnant.

Interviewer: Can you think of anything else that's important for us to know at this point?

Katherine: We feel very fortunate with everything. Mel's job is very secure now, which it wasn't when I last talked to you. We love the neighborhood, and the kids are all set for camp and playgroups, nursery school and kindergarten next year, and so all the physical things have been arranged, and we feel good.

It is clear from this interview that Katherine's pregnancy has allowed her to dismiss the anxieties she was experiencing as she contemplated moving into the world of work outside of the home, and she is very pleased about the prospect of having a new baby. We suspect that at some later point, when this third child begins school, Katherine will again consider going to work and will have to find another solution.

In the eighth month, Jane, who earlier felt so burdened emotionally and physically, continued to express many of the same feelings. Her adaptation was only moderately good.

Interviewer: How's it been going and how are you feeling?

Jane: It's been dragging and I've been dragging. I'm very uncomfortable and just wish it were over with. I feel like I'm tripping over my belly and I can't support the weight anymore. It's hard to stand up, and it's hard to sit down, and it's hard to lie down.

Interviewer: What about your moods? How are they?

Jane: I don't think my moods are normal, but I don't think they're as bad as the first time. I'm never tremendously happy and sometimes I get depressed.

Interviewer: Has the pregnancy been the way you thought it would be?

Jane: More or less. I knew it was going to be bad, but I don't think I thought it was going to be this bad. But it isn't that much worse than I thought it would be.

Interviewer: How does it compare to the last pregnancy?

Jane: It's similar in a lot of ways except that last time I was much sicker toward the end. But last time I could stay in bed and rest when I needed to and now I can't.

Although Jane's tone was negative, her husband Ralph saw things differently. In this interview he spoke of how well Jane has handled this pregnancy, that "you could hardly tell she's pregnant, she's been acting so normally." This marked discrepancy between Jane's unhappy experience and Ralph's perception of it may reflect just how much difficulty Jane had in expressing her feelings and stating her needs or it may reflect how much difficulty Ralph had in being empathic towards his wife. Both Jane and Ralph felt that they were getting along much better this time than during the last pregnancy when they were "at each other's throats much of the time."

Although Jane has difficulties in asserting her needs, she hopes that her new child will be assertive: "I hope the baby can compete with Mark and doesn't get lost in the shuffle because Mark's a very domineering child. It will be hard on me, but I hope it is an active child who can keep up with Mark and demand as much attention as he does."

Jane thus anticipated with some sense of excitement the approaching birth of her baby. In looking back over her pregnancy, however, she mentioned only negative feelings: "I go from one bad thing to another. The first two trimesters I was nauseous. The second trimester was better because it was in the summer and Ralph was at home more and we had a nice time. But then by the seventh month, I started getting tired all the time and that's been hard. And now, besides feeling exhausted I also feel like I can't carry the weight around. So each third has its problems. I can't say much good about it." Jane felt stuck. She wanted time for her own life yet was unable to arrange her life in a way that would give her some private time. She felt suffocated by the needs of her children, born and unborn, and angry at the lack of support provided by her husband. These difficulties resulted in a very stressful pregnancy, both early and late.

Summary

In sum, the findings from the eighth-month visit with our couples indicate strongly that pregnancy is indeed far more than just a biological event. In fact, the experience and comfort of pregnancy seem influenced by psychological and environmental variables which are unrelated to the actual biological situation. As we followed these couples through the postnatal period, we tried to ascertain the effects of these differences in adaptation to pregnancy on the newborn child and on the adaptation of each family member.

By integrating the clinical and quantitative data obtained from our women during their pregnancies, we discerned several trends as clearly important in the prediction of optimal adaptation to pregnancy.

First, of our four sets of predictor variables—the psychological, physiological, sociocultural, and marital—the most important in terms of predictive value at this early point are the psychological and the marital. A woman's general level of adaptation, how well she has coped with her life in the past, will predict how well she will cope with this particular stage of her life. Although our quantitative findings emphasize the negative effects of anxiety on a woman's adaptation to pregnancy, our clinical data and impressions suggest that a woman's ability to experience anxiety and yet not be overwhelmed by it has an important bearing on her general pregnancy adaptation. We suggest, as others have from previous research, (for example, Uddenberg, 1974) that total denial of all dysphoria in general, and of anxiety in particular, is not helpful to the pregnant woman. As our interview with Katherine so vividly suggests, every pregnancy, no matter how enthusiastically welcomed and experienced, requires the prospective parents to perform a significant amount of psychological "work" in order to prepare themselves physically and emotionally for the arrival of their new child. This work consists of personal change and growth and necessarily causes some amount of anxiety.

Closely related to this ability to accept change and the anxiety change causes is the need for the woman to accept an increase in her level of dependency—both psychological and physical. Our data show that the woman's acceptance of her new dependency can best be accomplished if she is able to ask for help and if her husband is able to hear that request and to respond appropriately. If he is unable to do so, she feels isolated, unsupported, and vulnerable—a situation that cannot but add to her psychological burden.

As stated before, our subjects were a strikingly favored group of couples, most of whom were quite physically and emotionally healthy, financially relatively comfortable, and most of whom wanted these pregnancies. And still differences emerged in the relationship of general and marital well-being to pregnancy adaptation. One can only imagine how much more striking these trends might be in a more diverse sample.

Perhaps this relative homogeneity in our sample helps account for the paucity of findings relating sociocultural factors and aspects of previous medical history to pregnancy adaptation. Very few of the predictor variables subsumed under these two dimensions seemed relevant in predicting the experience of pregnancy for our sample. However, different dimensions later emerged as important to women's subsequent adaptation.

Lastly, and perhaps most strikingly, our findings indicate the immense difference in the experience of pregnancy for first-time and experienced mothers. For the former, pregnancy does indeed seem to be a genuine crisis period requiring the marshalling of all one's resources, both intrapsychic and extrapsychic, for optimal adaptation. The task is not merely the making of a place in one's heart and in one's home for a new member (a weighty enough job) but also the adjustment to significant changes in a woman's view of herself, her role in her marriage, and her place in the larger context of the outside world. Our data indicate how consuming this work is for the first-time mother, while the experienced mother has already once sustained this reevaluation of her sense of self and her relationship to the world. For her, pregnancy seems to be a crisis of much smaller proportions. As such, she requires fewer resources and can pay more attention to other ongoing relationships and issues in her life.

Like so many findings of formal studies, these data would not startle mothers in our culture, many of whom can express the difference between their first and later pregnancies with much greater clarity than our data do. Our findings, however, do support the wisdom of creating and evaluating more educational and supportive programs for women and men who are about to become parents for the first time. In the past decade, there has been increased recognition of the needs of new parents. Our data suggest that this trend may well be important in helping prospective parents adapt more comfortably to pregnancy and parenting.

ᕽᕽ *3* ᕽ ᕽ ᕽ

Motivations for Childbearing

Sexually mature adults can now consciously choose to direct, with a high degree of success, most aspects of their procreative lives, for the technology exists whereby people can enjoy sexual intercourse and prevent conception. Yet as recently as the 1960s, estimates of unplanned first pregnancies in the United States ranged as high as 54 percent (Blau and others, 1963), indicating that the number of people who successfully control their reproductive lives is far fewer than the available technology permits. Evidence suggests that women who have unplanned or unwanted pregnancies tend to have more problems during and after their pregnancies (Grimm, 1969; Pohlman, 1969; Uddenberg, Fagerstrom, and Hakanson-Zaunders, 1976; Uddenberg, Nilsson, and Almgren, 1971). Consequently, a large number of pregnant women are constantly at greater risk for experiencing adjustment difficulties.

The systematic study of motivation to reproduce is still in its beginnings. Little is known about how the desire for ma-

45

ternity is first developed, later sustained, and finally expressed. In this chapter, we discuss both conscious and unconscious attitudes of women toward their pregnancies and look at the effect of these attitudes on pregnancy, labor and delivery, and postpartum adaptation.

Several psychoanalytic writers have theorized about the basis for a motivation toward maternity. Freud's (1959) phallocentric orientation led him to hypothesize that a woman's wish to have a baby is a substitute for her earlier wish to have a penis and that this substitute desire characterizes a mature and healthy woman. Deutsch (1945) agreed that in childhood, the girl's wish to have a baby indeed is a substitute expression of her desire for a penis. However, Deutsch postulated that the mature woman's wish for a child represents her desire to express tenderness and altruism, the integrative capacities of the mature female.

Benedek (1960) studied the daily hormonal fluctuations of female psychoanalytic patients and correlated these with aspects of psychological functioning, as revealed primarily in dream material. She concludes that certain hormonal regularities stimulate adult behaviors and memories leading to the woman's wish to have a baby and then to care for it. Kestenberg (1956a, 1956b) also emphasizes the biological component of the reproductive wish, but offers a different explanation by speculating that undischarged vaginal tensions create the reproductive motive, and are, in human beings, the biological equivalent of an animal instinct. She sees the preoedipal girl as struggling with the need to master and discharge vaginal tensions and seeking an object upon which to release these feelings. By identifying with her mother, she is able to choose a doll as a substitute for a baby. Though Kestenberg agrees with Freud that there is a phallic component to the maternal wish, which is later gratified by the performance of a growing child, she emphasizes a woman's early bond with her own mother as a major influence in the development of the wish for a child.

These theories all accept the significance of biological mechanisms, refer to some kind of modeling or identification of the girl with her mother, and emphasize the role of early influences in women's development of a maternal orientation. They do not describe the processes, or experiences, by which the maternal wish is sustained from early girlhood, nor how this wish is manifest in a variety of reproductive behaviors. These theories also say relatively little about the interplay of a variety of motivations for childbearing.

Much of the literature about individual motivations for childbearing is clinical and emphasizes the more pathological reasons for wanting a baby (for example, see Blitzer and Murray, 1964; Rheingold, 1964; Wenner and Cohen, 1968). Some motivations that have been described as pathological include a woman's wish to save her marriage, to restore her self-esteem, to be like other women, or to show her own mother how to better raise a child.

Normative data are less available. Whelpton, Campbell, and Patterson (1966) found that the most common reason people give for childbearing is liking children. Other popular reasons include seeking immortality through children (Swain and Kiser, 1953) and anticipating feelings of pride (Centers and Blumberg, 1954). Rainwater (1965) interviewed a large number of men and women who represented a cross-section of the American population and found that the most prevalent American value concerning family planning was that each couple should have as many children as they can afford and no more. At the time of his study, Americans considered it selfish not to have children. The strong social pressures to want children of course influence and distort responses given to direct questions concerning motivation for childbearing. Despite this substantial methodological difficulty, the effect of negative feelings on the physiological and emotional course and outcome of pregnancy has been the focus of considerable research interest. Goshen-Gottstein (1966) interviewed pregnant women and found that women who initially rejected their pregnancies had more fears about their babies. Zuckerman and others (1963), interviewing women during middle pregnancy, did not find any relationship between the women's attitudes towards the pregnancy and any outcome measure. However, they did find that women who had more conflicted and fearful dreams about the pregnancy had more physical symptoms during pregnancy. Thus in studying women's negative attitudes toward pregnancy, the researcher may consider both conscious and unconscious conflicts as expressed in fears, physical symptoms, and dreams.

Poffenberger and Poffenberger (1952), using retrospective questionnaire data, found that women who had tried to avoid their pregnancies and those who had taken no conscious action either way experienced more emotional upset in the first trimester than women who had planned their pregnancies. Klein, Potter, and Dyke (1950) found no relationship between attitudes towards conception and anxiety in a sample of lower-class women. However, women indicating less desire for the pregnancy had more physical symptoms. Several other researchers report that women with more negative attitudes towards pregnancy had more physical complaints (Brown, 1962; Chertok, 1969; Grimm, 1969; Uddenberg, Nilsson, and Almgren, 1971; Zemlick and Watson, 1953) and longer labors (Uddenberg, Fagerstrom, and Hakanson-Zaunders, 1976).

Several studies have focused on the effect of maternal ambivalence on later mother-child interactions. Ferreira (1960) found that women who had extreme feelings toward the pregnancy—positive or negative—had infants with lower levels of adaptation. Ferreira suggests that a mother's extremely positive feelings reflected her excessive concern due to her unconscious hostility towards the fetus. Zemlick and Watson (1953) found that mothers' attitudes towards their babies, assessed by a questionnaire given shortly after birth, were related to their initial acceptance or rejection of the pregnancy. Women who showed early negative feelings were likely to be overprotective after the birth. Zemlick and Watson, like Ferreira, consider a mother's undue attachment and concern as an expression of her repressed hostility toward the infant. A study of children born to Swedish women who were refused requests for abortion found that these children had a higher incidence of delinquency and psychiatric contacts than a matched control group of children (Forssman and Thuwe, 1966). In contrast, Grimm and Venet (1966) found judgments of maternal warmth positively related to acceptance of pregnancy and Leifer (1977) reports that women more positive about the pregnancy were more attached to their infants in the postpartum period.

The literature thus appears to support the view that negative attitudes towards the pregnancy adversely affect aspects of the pregnancy, labor and delivery, and the subsequent mother-child relationship. Other, more subtle questions remain unanswered; for example, are there differences in effect between more and less conscious negative attitudes? Also of interest are the possible effects of a woman's change in attitude towards the pregnancy as she approaches delivery. Improved attitudes as pregnancy progresses are reported in many studies (Goshen-Gottstein, 1966; Hall and Mohr, 1933; Klein, Potter and Dyke, 1950; Pleshette, Asch, and Chase, 1956; Zemlick and Watson, 1953).

In our study, we have attempted to untangle some of the issues concerning less conscious feelings and fantasies about having a baby from the more accessible "official position" of the woman. We have also attempted to examine the effect, if any, of a positive change in attitude on the course of and adaptation to pregnancy and the puerperium.

Within the context of the broader longitudinal study, two measures are particularly relevant to this discussion of motivation. One, a paper-and-pencil measure of the women's conscious motivation for this pregnancy, was given in the first trimester and at the eight-month contact. In addition, the women were given a modified TAT, based on a measure developed by Lakin (1957) which was scored for the women's emotional tone in their stories given in response to pictures of childbirth or early parenting. (At first we also scored whether women identified the woman on Card 2 of the TAT as pregnant, following Davids and DeVault (1962). Since no significant results were found—see Gofseyeff, 1977—the score is not included in this discussion.)

Motivation and Adaptation to Pregnancy

In general, the women in our study were highly positive about the pregnancy, as reflected in their conscious motivation score, with no difference between first-time and experienced mothers. Most spoke confidently when answering questions about their reasons for wanting a baby at this time. Nonetheless, we found some differences among women with varying attitudes toward the pregnancy at this time.

For the sample as a whole, women who in their first trimester described themselves as unambivalently positive about having the baby were also judged as better adapted to the pregnancy, and better adapted to their lives in general. These relationships were stronger among first-time mothers. The primiparous women who were most positive about having the baby had been married longer, described their marriages as more satisfactory, had less premenstrual tension, and less anxiety than women describing themselves as less happy about the pregnancy and coming birth. In contrast, only the number of children they already had was predictive for multiparous women; the more children they had, the less their conscious motivation for another.

In interpreting the results of the measure of conscious motivation, we found that the higher the individuals' scores on the motivation scale, the more they tended to be concerned about responding in a socially acceptable manner (as measured by a Social Desirability scale, see Appendix A). This relationship held for the sample as a whole and for experienced mothers in particular. In our culture, it is very hard for a woman to seem less than enthusiastic about a pregnancy and birth, even if her personal feelings are ambivalent. In contrast, when we elicited the women's less conscious feelings, a different picture emerged.

In our study, women indicating more ambivalent or negative feelings in their response to the modified TAT pictures were judged as better adapted to the pregnancy in the first trimester, and this was more strongly true for first-time mothers than for the sample overall. These findings seem consistent with the view expressed by Uddenberg, Fagerstrom, and Hakanson-Zaunders (1976) of the "work" required in early pregnancy. At this time, women need to come to terms with the role changes, both in fantasy and reality, occasioned by the pregnancy and impending birth. Perhaps those women actively working on these issues do experience—and express—some of the inevitable ambivalence about the changes. According to this view, those women not expressing or experiencing any ambivalence have not yet begun to do the necessary psychological work. It is not surprising that the finding is stronger for first-time mothers, since multiparous women have, by and large, already dealt with these changes in their earlier pregnancies.

Motivation at Eight Months

By the eighth month of pregnancy, the expressed conscious motivation for the pregnancy and baby was predicted best by the number of previous children and the length of the marriage. The more children a woman already had and the longer she had been married, the lower her conscious motivation. For first-time mothers, the motivation score continued to relate positively to marital adjustment and negatively to anxiety. For multiparous women, the pattern observed in the first-trimester measures again held: women whose expressed motivation was higher were those who had fewer children.

Some excerpts from both the first-trimester interviews and the responses to the modified TAT serve to illustrate the varying motivations of the women in our study.

When asked why they wanted a child at this point, our women responded with the statements such as:

"I have wanted children for some time. Having a family will lend meaning and continuity to my life and our marriage."

"At this time? My age."

"We wanted two children, and we were just ready to have a second child."

"We felt our first child was ready mentally to handle a sibling."

"Looking forward to creating a life and helping in its development."

"Young enough to start a family and still have a life of my own."

"We have one child and simply wanted another baby to share in our family love."

Perhaps somewhat more spontaneous and convincing are answers to two questions in the first-trimester interview about reasons for wanting to be pregnant and reasons for being particularly pleased about this pregnancy:

"Well, I wanted to be pregnant and being twenty-five and not really doing anything I had gone to school for, nor was I unhappy with myself in that respect, but felt it was time I started my family, and my husband wanted to. I don't feel I'm giving up anything for it."

"Yes, I'm pleased about it because I think it's going to be my last one. I feel like I'd just like to have the three and they can grow up together."

This second woman had a slightly lower level of conscious motivation than the first, but both were quite high, reflecting substantially positive views of the pregnancy.

This next woman received the highest possible score, and her enthusiasm is reflected in her interview: "You mean how is it different from before? Only that I know how it is to have children and love them and have them love you and how exciting it is and how much fun it is. And you have no way of knowing how you're going to enjoy a child until you have your own. I mean you can enjoy children and be with them, but my child excites me. It's a personal thing. I'm looking forward to the experimenting and everything else."

In contrast, this next woman received a very low score on her conscious motivation for this pregnancy, and indicated clearly she did not choose to get pregnant at this time: "I thought our first child—she's twenty-one months—was too young, and I said that to my husband. We thought we were using the contraceptive right, I thought I was protected. You know, it's one of those games people play with themselves. I was ambivalent about it." [Interviewer: "How old did you want your older child to be before the new baby came?"] "I thought from the reading I did that three would be right." ["Did you have questions about not continuing the pregnancy?"] "Yes, we did think about it. And then I didn't believe I was really pregnant. We got the tests back, and I went to the doctor, and I still expected him to say I wasn't pregnant." [She then described their thoughts on abortion and how she found she could not consider it for herself, even though she does not disapprove in principle.]

In slight contrast, these women's attitudes toward the maternal role, as reflected in their responses to the modified TAT, were slightly less positive, suggesting some ambivalence about pregnancy and childbirth. Again, there was no statistical difference between first-time and experienced mothers.

This first story, told by a woman who said she was pleased to be pregnant and who received high scrores for maternal aptitude on the TAT, was her response to a picture of a pregnant woman lying down, touching a ring on her hand—a picture most women interpret as a picture of a woman in labor. Her story was: "This lady looks like she's probably in labor, it could be. Her stomach's pretty big. She seems to be pretty controlled. I'm sure things work out well, she had her baby."

This next story was told by the same woman in response to a picture of a woman leaning over a crying baby in a bassinet: "Looks like the mother is picking up the baby, it's crying. The baby cried, and the mother came in and picked it up. The mother is composed, she's going to soothe the baby. The baby looks like he got up and felt strange and wanted her to comfort him."

This woman's third story was in response to a picture of a man and woman eating at the kitchen table, with a baby in a bassinet between them: "Looks like the husband and wife are having supper, the baby is in the kitchen, I guess. [Laughs.] Maybe it's very fussy, it must have been really bad to disturb the meal. I wouldn't do that. She'll calm him down and put him in his room. The husband isn't too happy. His wife is trying to soothe the baby."

Although this woman was rated as being highly motivated for this pregnancy, her stories still showed the amount of stress she anticipated. In her first story, she expressed no positive feelings, just a sense of everything being under control and manageable. Similarly, her second story emphasized composure and control, rather than enjoyment or happiness. In the third, she described the baby as fussy and the husband as unhappy about his wife's involvement with the baby.

In contrast, this next woman, also expecting her second child, expressed a low level of conscious motivation for this pregnancy and received a very low score on the TAT measure of unconscious maternal aptitude or readiness. In response to the picture of the pregnant woman lying down and fingering her ring, she said: "Well, this kind of looks like there was a vicious argument—looks like her husband got up and left. She's staying in bed looking and contemplating what can happen. This also doesn't look too encouraging. I think the end of the story would be—would just fade out, and you'd have to make your own conclusions after the fight as to whose side you'd take or whether they'd go back together."

Here, regardless of whether one accepts the interpretation that at some less conscious level she probably recognized that the woman in the picture was pregnant, her negative, rageful, and fearful feelings are clear, and were given by her after a long interview about her experiences of this pregnancy, in the context of a study about pregnancy and birth.

Even fewer interpretative inferences are required by her second story, in response to the picture of the woman bending over the baby in the bassinet: "I'd say this woman, um. I don't know if it looks like she's abusing the child or if she's trying to figure out if there's something wrong with him. Let's see, in the end she probably, she'll learn to live with the problem, but probably find it very difficult to accept it. But there's love there, she does love the child. It's funny, she has no expression one way or the other. I think the baby looks like it's hurting somehow. She's probably having a difficult time trying to accept the child, but she will. That's a strange picture."

Of the third picture, the couple eating and the baby in a bassinet, she said: "Oh, this, I have to laugh when I see this picture. It reminds me of our first baby. This is their first baby, and they're thrilled. But all of a sudden, they find that this child is taking over their lives. When he cries, they jump. Until a very good friend comes in and takes the baby out of her arms and back in the crib saying, 'Eat your dinner. He's dry.' The child cried for five more minutes, then went to sleep. He's a very well-adjusted child even though his mother put him back in the cradle that night. It's funny, it reminds me so much of when we brought Andy home.''

Here, even though her story concludes happily, it is based on the difficult time she had when her first child was an infant and her fears that she might somehow neglect or damage the child.

In some ways, the most interesting stories were from women who described themselves as strongly positive about the pregnancy and yet show marked negative or ambivalent feelings on this measure of less conscious attitude.

For instance, when shown a farm scene of a man plowing in the fields, a pregnant older woman in the background, and a young woman holding books, a woman who described herself as being entirely positive about this pregnancy and eagerly awaiting the baby told this story: "I don't know. It looks like it's a very poor family and the daughter looks like she is going to school and she's looking at her mother. She doesn't want to end up like her. She's leaning against the tree, she looks pregnant. That's probably where she'll stay. She'll have the baby there and then go back to work. It looks like the daughter has some pretty nice clothes. It looks like the parents are working so hard and sacrificing so she can go to school and not end up like them. Would be interesting to know what the artist was thinking of when he drew this."

This response to the picture stresses that the young woman desires to avoid the fate of her parents—poverty and, in the mother's case, pregnancy. Her story for the picture of the mother bending over the baby's bassinet shows her ambivalence more directly: "I can't really tell if this baby's . . . it looks a little as if he's crying, but I'd rather think he's laughing as his mother throws him up in the air. Oh, wait a minute! I had it [the card] upside down. She's either picking him up or putting him down for a nap."

This last story is told by another woman who indicated on the conscious motivation measure that she was delighted to be pregnant with this baby, but showed considerable ambivalence in her responses to the modified TAT. Looking at the picture of the mother bending over the baby's bassinet, she said:

"Looks like a mother picking up the baby, but the baby doesn't look regular to me. Not happy. The surroundings are stark, there are railings behind the baby's position, a hallway. I don't know what's the matter with the baby, but I don't think the baby is normal. The outcome? I don't think the baby's going to be right but somehow they'll all adjust."

Thus, women express some underlying feelings—ones that are less socially acceptable—on this projective measure, and it is clearly quite important for researchers to consider less conscious as well as more conscious aspects of a woman's motivation for pregnancy.

Motivation and Adaptation to Labor and Delivery

For the sample as a whole to a slight degree and more strongly for first-time mothers, the modified TAT scores, indicating the women's maternal interest or attitude, did predict significantly to a number of aspects of adaptation. Women who told more positive stories about the modified TAT pictures had significantly fewer obstetrical complications and were judged as having adapted better to the labor and delivery. This relationship held more strongly for primiparous women alone than for the sample as a whole. For first-time mothers only, the more positive their stories, the less likely they were to have a caesarean section.

Motivation and Postpartum Adaptation

For the sample as a whole, the women's conscious motivation reported at the first-trimester contact related *only* to marital adjustment at one year postpartum, and that relationship was quite small and at a low level of confidence. For first-time mothers only, their level of conscious motivation in the first trimester did relate to their level of anxiety and depression and their marital adjustment at one year; for experienced mothers, there were no meaningful relationships.

However, for the sample as a whole, women who reported themselves in late pregnancy as less positive about the pregnancy were more anxious and depressed at two months post-partum; they also had poorer marital relationships at one year postpartum. The relationships were even stronger when the primiparous women were considered separately. First-time mothers describing themselves as less positive about the pregnancy late in pregnancy were more anxious in late pregnancy, at two months postpartum, and at one year postpartum. They coped less well with labor and delivery, had a lower level of emotional well-being at two months postpartum, and had marriages that were more troubled at two months and one year postpartum. Few of those relationships held for experienced mothers. Thus a woman's description of her conscious motivation for childbearing at eight months of pregnancy is predictive, particularly for a first-time mother, of certain aspects of her condition after the baby has been born.

When we looked at changes in attitude over the course of the pregnancy, there were more women who became more positive in their view of the pregnancy than those who became more negative. A number of women whose attitudes had changed from negative to more positive by the eighth-month contact had forgotten or denied that they had held the earlier more negative view.

These findings suggest that a woman's attitude immediately prior to delivery is more important to her successful adaptation than her attitude earlier in pregnancy, when the baby is still largely a fantasy. Those women in our study, particularly first-time mothers, who were still not feeling positive by the last trimester were found to adapt less well to many of the ensuing stages of early motherhood. Ambivalent or negative feelings early in pregnancy are less predictive of postpartum difficulties and may merely reflect the woman's process of coping with the psychological "work" of pregnancy. It seems that pregnancy is indeed a time of preparation, both emotional as well as physical, and that women who by the end of pregnancy have come to accept more fully and anticipate more enthusiastically the birth of their baby will do better later on. The differences in the importance of this dimension of motivation between first-time and experienced mothers are consistent with much of the data re-

ported previously and suggest once again that the emotional experience of a first pregnancy is more complex, as first-time
mothers learn to accept the new role of mother, than later
pregnancies.

In sum, the large majority of these married women described themselves as pleased to be pregnant. This pleasure reflects the real feelings of this group of young, healthy married
women, most of whom planned to conceive. But, in part, their
strongly positive feelings reflect the pressures in our culture that
make it difficult for women to acknowledge any ambivalence or
negative feelings about pregnancy and childrearing. This underlying ambivalence is expressed in their TAT stories, which reflect less conscious feelings and attitudes.

The women's self-described conscious motivation, particularly at eight months, predicted to a remarkable extent how
things would be going at two and twelve months postpartum;
and as has been the case throughout the project, the relationships were stronger for first-time mothers than experienced
mothers. First-time mothers who indicated in the first trimester
that they were pleased about the pregnancy were less anxious
and depressed and more satisfied with their marriages at one
year. By eight months, women who were still feeling negatively
about the pregnancy—and many who started somewhat negatively had reconciled themselves to it—were those who would be
more anxious and depressed at two months postpartum and at
a year. These less positively motivated primiparous women had
a more negative experience of the labor and delivery and were
less satisfied with their marriages at every point. Of course,
women more satisfied with their marriages initially tended to be
more positive in their view of the pregnancy. These data do not
argue for a direct causal relationship between motivation and
later adaptation. They do support the predictive power of a motivation measure for later adaptation and more tentatively contribute to a theory that views motivation for maternity as
a major dimension of the psychological experience.

Less conscious aspects of maternal attitude, as reflected
in the TAT stories, predicted adaptation in these women, particularly to aspects of the labor and delivery. For all our women,

and more strongly for first-time mothers, women telling more positive stories had fewer complications of labor and delivery and were more positive about the experience.

Clearly, motivation for pregnancy is a fascinating, and important, dimension of the experience. Just as clearly, it is not a unitary, or single-faceted, concept.

✳ 4 ✿ ✿ ✿ ✿

Labor and Delivery

Intro

The birth of a baby is one of the most dramatic and emotional events in human experience. It represents the fulfillment of the biological goal of the species and, at the same time, it is an event with profound psychological implications.

For most people, an important aspect of growing up is being able to have their own family; they have anticipated the moment of their child's birth for many years. During the nine months of pregnancy that once distant prospect is becoming a reality, and the parents' hopes and anxieties become much more clearly focused. As a woman prepares to deliver her child, she experiences physical and psychological tension: Will her body respond in the appropriate way? Will she be able to cope with the painful aspects of labor and delivery? What will this child be like—will it be healthy, a girl or a boy? Will she be able to love and nurture it as she believes it should be loved and nurtured?

Particularly for a first-time mother, the labor and delivery period often becomes a highly charged focus of her fears and strivings. Although they are not always consciously aware of it, many women fear that their physical intactness is threatened,

60

that they will be ripped apart or destroyed during the process of giving birth, or that they will be out of control. Women whose self-esteem is very low and those who are highly ambivalent about the child may have grave doubts about their ability to produce a perfectly healthy baby. Other women see childbirth as a supreme moment of creative achievement; they invest a lot of self-esteem in their conduct as parturients; and many view their husband's role in the experience as an important test of the marital relationship. Although these issues are present in women who have previously given birth, many of their attitudes seem to be tempered by other concerns.

The outcome of childbirth may be viewed in both its physiological and its psychological components, and factors responsible for optimal outcomes in each sphere can be identified. Physiologically, an uncomplicated labor and delivery is the goal, but a large percentage of pregnancies do not end so perfectly. Obstetrical complications occur, ranging from a mild toxemia or slightly prolonged labor to maternal or infant death. In some situations the etiology of the difficulty is clearly mechanical or disease-related; in many other cases, the causes have not been determined, and the complications continue to occur despite advances in obstetrical skill.

The predictive value of various psychological variables in the course and outcome of pregnancy has been studied by a number of investigators and there appear to be some significant psychological differences between women who experience complications and those who do not (McDonald, 1968). In a study of women at risk for the development of toxemia, Glick, Salerno, and Royce (1965) found convincing personality differences between the women who did and those who did not develop the disorder. Sherman (1971) feels that the evidence taken as a whole supports the notion that psychological factors are important in the development of toxemia.

Anxiety is the psychological variable that has been the most consistently shown to be a predictor of physiological difficulty. Several studies have investigated the role of anxiety in the prediction of problems during labor and delivery. Davids, DeVault, and Talmadge (1961) found that those women judged more anxious in the seventh month of pregnancy had significantly more complicated deliveries than those who were less anxious. McDonald (1965) found that greater anxiety was related to later obstetrical complications. Gorsuch and Key (1974) measured anxiety monthly over the course of 118 pregnancies and found that the group with abnormalities of pregnancy, parturition, and infant status had significantly higher levels of anxiety during the third and fourth lunar months.

Taken as a whole, the evidence for a relation between anxiety in pregnancy and obstetrical complications is compelling. Results are more mixed when the focus of the study is the relation between anxiety and specific complications (Brown, 1964; McDonald, 1965; Zuckerman and others, 1963). Causal interpretation of such relationships is, of course, problematic since it remains to be determined whether anxiety affects physical symptoms, whether the presence of physical symptoms produces anxiety, or whether both are caused by some other underlying factor.

One specific abnormality that has been studied extensively is uterine dysfunction during labor (Crammond, 1954; Kapp, Hornstein, and Graham, 1963). In Rosengren's (1961) study of length of labor, he found that women who regard pregnancy as an illness and women of lower socioeconomic status tend to have longer labors. He also found significantly shorter labor times among the women whose views about pregnancy were congruent with those of their obstetricians.

Other studies suggest that a longer labor is more likely for women who have not done sufficient psychological work to prepare themselves to deal with the inevitable conflicts which arise around issues of childbearing. Uddenberg, Fagerstrom, and Hakanson-Zaunders (1976), in a study of primiparous women, found that those women who demonstrated more conflict about reproductive issues during pregnancy had shorter labor times. Investigating the dreams of pregnant women, Winget and Kapp (1972) found consistent data; namely, that women whose dreams showed less anxiety and threat were more likely to have longer labors due to inefficient uterine action. The anxious dreaming seems to be a way to work through pregnancy-related conflicts, which leaves the mother better prepared for delivery and a new baby.

Reality factors, such as various forms of environmental stress, also have an important effect on physical well-being and have been studied in relation to complications during delivery. Recent research has found a relationship between life stresses and obstetrical outcome, both physical and emotional. Life stress occurring in the six-month period prior to delivery was found to be significantly related to obstetrical complications in a study of low-income clinic patients (Gorsuch and Key, 1974). Nuckolls, Kasl, and Kaplan (1972) examined the relationship between social stress, psychosocial assets, and obstetrical difficulties and found that women experiencing greater recent social stress, in the context of having fewer psychosocial assets, had more obstetrical complications, although neither factor alone was predictive. Finally, Williams (1975) found more prenatal and pregnancy problems in pregnant women reporting greater life change.

Other studies have attempted to relate women's use of medication during labor to personality characteristics. Brown, Manning, and Grodin (1972) found that mentally healthier women and those whose adjustment to the pregnancy was better used fewer drugs regardless of their anxiety or pain during labor. Similarly, Yang and others (1976) found increased drug use during labor by women who had been judged during late pregnancy to have shown more irritability and tension, depression and withdrawal, and fears for themselves. It is, of course, too simplistic to assume that the amount of medication a woman receives is dependent only on her psychological characteristics; the amount of medication administered is the result of a complex interaction that includes the obstetrician's perception of the woman and his usual practice, as well as the woman's expressed needs. Less use of medication during childbirth has also been shown to relate to attendance at childbirth education classes (Enkin and others, 1972; Tanzer, 1967).

Over the past several years, more attention has been paid to the actual experience of childbirth; attempts have been made by those involved to enhance the event by making it less frightening, more comfortable, and more easily shared by the family. Home delivery is enjoying a renaissance, although this option is not endorsed by most obstetricians. Prenatal classes, the presence of the father at the birth, and awake-and-aware deliveries are now offered by most hospitals. That many such factors do influence how a woman feels about herself and the events surrounding the birth has been amply demonstrated.

In prenatal classes, women learn various psychosomatic methods as training for childbirth; almost all of these methods teach special patterns of breathing and methods of relaxation as well as provide information about what happens during labor and delivery. These classes include training for the husband or other attendant who will support and assist during labor and delivery (reviewed by Chertok, 1969). Studies indicate that attendance at childbirth education classes during which techniques for alleviating pain are taught positively affects the experience of giving birth (Chertok, 1969; Klusman, 1975). Psychotherapeutic prenatal counseling may also help adaptation at labor and delivery for some women. Shereshefsky and Yarrow (1973) found that women in their counseled group were more relaxed and viewed the experience as easier than those who did not receive counseling.

The importance of the husband's presence at the birth has been demonstrated by Doering, Entwisle, and Quinlan (1978) who studied 120 couples during the last trimester of pregnancy. When the husband was present at the birth, 63 percent of the women found the experience significantly enhanced.

In looking at obstetrical outcome, one cannot fail to be impressed by the strong effect of psychosomatic factors. Aspects of a woman's personality such as her anxiety level and how well she has worked through her conflicts, the amount of stress in her life, the support she has from attending prenatal classes and her husband's presence at the birth—all influence the physiological outcome of her labor and delivery and her perception of and reaction to this most significant of human events.

We studied eighty-nine women at the time of their labor and delivery. Nearly all the women had participated in childbirth education classes, in most cases with their husbands. Virtually all of the husbands were present at the labor and delivery. During the hospital stay after delivery, the mothers were interviewed, obstetrical data were gathered from the medical records, and the infants were tested. From these contacts, we obtained several measures of how the birth had gone for the mother and infant and of how they were doing a day or two postpartum. This chapter reports the experience of the mothers. Data about the infants will be presented in Chapter Nine.

Obstetrical Complications

One major outcome measure at this time was a rating of labor and delivery complications. Our rating of obstetrical complications evaluated the extent to which any complication was potentially life-threatening to mother or infant. Forty (45 percent) of our mother-infant pairs experienced no complications, thirty (34 percent) had mild to moderate complications, including uterine atony, cephalo-pelvic disproportion, caesarean section, and precipitous dilatation and descent. Nineteen (21 percent) had serious complications, including a neonatal death, abruptio placenta, birthweight below 2,500 grams, preeclamptic toxemia, and shoulder dystocia.

Most of the studies which define complications broadly report rates in the same range as our 55 percent rate (Davids and DeVault, 1962; Gorsuch and Key, 1974; McDonald, 1965; Nuckolls, Kasl, and Kaplan, 1972) but since there are no consistent criteria for defining complications, it is difficult to make meaningful comparisons. It looks then as if some degree of difficulty in the process of childbirth is normal. We feel that it is an unfortunate aspect of the current mythology of childbirth that most women today expect to have a problem-free delivery, whereas the majority have at least some complications.

In the present study, as expected, first births were more likely to be complicated ones. Age, however, was not a factor, perhaps because there were no very young or very old mothers in the sample. In addition, socioeconomic status did not predict to the physiological outcome at labor and delivery, although earlier studies have reported such a relationship. Most likely this

Table 1. First Trimester Variables Predicting Women's Adaptation to Labor and Delivery

	Complications			Caesarean Sections			Maternal Adaptation to Labor and Delivery		
	All Mothers[a]	First-Time Mothers[b]	Experienced Mothers[c]	All Mothers[a]	First-Time Mothers[b]	Experienced Mothers[c]	All Mothers[a]	First-Time Mothers[b]	Experienced Mothers[c]
Psychological dimension									
Life adaptation	.09	.05	.02	.09	.05	.18	.09	.16	.04
Anxiety	.22[a]	.24	.21	.18	.16	.10	-.20	-.19	-.08
Depression	.17	.18	.22	.14	.22	.13	.09	.07	.05
Conscious motivation	-.06	.13	-.21	.05	.07	.04	.04	.30	-.16
Modified TAT	-.24	-.36	-.16	-.17	-.30	-.05	.37[b]	.52[b]	.22
Adaptation to pregnancy	.03	-.01	-.09	.00	-.09	.08	-.17	.08	-.36
Religiosity	-.24[a]	-.43[b]	.01	-.34[b]	-.48[b]	-.12	.21	.23	.12
Physiological dimension									
Premenstrual tension	.11	-.13	.31[a]	-.02	.05	.02	.00	-.04	-.06
Medical risk	.18	.14	.17	.12	.10	.06	-.10	-.03	-.09
Sociocultural dimension									
Socioeconomic status	.06	.08	.12	-.08	-.08	.01	-.07	-.29	.09
Social support	.06	.14	-.02	-.02	-.01	.04	-.06	-.01	-.18
Life change	-.09	-.19	-.02	-.05	-.06	-.01	.05	.07	.03

Marital dimension								
Marital adjustment	.01	.06	-.11	.05	-.13	.11	.29[a]	.44[a]	.24
Sexual activity and satisfaction	-.17	-.09	-.25	-.07	-.07	.09	-.18	-.07	-.30
Marital style	.21	.05	.19	.21	.19	.06	.17	.11	.34

Note: These correlations are based on the following samples: For first-time mothers, N ranges from 24 to 39; for experienced mothers, N ranges from 28 to 43; for all mothers, N ranges from 52 to 84.

[a] $p \leqslant .05$, two-tailed
[b] $p \leqslant .01$, two-tailed
[c] $p \leqslant .001$, two-tailed

relationship did not hold for women in our sample because they received early prenatal care.

Several dimensions from the first trimester evaluation did predict complications of labor and delivery (see Table 1). Primiparous women whose scores on the projective task (modified TAT) reflected more negative and ambivalent feelings toward pregnancy, childbirth, and motherhood were more likely to have obstetrical complications. In addition, both first-time and experienced mothers with higher levels of anxiety were more likely to have complicated deliveries. These results lend support to the notion that the process of childbirth is complex and that the outcome is influenced by a broad interplay of factors—that it is not strictly a physiological event. Psychological factors, though not accounting for large amounts of the differences among women, do play a role in what must be seen as a complex psychophysiological situation.

Interestingly, those women who reported themselves to be more religious had fewer obstetrical complications in general and fewer caesarean sections in particular. Highly religious women in this study generally displayed lower levels of anxiety. It is possible that strong religious belief does work to some extent to protect believers from anxiety, and that this protection extends to psychophysiological events like childbirth. This interpretation is supported by the research of Katz and others (1970) who studied defensive patterns in women awaiting breast tumor biopsy and found that what they termed the *prayer-and-faith* group had significantly less psychological and physiological (steroid level) disruption. They felt that the religious defensive pattern contained strong elements that kept their subjects from reacting physiologically to the stress they were undergoing.

A final relationship from the first-trimester contact which was found in this study for experienced mothers only, was that those who had a history of premenstrual tension were more likely to have complicated deliveries. The nature of this relationship is not clear and deserves further investigation.

Few scores from the eighth-month contact predicted to complications of labor and delivery.

In addition to considering caesarean sections as a complication, we also looked at the effect of this kind of delivery on mother and baby. The rate of caesarean section in this sample was 23.7 percent with first pregnancies significantly less likely to result in normal vaginal deliveries. Across the country—and in other countries as well—rates for abdominal delivery have increased dramatically over the past ten years (Jones, 1976). The proportion of deliveries accomplished by caesarean section in medical facilities in this country ranges from 9 to 23 percent. The increase in caesarean sections seems to reflect the increased availability of techniques, such as fetal monitoring, which allow obstetricians to anticipate when vaginal delivery may prove dangerous to the fetus; rather than risk an unpredictable vaginal delivery, a caesarean section is performed. Discussion by prominent people in the field reflects the controversial nature of this obstetrical issue with some professionals praising the increasing rate of caesarean deliveries as an improvement and others pointing out the additional maternal risks, disability, and financial burden which abdominal delivery entails (Hibbard, 1976; Jones, 1976).

Certainly in terms of the experience of the birth and the early postpartum period, women who have caesarean sections have a more difficult time adjusting. Most had not expected this type of birth; their childbirth classes and obstetricians did not prepare them for it, and it carried additional postoperative discomfort and psychological tensions as well. One mother spoke of her difficulty as follows: "I wasn't connected to the process of giving birth. I wasn't that interested, just wanted to get out of there. It was such an artificial way to separate—very disjointed." During the postpartum period she felt she wasn't able to care for her daughter as well as she wanted to: "I've started to get discouraged. I can't really take care of her that well. Everything is such a bother, such an ordeal for me to get up out of bed and lift her. It's very frustrating."

Clearly, the postoperative pain and other physical after effects of a caesarean delivery contribute to additional difficulties during the postpartum period. The recovery from this major surgical procedure and any emotional disappointment put additional physiological and psychological stress on the new mother. In addition, the mother's postpartum condition may have detrimental effects on the very earliest mother-infant interactions and bonding patterns.

Among factors predictive of obstetrical complications among the women in this study, both psychological and physiological variables were of some importance, a finding consonant with that of Papiernik and Kaminski (1974). Our finding that anxiety is related to complications is also consistent with the literature; this finding is complemented by the negative correlation between religiosity—which may be considered a method of reducing or controlling anxiety—and complications. Of our findings on the physiological dimension, numerous previous studies have similarly reported that first births had more complications. Premenstrual tension has been linked in the literature with postpartum depression, but not with obstetrical complications.

Adaptation to Labor and Delivery

The second major outcome measure at this time was the mother's adaptation to labor and delivery, which was assessed from an interview taped in the hospital. We considered the situation to be optimal if the woman was positive in her view of how things had gone and how she had handled the experience, if she was pleased with the infant, if her mood was good, if she was not unduly anxious about being a mother, and if she had been satisfied with her husband's support during the birth.

Overall, the women were judged to have done moderately well during this period, with some women having had an extremely difficult time and others having been positively euphoric. Many of the mothers spoke very emotionally of how they had felt when their babies were delivered, of the joyous quality of the experience for them, and of their pleasure at how deeply moved they were to hold their infants close or to gaze down at them while they were sleeping. Others, however, had felt too exhausted to be very responsive, or were still reacting to unanticipated obstetrical complications. Women felt a wide range of emotions with a degree of intensity which often surprised them. They sensed the enormity of the physiological and psychological experience that they had just been through and felt extremely relieved that it was over.

Several factors emerged as influential in determining who adapted well in this early postpartum period. The single most important factor was a strong feeling of satisfaction with the marriage on the part of both husband and wife (see Table 1). The women who had rated their marriages highly were doing better in the early postpartum period. This finding was strongest for first-time mothers, although it was also true for the sample as a whole.

Another significant predictor of good adaptation at this time was a woman's more positive feelings toward maternity on the projective measure (modified TAT) we had administered early in pregnancy. Those whose responses to the TAT pictures were less negative or ambivalent in tone were doing better during their postpartum hospital stay. Again, this finding was stronger for the first-time mothers in the group.

Among the variables later in the pregnancy and their effect on the labor, delivery, and postpartum experience, the strongest predictor of difficulty was high anxiety at the eighth mongh. Women who had been more anxious late in pregnancy were not doing as well emotionally at the time of the birth. The other factor which was important, but only for experienced mothers, was the couple's preparedness at eight months, in both a practical and an emotional sense, for the new baby's arrival. The women who were adapting better after giving birth were those who, with their husbands, had seemed more prepared to welcome a new infant at the eighth-month contact.

Not surprisingly, a complicated delivery adversely affected adaptation. For example, in several instances where husbands were not present during a caesarean section, the women felt frightened and unsupported during the procedure. In addition, postoperative pain or concern about an infant who was having some problems were associated with postpartum anxiety and depression.

It is worthy of note that neither personality characteristics, nor sociocultural dimensions, nor physiological factors from the early contact predicted how the women in this study adapted to labor and delivery. Anxiety at eight months did predict the woman's adaptation to the childbirth and very early postpartum period as did the occurrence of obstetrical complications. For experienced mothers, the degree of the couple's preparation for the new baby was predictive of her adaptation to labor and delivery.

Several of the men's scores predicted the woman's adaptation to labor and delivery. Men who were highly anxious during the first trimester had wives who did not do as well during the childbirth and early postpartum period, and this finding was independent of the level of anxiety among the women. The quality of a man's overall life adaptation was not at all predictive of his wife's experience at labor and delivery, suggesting that there is something about his anxiety in itself that interferes with his wife's successful coping with this particular event. Perhaps, as suggested by such authors as Benedek (1970b), Jessner, Weigert, and Foy (1970), Lewis and Weinraub (1976), and Wenner and Cohen (1968), a central aspect of the husband's role during the stressful period of pregnancy and childbirth is to alleviate his wife's natural anxiety. If he himself is very anxious, he is less available to meet her needs and to calm her, and she, in turn, is less able to cope with the experiences in a comfortable and relaxed way.

Along the same lines, Doering, Entwisle, and Quinlan (1978) found that the degree of the husband's participation in the labor and delivery was significantly related to the quality of the woman's experience. It seems to be true that in our culture, for couples who have chosen to rear children within the context of a marriage, the husbands' participation makes a great deal of difference to the pregnancy and childbirth experiences of their wives.

Another interesting finding relating the man's experience to that of his wife was that men who were more satisfied with their marriages overall but who had lower scores on the sexual questionnaire (completed at the first-trimester contact) had wives who adapted better to labor and delivery. Clearly, pregnancy and the early postpartum period interfere with a couple's sexual relationship. Possibly those couples in which the husband is satisfied by a low degree of sexual contact have an easier time coping with the normal disruption of sexual activity caused by pregnancy.

The following excerpts are from interviews with the two couples whom we have followed in Chapter Two. Here they describe their experiences of labor and delivery.

Katherine and Mel, who were coping nicely at both previous interviews despite her continuing high level of anxiety, again did well at labor and delivery and seemed to be off to a good start with their new baby.

Interviewer: Tell me what happened.

Katherine: We knew I was in labor, but with me it goes slowly. We went to my doctor's appointment that day and sure enough, he said, "You're in labor. You can come into the hospital now, or better yet you can take a walk for a couple of hours with your husband, have breakfast, and then check yourself in." Which we did. It was delightful, a nice day. It was so pleasant, just walking. I knew I was in labor, and yet I didn't feel ready to be put into bed. Then we checked in at about twelve o'clock and the baby was born at six.

Interviewer: When did the speed of the labor increase?

Katherine: Even when I got here, things were pretty slow. Then, things picked up, they had me on an I.V., and the epidural was set up although they didn't give me any yet. And then the pitocin—Dr. Smith wanted me to have that, to speed things up. For me, they were going fast enough, but he wanted them to go faster. And then I was getting a little anxious. The girl who was putting in the epidural had some trouble with it. She tried four or five times, and she wasn't very nice about it. They say your husband can be with you, but during all these procedures they sent him away. That's the only criticism I have about the whole thing, that they sent him away. Anyway, they started giving me the pitocin, and things started going faster. And it felt like each contraction lasted about ten seconds, but it was really that I was just on top of them. And this went on for about an hour, with no complications, and I was ready to deliver, and then she came out and . . . oh!

[Pauses with a mixture of laughter and tears in her voice.] She's beautiful! And the doctor examined her yesterday and said that she's perfect, I'm fine and I can go home tomorrow. And I'm so thankful.

Interviewer: Do you see her as part of yourself or as a person outside of you?

Katherine: I see her as part of the family. I hadn't seen her as part of the family before. When she was big, the last couple of months, I started seeing her as a separate individual, but not knowing her, I didn't know where she fit in the family. But now I see her as one of us, as part of our family. She's just perfect, and she's just one of us. I just feel that, even before I see us all together.

Interviewer: I take it you're feeling fine?

Katherine: Yeah, I have some pains but they're all minor.

Interviewer: Is there anything else that you think would be useful for us to know?

Katherine: Just how close to her I feel already. She's just so sweet and precious and I feel that she's mine, even though I've known her for such a short time. She's just so special. [Laughs and cries.] She's just so calm and so nice. I don't have much milk yet; it's just coming in, and she's coping so well with that. She's nursing well and she seems to be content.

Katherine's adaptation represents what we consider optimal. The very real physical stresses of the delivery and the immediate postpartum period in no way interfered with her joyful appreciation of her new baby. She appeared in this interview to already have started to psychologically separate herself from her daughter and to integrate her into the family.

Jane, who earlier had difficulty expressing her needs and who was emotionally down during much of her pregnancy, reacted fairly positively to labor and delivery. For her, it was a time when she was experiencing something difficult and could thus legitimately ask for and accept the support and attention of those around her.

Interviewer: Tell me what it was like.

Jane: It went very fast. The contractions were coming faster and faster and stronger and stronger. In between I started shaking from nerves, uncontrollable shaking, so I had a shot of Valium to calm that. I was going through natural childbirth and the nurse was very helpful. You could study and practice for ninety years, but you need someone right there. I guess I was ready before they thought. The next thing I knew, my husband was in a yellow suit and everyone was wearing masks and garments. They put me into the delivery room and moved me onto the table. Sometimes I'd push well and other times I wasn't prepared enough. Finally she came and it was such a relief to have her out. It was a "zippo" compared to the first one. [Laughs.]

Interviewer: How *did* it compare to the first time.

Jane: This was much more painful and I wasn't in as much control, but it was so much shorter that it was better than the first.

Jane sounded mildly excited as she described these events and seemed very comfortable with how she handled herself.

Interviewer: What's the baby like?

Jane: She seems like a good baby. She doesn't cry much. She's a hungry baby, I guess, because of her size—she really gobbles the formula. When I heard she was a girl, I was delighted. I was just delighted in general—that it was finished, that she was a girl, that she was healthy.

Interviewer: What was your husband's role during labor and delivery?

Jane: Just having him in the room was very comforting. He held my hand and he brought ice chips,

which was very helpful. In the delivery room, he
helped with the breathing and he told me to
look when the baby was actually being born
so I wouldn't miss it. He was very supportive.
I think I would have panicked if he wasn't
there. When I needed him, he was able to do
whatever crazy thing I needed him to do. He
understood my gestures to do this or not do that
without my telling him.

This sensitivity to Jane's needs on the part of Ralph was
unusual in their relationship. It seemed to take an extreme situation like childbirth to bring the couple into close communication. Jane very much appreciated her husband's involvement
and felt good in general about how things went in the hospital.
She became more cautious, however, when thinking about the
future. When asked about her mood, she responded: "So far so
good. I don't know if it will be the same in a day or two. I don't
know what will happen. All I know is right now I'm all right."

Summary

It is noteworthy that not many factors from either early
or late pregnancy predicted obstetrical complications or maternal adaptation at the time of delivery. However, some of the factors which did predict more positive outcomes—lower levels of
anxiety, more positive feelings about motherhood, and a deeper
commitment to religion—raise provocative questions about the
integrated ways in which mind and body function.

The rather high percentage of caesarean births and of various kinds of obstetrical complications leads us to consider how
prepared women are for the realities of delivery: our data suggest that some degree of difficulty is at least statistically "normal" and to be expected. Obstetricians, obstetrical nurses, and
mental health professionals who see new mothers postpartum
must be prepared to deal with the women's feelings of disappointment and failure when the delivery has not gone smoothly.
Those who counsel or train women during pregnancy, instructors

of childbirth education classes, for example, might well be more frank about the realities of delivery today, so that women are better prepared.

In many ways, a birth is like a wedding. It is one of life's most important events and it is the focus of a great deal of emotional energy. It is the culmination of a period of planning and expectation and, at the same time, it is the beginning of a new phase of life. Those involved hope that all the details will fall into place and that the event will be a time of joyful celebration. However, just as the most wonderful wedding in the world is no guarantee of a good marriage, the effects of the delivery on the adaptation of the family, although still important at two months postpartum, are overshadowed and outweighed by other issues and concerns by the time the child is a year old.

⋙ 5 ⋘⋘⋘⋘⋘

Women at Two Months Postpartum

In our society, as in most, the arrival of a new baby is an occasion for celebration and ceremony, a time of renewal and expectation for the parents and for members of the extended family. However, the sense of specialness and awe contrasts quickly and sharply with the realities of the day-to-day care of the newborn. The period immediately following the baby's birth is a time of maximal upheaval and disruption, which is to be expected for several reasons. First, a newborn baby's physical needs and vulnerability make enormous demands on the parents' time, their emotions, and their energy. Second, because this helpless baby is also the newest member of the family, the other members must rearrange and change their own relationships in order to make room for him. For first-time parents, this adjustment, although exciting and wonderful in many ways, seems to be particularly difficult and absorbing, for the birth of their child represents a major disruption of the marital dyad. Parents with other children must cope with problems of sibling

78

rivalry and the increased number of demands on their finite resources.

Last, the period immediately after a baby's birth is often maximally disruptive and difficult because all of these adjustments, physical and emotional, follow so closely after another draining and difficult time, the last months of pregnancy and the delivery. Although a woman has been preparing herself for the impending birth for many months, the last stages of pregnancy, labor, and delivery are difficult times during which her emotional energy is often turned toward herself. In contrast, the postpartum period requires her to turn her energy outward, toward the new baby and toward the rearrangement of other family relationships. At a time of maximal fatigue and physical strain, this redirection of her emotions can indeed be a difficult and tumultuous undertaking.

Deutsch describes the psychological work of the postpartum period and the conflicts it includes in some detail: "After the unity [of pregnancy] has been split, two tendencies are present in the mother—one progressive, aiming at helping her ego to regain its rights, the other regressive, aiming at reunion with the child and the preservation of the psychic umbilical cord. . . . The fate of motherliness thus depends upon the result of the conflict of these opposite forces. An excess of fear of ego impoverishment produces flight from the child, failure of the bodily functions in the reproductive service, and inability to experience motherliness. On the other hand, excessive fear of losing the child will result in excessive devotion to him, too drastic a turning away from other interests, and a disposition to neurotic fears about the child" (1945, pp. 267–268). Pines (1972), in a sensitive and thoughtful elaboration of an aspect of the psychoanalytic perspective, emphasizes the importance of the mother's integration of her unconscious fantasies and the reality of her new baby.

With the exception of such theoretical statements from the psychoanalytic school, there is marked paucity of literature concerning the experience and emotional tasks of early motherhood. Up until quite recently, the main topics of research in this area were the effects on the infant of various maternal behaviors and the occurrence of severe postpartum depression or psychosis. Only recently have "normal" problems of adaptation to motherhood become an area of study (Rapoport, Rapoport, and Strelitz, 1977).

Incidence figures on postpartum difficulties are quite varied, ranging from one or two per one thousand births for psychotic reactions (Kaij and Nilsson, 1972) to as high as 65 percent (Pitt, 1968) for milder depressions or blues. Considerable debate continues about the etiological factors of postpartum difficulties, with some researchers arguing for the primacy of hormonal factors (Hamburg, Moos, and Yalom, 1968; Hamilton, 1962; Horsley, 1972; Melges, 1968; Tetlow, 1955), while others have placed more emphasis on psychosocial variables (M. B. Cohen, 1966; Deutscher, 1970; Gordon and Gordon, 1959; Gorsuch and Key, 1974; Nuckolls, Kasl, and Kaplan, 1972).

Studies of the normality of crisis and disequilibrium in the postpartum period, especially for first-time mothers, include Deutscher (1970), LeMasters (1957), and Rubin (1975). Shereshefsky and Yarrow (1973) judged around one third of the women in their sample to be having special difficulty postpartum, including such feelings as excessive anxiety or depressive feelings about their abilities to mother, overreaction to realistic problems, and hostile or punitive attitudes toward the infant. Factors which were predictive of more adequate postpartum adjustment included previous interest in and experience with children, visualization of self as a mother, and adaptation to each stage of pregnancy. During the postnatal period, the most important correlates of maternal adaptation were the current marital relationship and measures of the woman's nurturance and ego strength. In a similar vein, Meares, Grimwade, and Wood (1976) found anxiety and neuroticism during pregnancy to predict postpartum depression.

Finally, Leifer (1977), in her study of nineteen middle-class primiparous women, reported that immediately postpartum, her women were elated and euphoric, but quickly felt varying amounts of depression and anxiety. They described the first two months postpartum as extremely stressful; for more than two thirds of her sample, their dominant mood during this time was moderately to extremely negative.

From our conceptual perspective and with the literature in mind, we looked at our families at two months postpartum, intending to describe their situation and to relate aspects of their adaptation to their previous experience.

The Two-Month Postpartum Contact

At the two-month postpartum visit, we interviewed the parents individually, asking about their experience with their new baby, their feelings about themselves, and their feelings about their performance as parents. We also repeated several of the paper-and-pencil tests administered earlier, measures of anxiety, depression, and marital satisfaction. In addition, we tested and observed the infant's functioning and interaction with each parent during play and with the mother during a feeding.

The situations we observed at this time bore out our predictions about the difficulties and joys of the early postpartum period. The typical picture which we encountered was of a family in the process of reconstituting itself. Most of the emotional energies of the women, and to a somewhat lesser extent of the men, were still directed toward the care of the new infant. At the same time, we saw signs that the women were becoming aware, however dimly, once more of the world outside their homes. They commented about how involved they had been with the baby to the exclusion of their husband or other children, but that the situation was now returning to normal. Many women described vividly the difficulty of the time since delivery, but carefully stated that they felt "out of the woods" now. The research team often sensed that this was not quite true yet and that the emotional disequilibrium occasioned by the birth was still very much in evidence. We often felt that the women's premature attempt to present an image of complete recovery stemmed from the cultural stereotype about this period: that a well-functioning family experiences only the joys of having a newborn and is easily able to incorporate the arrival of a new baby. To have difficulty doing so, as most of our families had to

varying degrees, arouses the couple's fears of being a dysfunc-
tional family or the woman's fear that she is having an unnatural
psychopathological reaction. The cultural expectation that a few
months are sufficient for recovery from one of the most powerful experiences of life further burdens the new parents in their
struggle to readjust.

Regarding the mother at two months postpartum, we
were interested in exploring her sense of her own well-being, her
perceptions of her marriage, and her adaptation to her mothering role.

Psychological Adaptation

We appraised each woman's postpartum psychological
health in each of three categories: emotional well-being, anxiety,
and depression. These evaluations were based on the women's
scores on the repeated measures of anxiety and depression and
our clinical judgment of an interview with the mothers. During
the interview, we ascertained the mothers' current mood, level
of physical energy, sense of comfort with themselves, and awareness of themselves as separate from their babies. Table 2 shows
the correlations between the three aspects of the women's psychological adaptation—emotional well-being, anxiety, and depression—and various measures obtained at the first-trimester
contact, the eight-month contact, and the hospital contact.

Our findings indicate that, at two months, the women's
anxiety tended to be higher than at any other contact, although
still relatively low in an absolute sense. The depression scores
were lower for the group as a whole than they had been early in
the pregnancy. This is a puzzling finding in that both our clinical observations and the literature suggest that women are more
depressed at two months postpartum than they are during
pregnancy.

Both anxiety and depression at two months postpartum
were most related to the predictor variables that measure general psychological health and earlier marital satisfaction. As
expected, there is a high correlation between anxiety and depression in the first trimester and in the postpartum period;

similarly, there is a strong negative correlation between high scores on life adaptation, measured in the first trimester, and postpartum anxiety and depression. In addition, for the group as a whole, a higher degree of motivation for the pregnancy, as measured both in early and late pregnancy, predicted less postpartum anxiety and depression. We also found that those women we judged to have done well during the labor and delivery felt significantly less anxious and depressed two months later. Socioeconomic status was also related to postpartum adjustment, particularly for experienced mothers: women having more money and formal education felt less anxious than those having less. Current as well as previous marital satisfaction was also predictive of postpartum ease for the entire sample.

The clinical rating of a woman's emotional well-being, judged from the interviews, corroborates the findings obtained from the self-rating measures of anxiety and depression. The three background variables of the women predicting postpartum well-being were life adaptation, anxiety and depression levels throughout the pregnancy, and marital satisfaction.

Besides these findings concerning the group as a whole, there were some interesting differences between first-time and experienced mothers in their postpartum adjustment. These differences were most apparent in the interview scores. For first-time mothers, more variables concerning previous psychological and marital adjustment were predictive of our clinical rating of greater postpartum well-being. In addition, two psychological issues specific to the childbearing situation, motivation for the pregnancy measured at eight months and adaptation to labor and delivery, were predictive of adaptation at two months for first-time mothers only.

The emotional task of adjusting to one's first baby is an enormously difficult one, at least partially because a woman must enlarge her identity to include the role of mother and integrate this new role into her sense of herself. This change in basic sense of self is not required of a woman who is already a mother and adds another child to her family. Although the experienced mother must cope with the physical work required by her newborn, her psychological work does not include the

Table 2. Women's Psychological Adaptation at Two Months Postpartum

	Emotional Well-Being			Anxiety			Depression		
	All Mothers[a]	First-Time Mothers[b]	Experienced Mothers[c]	All Mothers[a]	First-Time Mothers[b]	Experienced Mothers[c]	All Mothers[a]	First-Time Mothers[b]	Experienced Mothers[c]
First trimester									
Psychological dimension									
Life adaptation	.33[c]	-.36[a]	.32	-.28[a]	-.28	-.29	-.38[c]	-.40[a]	-.37[a]
Anxiety	-.31[b]	-.48[b]	-.27	.63[c]	.65[c]	.61[c]	.56[c]	.63[c]	.52[b]
Depression	-.38[c]	-.37[a]	-.38[a]	.42[c]	.37[a]	.48[c]	.48[c]	.58[c]	.41[a]
Conscious motivation	.14	.28	.01	-.23[a]	-.18	-.29	-.22[a]	-.21	-.25
Adaptation to pregnancy	.22	.16	.28	-.18	-.22	-.14	-.16	-.20	-.14
Physiological dimension									
Premenstrual tension	-.18	-.09	-.20	.30[b]	.24	.38[a]	.22	.20	.27
Sociocultural dimension									
Socioeconomic status	-.02	-.08	.02	.28[a]	.08	.39[a]	.18	-.06	.31
Years married	-.01	-.31	.14	.06	.38[a]	-.20	-.05	.26	-.26
Social support	-.20	-.36[a]	.02	.16	.15	.19	.16	.23	.12
Age	-.03	.08	-.19	-.08	-.03	-.19	-.14	-.01	-.27
Marital dimension									
Marital adjustment	.22	.56[c]	-.06	.38[c]	-.60[c]	-.21	-.37[c]	-.57[c]	-.24
Marital style	.12	.20	.11	-.14	-.16	-.09	-.16	-.22	-.16

Eighth month of pregnancy									
Anxiety	-.35[b]	-.42[b]	-.46[b]	.65[c]	.58[c]	.74[c]	.52[c]	.48[b]	.55[b]
Symptoms	-.13	-.19	-.09	.34[b]	.28	.40[a]	.23	.16	.29
Adaptation to pregnancy	.15	.21	.05	-.03	.00	-.08	-.10	-.17	-.01
Life change	-.15	-.11	-.35	.21	-.04	.53[b]	.18	-.02	.40[a]
Conscious motivation	.17	.44[b]	.01	-.37[b]	-.50[b]	-.29	-.35[b]	-.36[a]	-.37[a]
Couple's preparedness	.19	.31	.18	-.08	-.06	-.16	-.30[a]	-.27	-.34
Labor and delivery									
Complications	.01	-.12	.13	.12	.24	.11	.02	.06	.01
Caesarean section	.00	-.19	.14	.19	.32	.20	.06	.21	-.11
Adaptation to labor	.15	.41[a]	.01	-.39[b]	-.56[b]	-.20	-.31[a]	-.38	-.22

Note: These correlations are based on the following samples: For first-time mothers, N ranges from 23 to 37; for experienced mothers, N ranges from 21 to 38; for all mothers, N ranges from 50 to 74.

[a] $p \leq .05$, two-tailed

[b] $p \leq .01$, two-tailed

[c] $p \leq .001$, two-tailed

stressful task of changing and reorganizing her basic identity. We are speculating that for this reason psychological health at two months postpartum related so strongly to a number of general psychological measures, as well as to pregnancy-related characteristics, for first-time but not for experienced mothers. Similarly, previous marital satisfaction in early pregnancy correlated to well-being for first-time but not for experienced mothers in our sample. This finding concurs with and expands on conclusions reached by Wenner and Cohen (1968) and Wenner and others (1969). In those two studies of first pregnancies, they found that a strong marriage was an essential prerequisite for an adaptive pregnancy.

As compared to first-time mothers, experienced mothers seem more vulnerable to external pressures and factors, as shown by our finding that socioeconomic status and recent life stresses measured at eight months were predictors of anxiety or depression postpartum for experienced but not for first-time mothers. One wonders if the primiparous women are so engrossed in their efforts to adapt their self-image and to learn the complex mothering tasks that they are somehow insulated, in these first few months, from effects of external factors. The experienced mothers appear to be less occupied by such internal issues and might have more available energy and attention to notice and to respond emotionally to external issues.

Although a discussion of the data about the husbands is reserved for Chapters Seven and Eight, it seems appropriate to mention several findings here since aspects of the husbands' behavior during pregnancy related to the postpartum adaptation of their wives. Men who were initially more anxious (although not necessarily coping less well with the tasks of adulthood) had wives who themselves were significantly more anxious and depressed at two months. Even when the wives' initial anxiety levels were statistically controlled, the husbands' anxiety during the first trimester predicted significantly the women's anxiety at two months. Similarly, a husband's level of anxiety at the eighth-month interview predicted to his wife's depression and anxiety in the early postpartum period, even when the wives' eighth month anxiety levels were statistically controlled. Pragmatically, then, a husband's early anxiety level is a strong predictor of his wife's postpartum adjustment. As we found at labor and delivery, a man's ability to support his wife through pregnancy and childbirth is of central importance to her postpartum adjustment.

Thus we found significant relationships between a woman's psychological adaptation at two months postpartum—as measured by anxiety, depression, and well-being—and predictor variables from each of the major dimensions measured early in pregnancy—the psychological, physiological, sociocultural, and marital. The following excerpts from two postpartum interviews depict the daily situation of the families and illustrate some of the differences between first-time and experienced mothers.

Katherine, whom we have introduced in previous chapters, already had two children, aged three and five, when her third child arrived. As mentioned before, although she was originally considering returning to work, when she discovered that she was pregnant, she anticipated the birth of her child with pleasure. As the interview illustrates, she greatly enjoyed her other two children and also felt a great deal of support from her very attentive and involved husband. At two months postpartum, we found Katherine very busy coping with everyone's needs, yet cheerful and pleased with her life and her expanded family. As our data suggest, as a multiparous woman she did not seem to have to devote much emotional energy to the readjustment to herself, her identity, or her marriage. Her sense of herself as a mother was already so firmly established that she seemed able to devote herself fully to the practical demands of her family. Although she was not able to attend to her husband with as much devotion as previously, she had a sense, shared by many of our experienced mothers, that the upheaval caused by her new baby was temporary and that she, as well as the others, would adjust, survive, and grow as a family.

Interviewer: What's it like having another child in the family?
Katherine: It's great! I'm enjoying her very much. The first two or three weeks weren't such fun. I had a re-

lapse and was confined to bed for three or four days, bleeding heavily, and I had to take ergotrate. The doctor didn't say I had to stay in bed. I think I overreacted a little bit, so it was very hard on everyone. It was tense for a couple of weeks, but once that was over, it just kept getting better and better, and now it's fine.

Interviewer: Are you physically recovered?

Katherine: Physically feeling well. I'm still fat. [Laughs.]

Although she said this laughingly, her weight did bother Katherine, as it does most women, and only many months later was she able to address her weight problem and to begin to feel good about her body. Pregnancy is a major assault on a woman's body and her physical self-image. For women in our culture, with its emphasis on physical attractiveness, returning to their former weight and shape represents a major step in the postpartum recovery.

Interviewer: But you're not tired anymore?

Katherine: No. I'm tired if I get up at night with her, but otherwise, no.

Interviewer: What do you do about that?

Katherine: I go to bed when she goes to bed, at eight or nine o'clock. But things are really good. It's easier than I thought, cause she's a good girl. And the other kids are so great with her.

Interviewer: Would you say that things are back to normal in the household, some new routines established?

Katherine: Almost back to normal. I think what's hard on my other kids is that we used to go out a lot, to playgrounds or lakes, almost every day, and we've had to slow down on that a lot. When Mel comes home, if she's screaming, that's her fussy time, then things will get tense. But we're trying to do what we normally have done, and she's good. So I guess things are pretty well back.

For Katherine, as for other experienced mothers, there was at least the possibility of a return to what feels normal and customary, whereas for first-time parents there is a sense that what used to be "normal" for them is irretrievably behind them.

Interviewer: How is it for Mel seeing you with another baby?

Katherine: I think he's happier than he thought he would be, too. Sometimes he'll get a little irritated, like when he comes home and wants to talk about work and I'm just so effusive about Lenore and what the other kids are doing. If anything, I'm too much into her and I haven't been able to give enough to the other kids and to Mel.

Interviewer: I was going to ask you that; how do you juggle your responsibilities as a mother of three and as a wife?

Katherine: I find it hard, especially now that I recognize that I haven't been neglecting Lenore—if anything, it's the other kids—and Mel's on the bottom.

Interviewer: Do you have any help with work around the house?

Katherine: For the first two weeks, I had a homemaker, full-time. Then she came one day a week after that, but that's mainly for babysitting so that I can go out and do errands.

Interviewer: Do you have any time for yourself?

Katherine: We were just talking about that. I don't have any teenage baby sitters that I would leave Lenore with, so it's a problem. Now it's getting better. She's on a better schedule at night, so I'll be able to leave her then, and during the day I can have a high school student take her for a walk. Then I can be with the other kids and do something.

Interviewer: Do you mind not having time for yourself?

Katherine: Well, the weather's been so good, that I haven't minded it too much. And Mel has been so great.

	He'll come home and take over, and I can get out for a couple of hours.
Interviewer:	What do you do with that time?
Katherine:	[Laughs.] Well usually, it's errands, like grocery shopping or clothes shopping. I haven't been to meetings or to anything else.
Interviewer:	What was it like the first time you left Lenore with somebody else?
Katherine:	I felt good. I remember calling to see if she was ready to be nursed yet, but I felt so fine being out and feeling good. I went to a little art gallery and that felt really good.

Katherine has been able to adjust quite well to having a new baby. She seemed to be directing a special kind of emotional attention toward her new daughter in order to establish a close and individualized relationship with her. She knew that she has had to neglect her relationships with the other family members but she seemed to feel that her family could tolerate this temporary diversion of her attention. Although Katherine has not had much time for herself and she used what little time she had for the family's errands, she took this in stride, knowing that this was a temporary state of affairs and therefore one which she need not struggle against. Her acceptance of this temporary upheaval seemed to enhance her ability to enjoy her new baby and to devote herself rather unambivalently to her.

The next excerpt presents a less rosy picture and is not atypical of normal families in the postpartum period. This couple was quite articulate in describing their distress; we sense that many of our families could not express, but shared, at least some of their feelings.

Pamela and Al were first-time parents who had felt ambivalent about having a child before and during the pregnancy. Pamela had been very involved in her work and expressed concern about the effect a child would have on her career. Neither parent strongly desired to have children of their own and yet, at the same time, they both, and especially Al, seemed to feel that they *should* have at least one child.

At the two-months postpartum interview, we found Pamela able to talk readily about her continued distress and ambivalence about being a mother. She described vividly her sense of being overwhelmed and upset by her new role and the amount of work it entailed. At that time, the researchers observed her behavior with her baby and rated her as doing about average. Her other scores, however, reflected how great her distress was relative to the other mothers. Her struggles with her new baby and her attempts to master her anxiety are evident in the interview.

Interviewer: In general, how's it going?

Pamela: It has been really incredible, it's really rough. I really think I was ill-prepared for the intensity of having a demanding, needy infant twenty-four hours a day. I came home [from the hospital] not feeling particularly well in the beginning, I felt really disoriented. It's getting better now that some of the physical problems are being resolved—they're not really problems, but just the care, like twenty bowel movements a day. I could change his diaper four times in the space of fifteen minutes. You learn not to kill yourself that way. And the breast-feeding took a long time to establish itself, and just now I'm beginning to feel that it's more worth it than not. For a long time, it just seemed to be not worth the hassle and I was feeling "Why did I do this, I must be crazy." It didn't seem to be helping him and I wasn't physically feeling well, I felt drained and I was leaking and engorged a lot. So just now, in the past week, I've been feeling better and happier and less harassed. But I can't say that it's been a joyful experience. Everyone says it's wonderful and that the child brings so much joy but it's hard to see that joy in the first few months.

Interviewer: Are you still feeling tired?

Pamela: Yes. I don't get enough sleep. I don't take naps, and that's a problem, but I feel that I can't. When he's sleeping, I have to use that precious time to take care of things I need to do. So I just sleep at night which is part of it; I'm still tired.

Interviewer: What are you doing to help yourself to feel better?

Pamela: One thing is to get someone to come in to help one day a week. I started going back to work one day a week for a six-hour stretch and that helped mentally—just getting out and not having the feeling that he's utterly dependent on me. And just doing something productive besides being with the baby. It's made a lot of difference and I feel much better about it. Physically, I'm more tired after working when I come home, but it's helping mentally. That's the main thing I've done to help myself feel better.

Interviewer: Who's doing what in the house?

Pamela: I'm doing most of the feeding, although Al gives Tommy a supplementary bottle. The other things like diapering and putting him to bed, we sort of share. But Al is home much less than I am, so of course most of the responsibility falls on me. Nobody takes care of the house and Al does most of the food shopping and dinners.

Interviewer: How do you think it's been for Al seeing you as a mother?

Pamela: I know it was hard for him in the beginning, not so much seeing me as a mother but seeing me so anxious and tense. I was really in bad shape for about three or four weeks. I really didn't believe in postpartum depression. I thought you could avoid it if you're smart and you know enough about it. And that was hard for him because he's used to seeing me cope, and I wasn't coping. Him seeing me as a mother? Sometimes I think that he's a little disappointed that I'm not more motherly and maternal. Sometimes I think that he worries that I don't love Tommy as much as I should. And that's [the love] been slow in coming, the maternal feelings of joy and love for this child who, to this point, has just been taking and taking and taking. I think he's a little disappointed in that but he hasn't said that.

Interviewer: How have things changed for you since having the baby?

Pamela: Just that all my energy is going into this child, and there's nothing left over to even think about anything else. I've always thought of myself as someone with a lot of interests, but they've all fallen by the wayside right now. And not having any predictable time is a change for me; I'm used to having that. And it's upset me.

Interviewer: How are you juggling your responsibilities as a mother and as a wife? Do you feel a conflict?

Pamela: Yes, I do. And I feel bad about that. Right now Al has been displaced, not only by the time I spend with Tommy but also by what I'm thinking about. Al will come home and want to talk about work and all I want to talk about is the latest thing with the baby and I feel there's been some deterioration in that sense of our couple-ness. It bothers me, and I don't know what we're going to do about that. I think that it's something that you get back to after a while, but at this point there's been a real displacement and it's not one that I wanted to make. It's not like I love the baby more than Al, but just that he's so needy and demanding that there's no energy left over for anything else.

Interviewer: Do you have any time for yourself?

Pamela: Very little, except for the day that I go to work. But that's work time and it's different from time to sit down and read a magazine, and I have very little of that. [She then says that they have been seeing friends, and feels that they've been doing too much of that too soon, thereby aggravating her exhaustion.]

Interviewer: Now, you say you're working one day a week?

Pamela: This week, I'm going up to two days. And that's important, it's really liberating. I can see that everyone's still living their lives and that there's a world out there. That's helpful to remember. Your world becomes so tiny and so narrow and you forget that there's a functioning world out there.

Interviewer: How did you feel leaving the baby the first time?

Pamela: I had no conflicts about it at all. I wanted to. And that's something I wonder about, that I had no qualms at all about leaving him. I just wanted to get out. That's when I think Al is a little disappointed in me for not feeling more for Tommy, not being more maternal.

Interviewer: Do you worry about how the baby's doing?

Pamela: No, I just assume he's doing everything at the right time and that he's all right.

Pamela's description of her feelings suggests that she is most comfortable when she is involved with external reality and the "world outside" and that the regressive pull of new motherhood is acutely distressing to her sense of herself as a competent individual. In an effort to preserve her own identity, she seems to be actively struggling against the "psychic umbilical cord" which Deutsch (1945) describes. This struggle is most evident in her decision to double her time working outside the home in spite of her acknowledged exhaustion and sense of being overwhelmed by the demands of her baby. Pamela needs to be able to feel more comfortable about herself in the context of her relationship with her child and to understand emotionally that an intense closeness with her child need not necessarily require the destruction of her own ego.

Marital Adaptation at Two Months Postpartum

At the two-month visit, as at all previous visits, we were interested in finding out how our participants' marriages were faring. At this time, we again administered the marital adjustment scale, and during our clinical interview we asked the women how they felt about their husbands at that time and how comfortable they were with issues such as their division of domestic chores, the amount of time they had for each other, and the state of their struggle to maintain some sense of "coupleness" while integrating a new baby into the family.

Overall, the marriages were going well, as they had been before. First-time and experienced mothers were not different from each other in their evaluation of their marriages, in contrast to their assessments at previous contacts. At the beginning of the pregnancies, first-time mothers had rated themselves as more satisfied with their marriages than had experienced mothers, but by two months postpartum, the first-time mothers felt less satisfied and the experienced mothers somewhat more satisfied, thus reaching an approximately equivalent level.

Looking at the sample as a whole, at least one major variable from each of the four predictor dimensions related significantly to marital adjustment at two months postpartum (see Table 3). Women who were judged in the first trimester to have better life adaptation, and less anxiety, and who used more stereotypically feminine adjectives to describe themselves—all variables from the psychological dimension—were more satisfied with their marriages at the two-month contact. In addition, women with lower levels of premenstrual tension, higher socioecnomic status, and higher marital adjustment early in pregnancy, also had a better marital adjustment at two months. In short, marital happiness seems to be a relatively sensitive barometer for other assets and liabilities in a woman's life. Not surprisingly, then, pregnancy-related symptoms measured in the last trimester, adaptation to labor and delivery, and the two-months postpartum measure of the mother's emotional well-being, anxiety, and depression all were related significantly to her marital satisfaction.

Table 3. Women's Marital Adaptation at Two Months Postpartum

	Marital Adjustment			Adaptation to Spouse		
	All Mothers[a]	First-Time Mothers[b]	Experienced Mothers[c]	All Mothers[a]	First-Time Mothers[b]	Experienced Mothers[c]
First trimester						
Psychological dimension						
Life adaptation	.27[a]	.18	.44[b]	.18	.33	-.07
Anxiety	-.31[b]	-.25	-.42[b]	-.06	-.20	.02
Depression	-.22	-.23	-.23	-.08	-.02	-.12
Masculinity	.22	.19	.31	-.02	-.17	.21
Femininity	.23[a]	.14	.37[a]	-.04	-.10	.04
Adaptation to pregnancy	.16	.06	.28	.32[b]	.30	.35
Physiological dimension						
Premenstrual tension	-.31[b]	.00	-.40[a]	-.01	-.24	.03
Marital dimension						
Marital adjustment	.49[c]	.77[c]	.25	.24[a]	.35[a]	.11
Sexual activity and satisfaction	.06	-.19	.45[b]	.13	-.28	.07
Marital style	.10	.23	.10	.28[a]	.28	.29
Sociocultural dimension						
Socioeconomic status	-.46[c]	-.42[b]	-.55[c]	-.14	-.04	-.24
Women's occupation	-.35[b]	-.30	-.61[b]	.06	.09	.04
Age	.15	.18	.04	.15	.35[a]	-.01

	1	2	3	4	5
Eighth month of pregnancy					
Anxiety	-.21	-.40[a]	-.03	-.18	.03
Symptoms	-.37[b]	-.42[a]	-.05	-.15	.07
Conscious motivation	.19	.06	.15	.44[a]	-.11
Labor and delivery					
Maternal adaptation to labor and delivery	.28[a]	.02	.05	.28	-.15
Individuation	-.05	.33	-.06	-.06	-.17
Two months postpartum					
Mother's emotional well-being	.29[a]	.05	.29[a]	.43[b]	.10
Anxiety	-.48[c]	-.43[b]	-.15	-.35[a]	.09
Depression	-.42[c]	-.39[a]	-.33[b]	-.44[b]	-.26
Marital adjustment	—	—	.26[a]	.31	.18
Adaptation to spouse	.25	.18	—	—	—
Observed maternal adaptation	.05	-.34	.04	.20	-.13
Interview measure of maternal adaptation	.12	.00	.26[a]	.44[b]	.03
Reciprocity	-.08	-.30	.07	.38[a]	-.38[a]

Note: These correlations are based on the following samples: For first-time mothers, N ranges from 23 to 37; for experienced mothers, N ranges from 31 to 36; for all mothers, N ranges from 49 to 72.

[a] p ≤ .05, two-tailed
[b] p ≤ .01, two-tailed
[c] p ≤ .001, two-tailed

There are some interesting differences at this point between first-time and experienced mothers. Factors predicting only to the former's postpartum marital adjustment included marital adjustment (first trimester), conscious motivation for the pregnancy (at eight months), adaptation to labor and delivery, and a woman's emotional well-being (at two months postpartum). In contrast, for experienced mothers only, their anxiety at both the first trimester and later in pregnancy, their general life adaptation, their femininity, their levels of premenstrual tension, and their sexual activity and satisfaction measured early in pregnancy—but not their marital adjustment— were related to postpartum marital adjustment.

These data support our observation that the pregnancy-related variables are the primary predictors of marital adjustment for first-time mothers, whereas for the experienced mothers, factors reflecting more enduring personality characteristics are more important to the marriage at two months. These data thus also support our speculation that for first-time mothers, pregnancy and birth are more emotionally consuming and affect the woman's adjustment to her marriage as well as to herself, at least as soon after the birth as two months. In contrast, for women who have previously experienced childbirth, the more enduring variables such as anxiety, general psychological adaptation, and femininity are more predictive of postpartum marital adjustment. In other words, the psychological reverberations of the pregnancy and delivery themselves seem to have less effect on multiparous women than on primiparous women.

It is somewhat surprising that for first-time mothers, their psychological health measured early in pregnancy did not predict their marital adjustment at two months postpartum. For this sample, comprised primarily of relatively healthy women, the crisis of becoming a mother seems sufficiently consuming that factors relating exclusively to the pregnancy are most important to adjustment in the early postpartum period. It seems likely that once the crisis has passed, more enduring characteristics would begin to exert their influence on the women's adaptation.

The second measure of the quality of the marriage at two months, adaptation to the spouse, was determined from the interviewers' clinical ratings of how the women felt about their own and their husband's adjustments to the parenting tasks at this early point.

Although several measures predicted adaptation to the spouse for the sample as a whole, when the first-time and experienced mothers are looked at separately, scores on this variable were predicted by earlier measures only for the first-time mothers. There are no relations to any other variables for the experienced mothers (see Table 3, "Adaptation to Spouse"). Again, it seems that for experienced mothers, issues related to parenting have already been essentially settled and are now relatively independent from other issues. For first-time mothers, in comparison, the role of parent is a new one and the style and quality of that role seems to depend more strongly on the psychological and experiential resources (or lack of them) with which the woman and her husband approach it. Of the primiparous women, those who were older, those with greater marital satisfaction in early pregnancy, and those with greater motivation for the pregnancy at eight months reported themselves happier with their husbands at this time.

In sum, marital adjustment seems to be jostled considerably by the first pregnancy and birth. In light of the distressing current divorce statistics, it seems reasonable to suggest that well-planned programs of support and education in parenting offered to first-time parents should attempt to mute those stresses and vicissitudes by encouraging couples to be mutually supportive, rather than destructive, during this difficult and crucial time. Shereshefsky and Yarrow (1973) and Cowan and others (1979) report substantial success in their work with couples from early in the first pregnancy to sometime in the first postpartum year.

The two-month postpartum interview with Pamela shows more dramatically than do our quantitative data the changes in her marriage caused by the birth of her first child. Like most of our couples at this time, Pamela and Al found little time to be together as a couple. They felt this period to be a disintegration, albeit temporary, of their relationship.

Interviewer: What's your husband like as a father?

Pamela: I think he's pretty good. I'm disappointed that he hasn't taken as much responsibility as I had hoped. But that also has to do with my not letting him, you know, I know the best way to put on the diaper and to do other things. He's pretty good. I thought he'd be much more squeamish about picking up the baby and taking care of him, but he's not. And I feel relieved about going off and leaving the baby with him. And I actually feel he's more sensitive than I am to a lot of Tommy's stages and what he's going through and stuff like that.

Interviewer: How do you think he's feeling about having the baby?

Pamela: Oh, I think he's very pleased. Except, like myself, neither of us had realized the amount of work and energy that it would consume, and I think he's been thrown by that too.

Interviewer: What's it like for you as a couple?

Pamela: Oh, difficult. We haven't had much time together; we haven't gone out in the evening yet together. I think our coupleness has disintegrated—temporarily—but without time for ourselves, it's really hard. We just don't sit down anymore and talk about what's happening. He's had a lot of changes at work, and I haven't been able to listen and talk about it. And I'm mad at myself about it too because I had thought that wouldn't happen with us, and it has.

Interviewer: Have you had intercourse yet?

Pamela: No, I need to get birth control, but also there's some resistance to it.

Interviewer: Would you say you've been experiencing strain in your marriage?

Pamela: No, it's not strain. It's that I miss the closeness we had as a twosome; there's a third person around now. I miss something that we had that's missing with a third person. Sometimes I wonder if it will come back, because the two of us are focusing on him a lot instead of each other.

Katherine and Mel seemed to be experiencing a similar overload in their commitment to their children and a similar absence of time available for each other. But Katherine's interpretation of this state of affairs was quite different from Pamela's in that, although she and her husband spent less time together, their basic emotional commitment to each other remained intact. As an "old hand" at parenting, Katherine knew from experience that things would change and they would have more time for each other again.

Interviewer: What's your husband been like with the baby?

Katherine: He's enjoyed her. He gets up in the middle of the night and changes her and brings her to me for nursing. I've left him with the three children and he manages okay. Oftentimes, when I leave the baby with him, she's fussy, and I can always nurse her and he can't. So I don't think he sees her as being as good as I see her. She can be great all day, and when he comes home, she might fuss for half an hour and the whole family will be crazy.

Interviewer: Is his role with her about the same as it was with the other kids when they were this age?

Katherine: I think he was more involved with the other kids when they were babies, cause there was more time. Now the other kids make demands on him. He'll try to hold Lenore, but it seems when we're both here, I'm spending time with the baby and he's with the older kids.

Interviewer: Are you comfortable with his degree of involvement?

Katherine: Yes.

Interviewer: Have you two had any time together yet?

Katherine: No, we played tennis one morning, but that's all. That's why we're going away for a week. It will be more relaxing and he won't have to work.

Interviewer: Are you two experiencing any strain in your relationship?

Katherine: I'd say it hasn't been ideal yet, since the pregnancy. It's been so hectic. I think I'm happier than he is. He works hard all day and comes home and the whole family converges on him and he's so good and so devoted to us that he's exhausted as a result. And when he has ten minutes of his own at home, he has his office work to do. We make so many demands on him. So I think he's not enjoying the situation as much as I am. I have the days that are so relaxing, as you can see, and he doesn't have that.

Interviewer: Are you doing anything about the strain he's experiencing?

Katherine: I'm trying. I say, "Leave Daddy alone, he's tired", or "Go play, Daddy and I have to talk." Or we'll close the door on Lenore. We both wish we had more time together, and we wish we weren't so tired. It's getting better and certainly our relationship hasn't changed. We're still very kind and good to each other and very communicative. But sometimes I feel like I can't listen to him. He'll come home and want to talk about what's going on in the office, or the world, and I'm talking about Lenore. But I'm coming out of it now.

Maternal Adaptation

Distinguishing the two-month postpartum visit from the previous ones was, of course, the presence of the babies. All the families were actively involved in the task of integrating their new offspring into the family, and at this visit we were able to observe closely the vicissitudes of this complex, and at times trying, task. We chose to visit the families at two months in order to observe them after the initial upheaval had passed, yet before they had settled into comfortable routines. We felt that observations at this time would yield valuable insight into the crisis of childbearing.

Besides readjusting her own self-image and relationship to her husband, the postpartum woman also must establish a relationship with her new baby. We measured the quality of this relationship in three ways. From observing the mother's interaction with the baby, we assessed the quality of her mothering on a number of subscales, including her acceptance of the infant, her sensitivity to its needs, her apparent affect while she was handling the baby, and the like. Second, we observed a feeding—bottle or breast—and rated the reciprocity between mother and infant. This reciprocity score is made up of nine subscales, including evaluations of the locus of control during the feedings, the mother's timing of stimulation during the feeding, and other such factors. Third, we conducted a rather extensive clinical interview concerning the mother's feelings about her child and how well she felt she was coping with the baby. These interviews were evaluated on the same subscales as the observation. From these measures we obtained a rather full picture of each woman's maternal functioning. The women were enjoying their infants, by and large, and showed themselves to be skilled at mothering. On the whole, they were loving and empathically sensitive, and at least moderately confident about their abilities to nurture their new infants.

Table 4 presents the correlations between variables measured earlier and our three measures of maternal adaptation. What is most striking is that, for the group as a whole, none of the earlier variables is significant in predicting observed adaptation. Of the measures obtained at two months postpartum, only the woman's maternal adaptation, as judged from her report during the interview, and the degree of reciprocity maintained with the infant during a feeding related to observed adaptation.

A few relationships appear when data for first-time and experienced mothers are looked at separately. First-time mothers who were more depressed early in pregnancy or at the two-

Table 4. Women's Maternal Adaptation at Two Months Postpartum

	Observed Maternal Adaptation			Interview Measure of Maternal Adaptation			Reciprocity		
	All Mothers[a]	First-Time Mothers[b]	Experienced Mothers[c]	All Mothers[a]	First-Time Mothers[b]	Experienced Mothers[c]	All Mothers[a]	First-Time Mothers[b]	Experienced Mothers[c]
First trimester									
Psychological dimension									
Life adaptation	.00	.10	-.02	.01	.15	-.18	.12	.44[b]	-.20
Anxiety	.07	-.17	.23	-.10	-.28	.10	.01	-.15	.09
Depression	-.17	-.39[a]	-.01	-.13	-.14	-.14	-.12	-.23	-.01
Masculinity	-.16	.18	-.51[c]	-.08	-.16	.01	-.02	.03	-.08
Femininity	.03	.09	-.03	.16	.19	.12	-.02	-.14	.10
Marital dimension									
Marital adjustment	.02	.26	-.15	.14	.10	-.03	.08	.05	.08
Sexual activity and satisfaction	-.13	-.05	-.20	-.10	-.12	-.09	-.33[b]	-.41[a]	-.26
Marital style	-.13	.30	-.36[a]	.05	.05	.03	.14	.41[a]	-.10
Years married	-.08	-.29	-.23	-.10	-.31	.12	.01	-.11	.14
Sociocultural dimension									
Socioeconomic status	.14	.00	.21	.17	.16	.20	.10	-.01	.18
Age	.14	.36[a]	-.16	.03	.10	.00	.30[b]	.47[b]	.22
Eighth month of pregnancy									
Anxiety	-.11	-.15	-.07	-.33[b]	-.38[a]	-.25	-.07	-.18	-.06
Symptoms	-.08	-.30	.14	.03	-.05	.15	-.15	-.41[a]	.13
Couple preparedness	.03	-.15	.16	.03	.12	-.07	-.23	-.36[a]	-.03

Labor and delivery									
Maternal adaptation to labor and delivery	.26	.39	.16	.46[c]	.62[c]	.24	.23	.10	.45[a]
Two months postpartum									
Emotional well-being	.23	.32	.17	.49[c]	.56[c]	.49[b]	.15	.36[a]	-.07
Anxiety	-.10	-.28	.03	-.32[b]	-.42[b]	-.20	-.12	-.27	-.01
Depression	-.23	-.50[b]	-.04	-.46[c]	-.58[c]	-.32	-.11	-.44[b]	.11
Marital adjustment	.05	.30	-.34	.12	.20	.00	-.08	.09	-.30
Adaptation to spouse	.04	.20	-.13	.26[a]	.44[b]	.03	.07	.38[a]	-.38[a]
Observed maternal adaptation	—	—	—	.48[c]	—	—	.63[c]	—	—
Interview measure of maternal adaptation	.49[c]	.45[b]	.55[c]	.44[c]	.43[b]	-.49[b]	.63[c]	.43[b]	.49[b]
Reciprocity	.63[c]	.69[c]	.61[c]	.44[c]	.43[b]	.49[b]	—	—	—

Note: These correlations are based on the following samples: For first-time mothers, N ranges from 23 to 36; for experienced mothers, N ranges from 23 to 39; for all mothers, N ranges from 50 to 72.

[a] $p \leq .05$, two-tailed
[b] $p \leq .01$, two-tailed
[c] $p \leq .001$, two-tailed

months contact and those who were younger appeared to be doing less well with their infants. For experienced mothers, a greater degree of self-reported masculinity and a more egalitarian marital style are negatively correlated with the quality of their observed mothering.

Possibly, more feminine and more traditional women approach more closely the cultural stereotype of good mothering, with the required selflessness and relative lack of differentiation at two months, than more masculine women and women who have negotiated more egalitarian marriages. Whether this latter style is less adaptive at later stages of childrearing remains to be seen.

More significant findings emerged from the interview measure of the women's maternal adaptation. The women's descriptions of themselves, of course, reflect their own definitions of the qualities of good mothering, their self-images, and their individual styles in describing themselves. For the group as a whole, none of the variables from the first contact predicted maternal adaptation as judged from the interview. From the eighth-month measures, those women who had been more anxious and those who experienced more anger toward their fetuses were judged to be less adequate at mothering at two months postpartum. Of the measures taken after delivery, those women who felt they had handled the experience less well were later rated as handling their babies less well also. This is consistent with Leifer's (1977) finding that women who are more negative toward the fetus during pregnancy appear less attached in the postpartum period. No variable relating to general psychological health was found to relate to postpartum maternal adjustment for the group as a whole.

Several aspects of the women's adaptation measured concurrently at two months related to the interview measure of maternal adaptation. For the group as a whole, maternal adaptation was correlated with emotional well-being, absence of anxiety and depression, good marital adjustment, and the physiological health of the baby. From these findings, we cannot determine whether a woman's good feelings about herself enable her to better handle her baby or whether competency at handling her baby affects her emotional well-being. It seems most likely that each aspect of the system—mother, baby, and couple —both enhances and is enhanced by every aspect. Conversely, when one aspect, such as the marriage or the baby's temperament, is somewhat troublesome, all other aspects of the system are affected.

For first-time mothers only, their adaptation to labor and delivery was strongly predictive of better maternal adjustment at two months, as assessed by the interview. Neither this nor any other variable from the early contacts predicted for experienced mothers.

For our third measure of maternal adaptation, the reciprocity the mother maintained with her infant during a feeding, once again more variables related for first-time than experienced mothers. For the group as a whole, and for first-time mothers, older women and women who were less sexually active and satisfied early in pregnancy showed greater mother-infant reciprocity at two months postpartum. In addition, first-time mothers whose general life adaptation was better, those who had more egalitarian marriages, and those who felt better about themselves and in their new role at two months postpartum were judged to be relating more closely and reciprocally at two months. For experienced mothers, favorable adaptation to labor and delivery, and unfavorable adaptation to their spouse at two months postpartum predicted higher levels of reciprocity.

Both this last finding, as well as the one relating to sexual activity in first-time mothers, are consistent with Baxter's (1974) finding that women who breast-fed their infants had a lower frequency of sexual intercourse and orgasm in the early postpartum months. Similarly, Fox (1979) found that single women having babies felt less stress in the early postpartum weeks if they were less involved with a man. Clearly a certain kind of merged closeness with one's infant is incompatible with an intense closeness with one's husband. Indeed, these data seem to support Deutsch's (1945) view that motherliness represents a sublimation of sexuality and is affected if that sublimation does not occur. It is impossible to specify what degree of closeness is optimal for a mother and child in our culture, but it is clear from our data that some women must choose between their husbands and their infants.

As a final note, we found no differences in maternal adaptation related to the sex of the infant. This finding contradicts much of the literature (for example, Will, Self, and Datan, 1976) which reports differential behavior of mothers with boy and girl infants. We suspect that mothers of several children are not aware of the different ways they respond to the sex of their children and probably would not be comfortable telling us if they were.

Looking at the relations between characteristics of the fathers' and mothers' adaptation to the infant, we found that men who were initially more anxious had wives who were observed as handling the baby less skillfully and warmly, and were less reciprocal in their style of feeding the baby. Even with the wife's initial anxiety level statistically partialed out, the husband's anxiety continued to predict the observed quality of her mothering at two months.

Excerpts from the interviews with the two mothers quoted previously in this chapter serve best to illustrate different styles of perception and motherliness.

When questioned about her new baby, Pamela was again ambivalent and readily able to express her difficulty relating to her baby.

Interviewer: What kind of baby is he?
Pamela: I think he's a little tense, a little fretful. He has a hard time relaxing and falling asleep. At first, I thought he was sweet—that was the word I would use then. I don't feel that way anymore. I think he's cute, I like to look at him. He's alert and responsive. But I wouldn't describe him as a placid baby; he's more tense, and colicky sometimes.
Interviewer: Does he get upset easily?
Pamela: Yes. He doesn't seem calm and contented for long periods of time.
Interviewer: What's his usual mood?

Pamela:	That's hard to answer. When he's alert and physically comfortable, he seems fairly happy, but he's also often fretful, fussy—that's the only word I can use.
Interviewer:	Does he cry a lot?
Pamela:	Yes, I would say so. It's getting better now, but we've watched him cry for two hours at a time.
Interviewer:	Is he interested in people?
Pamela:	Yes, he likes to look at faces and he is interested in people. For such a long time he was oblivious to everything, just this week he's starting to become more interested, in people, things that make noise, and bright things.
Interviewer:	What do you do when he's crying and he's not hungry or wet?
Pamela:	I first pick him up and try to cuddle him. If that doesn't work, I give him a pacifier, and if that doesn't work either, I'll nurse him again. I try not to do that if I've just fed him but sometimes I do. [She then talked about how she enjoyed holding him and having physical contact, and mentioned that she does not worry about spoiling him.]
Interviewer:	How do you feel about his sex?
Pamela:	I was very relieved that he was a boy because I'm probably only going to have one child and Al wanted a boy. If he turned out to be a girl, there probably would have been pressure on me to have another one.
Interviewer:	How do you feel about his temperament?
Pamela:	I would like it if he were more placid and easier to pacify.
Interviewer:	How do you feel about taking care of his physical needs?
Pamela:	I have mixed feelings about it. I don't particularly enjoy the feeding—well, I guess I do; it's relaxing and sensual for me too. The diapering and things like that I don't really enjoy. It's an obli-

gation because he's my child, and I do it well,
but I don't really like to do it. I have real mixed
feelings about the physical demands, and the
enormous amount of time required, and I really
resent it.

Interviewer: Is there anything else about the baby that you
think we should know?

Pamela: Well, just that I really feel that there has to be
a way to prepare new parents for what the experience is really like. No matter how much
I read, it just didn't prepare me for it. I found
myself not coping and tense all the time, and
I even thought I was having a nervous breakdown
at one point. I was crying all the time, that still
happens occasionally, and I was overwhelmed by
my feeling. I was just not prepared for this experience at all. My feeling is that if I had known
more about infants and what they were really
like, it might have helped.

In contrast, Katherine seemed to be very comfortable in
her relationship to her new baby, although her baby did not
seem markedly different from Pamela's. But even in Katherine's
interview, one can hear an echo of the difficulty that she also
experienced previously, when she herself was coping with her
first child.

Interviewer: What's Lenore like?

Katherine: She's very sweet and not terribly demanding.
When she's fussy, I think it's really because she's
uncomfortable. I never feel that she's fussing to
irritate me. With my first, I used to take it so
personally if I couldn't comfort him, but with
her I know she's just uncomfortable. She is
colicky at times and those times are hard, but in
general, when she's feeling all right inside, she's
a lovely person.

Interviewer: Is she more active or passive?

Katherine:	She's more active than my other two, she wiggles on the changing table.
Interviewer:	How do you feel about her being a girl?
Katherine:	When she was first born, I was disappointed, because I wanted to give Mel another boy. And now I love her so much, it's all right. And in our family I think it's better that she's a girl, because she and Amy are closer in age.
Interviewer:	Is there anything else you think we ought to know about Lenore?
Katherine:	Just that I think she's going to be the most adaptable one in our family. And I think there's a real advantage to having an older brother and sister, and a relatively calm mother. She's been really good and we enjoy her.

Summary

In summary, we found the postpartum period to be a time of considerable stress as well as considerable pleasure. For all the mothers, the upheavals caused by the caring for a newborn were accompanied by some level of disorganization and turmoil. In addition to the physical work of caring for the baby, the mothers had to shuffle and reorder the relationships among the family members in order to create an emotional place in the family for the new baby.

In general, we found that various psychosocial aspects of the pregnancy affected the mother's emotional comfort in the postpartum period. Specifically, aspects of a woman's general psychological adjustment and aspects of her husband's adjustment had a bearing on early adaptation to mothering. In particular, the variable of anxiety, in both wife and husband, seemed to be especially important in its persistence over time and in its predictive nature for later outcome. Also, the dimension of marital satisfaction seemed to be a particularly sensitive predictor and barometer of adjustment in the postpartum phase. The degree of earlier marital adjustment was very important to the subsequent emotional adjustment of the new mother. Also, the postpartum marital adjustment reflected many of the stresses experienced in the preceding months of pregnancy and how well the couple resolved those stresses.

Perhaps the most striking of our findings concerning the postpartum phase are the considerable differences which appeared between first-time and experienced mothers. These differences are apparent in our data concerning the earlier experience of the pregnancy. At two months postpartum they are still very much in evidence and consistent with our earlier findings.

Specifically, first-time mothers again seemed to be much more consumed and emotionally involved in the pregnancy and in its meaning to them than were experienced mothers. While several dimensions concerning general emotional adaptation were predictive of postpartum ease for both first-time and experienced mothers, the relationships were more strikingly evident for first-time mothers. In addition, issues concerning specific aspects of the pregnancy and delivery seemed to be more important for first-time mothers than for experienced mothers in their postpartum adjustment. Marital adjustment seemed more crucial to the first time mothers' adaptation than to experienced mothers. In contrast, issues more external to the woman herself and to her immediate family seemed to have more impact on the experienced mothers.

It is as if the experienced mothers have read the story before and know that this is just one of many chapters, whereas the first-time mothers have not, so they can only worry and wonder how it will all turn out in the end.

6

Mothers of
One-Year-Olds

A child's first birthday marks the official end of the period of infancy. For the child and the parents each such maturational step presents adaptive challenges. For mothers, the adaptive tasks at one year are different from what they were a few months earlier. The child who was once such a very close part of her is becoming an increasingly independent individual; most one-year-olds can walk (or at least crawl very quickly) away from mother. Adjusting to this separation, finding a balance between holding on and letting go, is perhaps the major emotional task for the mother and the child during this phase (Mahler, 1974). At this time, too, many women are shifting the balance in their lives from a nearly total involvement with the child to a pattern that reflects increased emotional freedom to be involved in their marriages, their work outside the home, and their personal interests.

Recent studies on motherhood recognize motherhood as a developmental process for a woman and consider the mother not only as a mother but also as a woman with her own identity, needs, and development (Rapoport, Rapoport, and Strelitz, 1977). In contrast, earlier psychoanalytic theorists discussed the mother primarily as the major determinant of her child's psychological development (Bowlby, 1969; Winnicott, 1949) and focused on such issues as maternal deprivation (Bowlby, 1969; Spitz, 1945) and of maternal overprotection (Levy, 1943).

While most researchers have considered the mother primarily as the provider of her baby's needs, several have spoken about the woman herself, most notably Deutsch (1945) and Benedek (1960, 1970b). Erikson's (1963) discussion of the life cycle as a developmental process led to a new interest in parenthood as an important developmental phase for the parents (Group for the Advancement of Psychiatry, 1973; LeMasters, 1957; Rapoport, Rapoport, and Strelitz, 1977). Such studies evidence a greater appreciation of the context of parenting and discuss the woman not only in terms of her intense relationship with the infant but also as a wife, a working person, and someone with her own separate interests and needs for satisfaction.

Rossi (1968) judges the transition to parenthood to be more difficult than the transition from being single to being married because of its tangible effects and also because parenthood is an irrevocable state. She found that parenthood does not necessarily effect a higher level of maturation. Rather, many women suffer from a depressed sense of self-worth, perhaps, Rossi suggests, because the requirements of motherhood in American family life exact too high a price for those women who were raised with an eye to the larger society.

Another very important and new aspect of the study of mothers is the interest in understanding how the infant's behavior may facilitate or hinder his mother's adaptation to parenthood. No longer do researchers view the infant as a blank and totally impressionable being in a world composed of only mother and baby, but rather they recognize that infants come into the world with individual needs, styles, and demands which are stable over time (Bell, Weller, and Waldrop, 1971; Brazelton, 1973; Korner, 1971; Thomas and others, 1963). Some of these characteristics have been demonstrated to relate to differences in parental behaviors (Brazelton, 1961; Osofsky and Danzger, 1974; Pedersen, 1975; Sander, 1975). Such studies consider the interactions between mother and infant, father and infant, and father and mother as components of a complex system to which all three partners make contributions and by which all are affected.

Motherhood is certainly a major adaptive task for a woman, and many factors help determine what kind of adaptation she makes. Her psychological health, the sociocultural context in which she lives, the quality of her marriage, and the baby's characteristics—all would be expected to play a role in her adaptation. In our study, we looked at these dimensions at one year postpartum in order to assess which factors contribute to adaptive success.

During labor and delivery, as we have described, the single most important factor in predicting good adaptation for the women in our study was their satisfaction with their marriages. This phase of the childbearing process was also less stressful for women who were less anxious during pregnancy, those who looked forward to motherhood without a great deal of conflict, and those who had a relatively uncomplicated labor and delivery.

At two months after the birth of the child, most families in this study were still experiencing a considerable degree of upset in their lives. Our most consistent findings concerned the differences between first-time and experienced mothers. The adjustment of first-time mothers seemed to depend most heavily on their general psychological health and on the quality of their marriages. Experienced mothers were less vulnerable to these factors, and their coping was more apt to reflect a broader range of issues and concerns in their lives.

With this background, we approached the visit at one year postpartum, wondering whether there were still marked differences between first-time and experienced mothers and whether anxiety would continue to play such a major role in predicting which women would be adjusting well. We were also interested in seeing whether there was more variability in how well women were adjusting at one year postpartum than there had been at two months, at which time we saw no extreme highs or lows.

Everyone seemed to be disrupted to at least a moderate extent and yet we felt, in general, that people were managing relatively well. By one year, we expected the crisis to be past and we were curious about the range of functioning.

Psychological Adaptation at One Year Postpartum

When we visited the families near the time of the baby's first birthday, we again interviewed the women and men individually. We asked the mother about her physical and emotional health, her marriage, and how things were going with the baby. We observed her interacting with her child and asked her to fill out another set of our paper-and-pencil measures. For women who were working, we were interested in determining the effects of her working on her and on her family.

At this visit we had the strong impression that the turmoil and disorganization had passed. The women were accustomed to having a baby around the house and their anxiety about the fragility of the child was markedly reduced. The mothers' involvement in the world outside their homes was definitely on the increase. Some had returned to work and others were thinking about it. Couples were returning to their former patterns of social activity. By and large, the mood of the women was good and they were feeling healthy and energetic.

Our judgment of a woman's psychological health at one year postpartum was based on measurements of her anxiety and depression as evidenced by the questionnaires and the part of the interview that probed how she was feeling about herself— what we termed *emotional well-being*. Overall, we found our women to be doing rather well. They were less anxious and depressed than they had been at all previous contacts. The peaks of anxiety for the group as a whole came at the eighth month of pregnancy and at two months postpartum. Depression was highest in the first trimester and declined at each subsequent contact. Looking first at the women's levels of anxiety and depression, we found, as we had at two months postpartum, that a woman's psychological health at one year was more closely related to her previous levels of emotional integration than to her reactions to pregnancy, childbirth, and motherhood (see Table 5). Previously well-functioning women tended to continue to function well and those who were more anxious and depressed at the initial contact, late in pregnancy, and at two months postpartum were still more distressed at one year. Women of lower socioeconomic status were more anxious and depressed at one year, as they had been all along, than women who had more money and formal education. Those women who had reported themselves are more satisfied with their marriages were better emotionally adjusted at one year.

Interestingly, none of the measures from the labor and delivery period related to a woman's anxiety or depression at one year for the group as a whole, although there had been several relationships between these measures and adjustment at two months postpartum. The finding that these relationships were no longer significant at one year suggests that a woman's experience of childbirth itself has only short-term effects, at least for generally well-functioning married women. Perhaps a woman's adaptation to these events is much more influenced by the demands and vicissitudes of the immediate situation rather than by enduring psychological characteristics. Neither positive nor negative childbirth experiences seem to influence a woman's psychological health a year after the event, at least on these dimensions.

Within these broad outlines, we observed some differences between first-time and experienced mothers. For first-time mothers, some pregnancy-related measures were predictive of their later intrapsychic adaptation as reflected in their levels of anxiety and depression. For example, those whose conscious motivation for pregnancy was higher were doing better at one year postpartum. In addition, those who had more gynecological or medical problems during pregnancy tended to be more anxious and depressed. A positive overall adaptation to the pregnancy itself at both the first-trimester visit and the eighth-month visit predicted positive psychological health at one year for the first-time mothers.

In contrast, the earlier measures of adaptation to pregnancy did not predict the psychological state at one year of

Table 5. Women's Psychological Adaptation at One Year Postpartum

	Emotional Well-Being			Anxiety			Depression		
	All Mothers[a]	First-Time Mothers[b]	Experienced Mothers[c]	All Mothers[a]	First-Time Mothers[b]	Experienced Mothers[c]	All Mothers[a]	First-Time Mothers[b]	Experienced Mothers[c]
First trimester									
Psychological dimension									
Life adaptation	-.17	.13	.33[a]	-.42[c]	-.47[b]	-.39[a]	-.38[b]	-.38	-.36[a]
Anxiety	-.26[a]	-.33	-.26	.53[c]	.59[c]	.52[b]	.43[b]	.29	.60[b]
Depression	-.29	-.24	-.36[a]	.45[c]	.38[a]	.51[b]	.42[b]	.27	.59[c]
Femininity	-.12	-.38[a]	.16	.08	.31	-.09	.04	.10	-.02
Adaptation to pregnancy	.18	.37[a]	.05	-.21	-.51[b]	-.02	-.07	-.41[a]	.04
Conscious motivation	.07	.03	.13	-.17	-.34	-.06	-.18	-.39[a]	-.05
Physiological dimension									
Premenstrual tension	-.28[a]	.01	-.47[a]	.39[b]	.40[b]	.39[b]	.35	.18	.49[b]
Medical risk	.09	.01	.14	.14	.36[a]	-.01	.09	.43[a]	-.11
Sociocultural dimension									
Socioeconomic status	-.17	.08	-.29[a]	.37[b]	.29	.40[a]	.40[b]	.11	.61[c]
Marital dimension									
Marital adjustment	.12	.13	.12	-.29[a]	-.23	-.31[a]	-.44[c]	-.37	-.48[b]
Sexual activity and satisfaction	-.21	-.27	-.10	.23	.48[b]	.08	.19	.40[a]	.05
Marital style	.04	.38[a]	-.15	-.12	-.40[a]	.05	-.16	-.13	-.17
Years married	.03	-.17	.17	-.21	-.37[a]	-.30	-.11	-.24	.25

Eighth month of pregnancy									
Anxiety	-.31[a]	-.53[b]	-.14	.48[c]	.44[b]	.52[b]	.29[a]	.39	.22[b]
Symptoms	-.15	-.07	-.24	.51[c]	.55[b]	.47[b]	.44[c]	.35	.54[b]
Life change	-.01	.18	-.30	.28[a]	.15	.51[b]	.16	.04	.44[a]
Labor and delivery									
Complications of labor and delivery	-.09	-.05	-.16	.11	-.02	.26	-.05	-.25	.16
Caesarean section	.00	-.12	.08	-.05	-.03	-.05	-.22	-.11	-.31
Adaptation to labor and delivery	.14	.27	.03	-.20	-.14	-.24	-.19	-.26	-.14
Two months postpartum									
Psychological adaptation									
Emotional well-being	.55[c]	.42[a]	.65[b]	-.25	-.16	-.36[a]	-.33[a]	-.26	-.41[a]
Anxiety	-.37[b]	-.32	-.44	.53[c]	.32	.74[c]	.44[b]	.24	.68[c]
Depression	-.51[b]	-.48[b]	-.52[b]	.55[c]	.16	.72[c]	.63[c]	.48[a]	.77[c]
Marital dimension									
Marital adjustment	.02	.02	-.02	-.27[a]	-.17	-.38[a]	-.20	-.23	-.16
Adaptation to spouse	.22	.44[b]	.00	-.07	.02	-.18	-.17	-.12	-.22
Marternal adaptation									
Interview measure of maternal adaptation	.33[b]	.44[b]	.29	.04	.09	-.01	-.14	-.28	-.04

Note: These correlations are based on the following samples: For first-time mothers, N ranges from 22 to 34; for experienced mothers, N ranges from 22 to 33; for all mothers, N ranges from 41 to 67.

[a] $p \leqslant .05$, two-tailed
[b] $p \leqslant .01$, two-tailed
[c] $p \leqslant .001$, two-tailed

experienced mothers. The only distinguishing finding for this group was that those women who felt better about themselves at two months postpartum were less anxious and depressed at one year. Once again the difference between the first-time and experienced mothers is a marked one.

As mentioned, the other measure of the woman's psychological health at one year came from her statements during the interview about how she was feeling. We asked about her mood, her energy level, and self-image. We also explored how she divided her time between family, outside interests, and friendships. To a considerable extent, a positive rating on this dimension was related to the more general ratings of psychological functioning. Those women who felt better about themselves at one year postpartum were those whom we had rated as less anxious and depressed both at one year and at the previous contacts (see Table 5, "Emotional Well-Being). Self-image also strongly reflected the general family situation. For example, women who experienced a great deal of stress during the previous year tended to have less positive self-images. A positive sense of emotional well-being was very much related to how things were going with the child or children, with her husband, and for a woman who was working outside the home, with her job.

In addition to these predictors of a woman's adaptation, certain personality characteristics and adaptive patterns of her husband related to her psychological health at one year postpartum. We saw earlier that a man's anxiety level was a major predictor of how well his wife would adapt to labor and delivery and also to early parenthood, as assessed by us at two months postpartum. We speculated that a major role of the husband during the period of pregnancy and early childcare is to reassure his wife and support her, in the face of her inevitable anxieties.

Concerning the women's psychological health at one year postpartum, as reflected in levels of anxiety and depression, and emotional well-being as assessed from the interview, two dimensions concerning the husbands emerged as important. Men who strongly identified with and positively perceived their own mothers and those of higher socioeconomic status had wives who were less depressed and anxious. At the research contact in late pregnancy, men with stronger identification with their mothers were adapting better to the pregnancy, independently of their general life adaptation. These correlations suggest that a man's sense of having been well-mothered and his feeling himself to be in some ways like his mother are important dimensions in his ability to relate to his wife as she carries a child and later nurtures it.

When we looked at the experienced parents and first-time parents separately, some interesting differences appeared. First-time mothers with more anxious husbands had less positive feelings about themselves at one year, and the husbands' marital and paternal adaptation at two months postpartum strongly predicted to the women's level of depression and anxiety at one year. The man's marital satisfaction at two months also predicted to the woman's psychological health at one year. In other words, for couples having their first child, the husband's anxiety level and the manner in which he treats his wife and child in early infancy are very important to his wife's health and well-being at one year postpartum. Because the marital system is a tightly interconnected one, the husband's behavior and attitude make an important difference in the overall adaptive picture.

In contrast, for experienced couples, neither the man's earlier anxiety level nor his effectiveness in relating to his family at two months was predictive of his wife's condition at one year. Only his age, the degree of his identification with his own mother, and his job status predicted. That is, older men with stronger identification with their own mothers, and higher-level jobs had wives who were less depressed and less anxious at one year.

It is intriguing to speculate why the husband's anxiety does not disrupt the wife as much in couples who are experienced parents. Possibly the wife's anxiety level is down, at least regarding the baby, because of her previous experience, and hence she is not in as much need of her husband's reassurance. It is also possible that the couple's system is much more open in families with at least one child, so that the husband and wife are not as inevitably influenced by their spouse's anxieties and concerns.

Several interview segments illustrate the struggles these women had over the year and how they were feeling about themselves.

Katherine, whom we have followed throughout and for whom this child was her third, clearly derived great pleasure from her family. However, she was also struggling with a feeling at times of losing herself amidst the concerns and responsibilities of motherhood. At the time of the interview, she seemed to be moving toward a workable balance. All through our contact, Katherine impressed us with her resilience, as well as with the strength of her marriage.

Interviewer:	How has the year been?
Katherine:	I was just coming out of it a couple of months ago. I was in all winter and gained some weight and felt awful about myself. Now it's better because I'm going to Weight Watchers and doing something about it.
Interviewer:	Do you have time for yourself?
Katherine:	Not so much yet, but I can see a time when I'm going to. I've been playing some tennis and I'm going to take a macrame course. Sometimes I feel it more. There were a slew of kids here all day, and I was making peanut butter sandwiches and turning on the sprinkler. By the end of the day, I was going crazy. Sometimes I feel my identity is so caught up in the kids that when I go out socially it takes me a while to lose the motherhood role.

Katherine had always been able to talk about her worries and concerns. It is not as clear from this interview segment as it is from a more overall view of her adjustment that although Katherine did not deny her negative feelings, she in fact handled things very well. She felt basically good about herself and in control of what happened to her. At one year postpartum, her anxiety and depression scores were low and her sense of self very positive.

Martha, a middle class woman for whom this child was her second, had had a somewhat stressful year since the baby's birth. Her infant was sick for two months and, at present, she was trying to sell their house.

Interviewer: Are there things you would have done differently in this past year if you had it to do over again?

Martha: Yes, I have regrets. I would have wished I had a different threshold—could have controlled myself better. I couldn't enjoy her until she was ten or eleven months old. She screamed so much—it'd drive you crazy.

Interviewer: Have you changed in your feelings about yourself over this past year?

Martha: I feel like I've aged a lot. I'm a lot more tolerant about things that used to bother me. I've grown up. I had it so easy with Sharon [her first child]. I used to think it was me, but it was the child's basic personality. It's not all the mothering. You learn a lot about yourself, especially when you go through ordeals. When Alison had bronchitis, I fell apart. My perspective now is on getting through the next couple of years.

Overall, Martha was in more emotional difficulty at one year than when we saw her early in pregnancy. At that time, we had rated her anxiety and depression as extremely low and her overall psychological functioning as quite high. Her score on marital satisfaction was very high as well. We considered her adjustment to labor and delivery to be quite good. By two months postpartum she had slipped to below average in her emotional well-being and she returned none of the paper-and-pencil questionnaires, although we went to considerable lengths to pursue delinquent material. At one year postpartum, Martha was considerably more anxious than she had been before the baby was born, whereas the pattern for most of the women in the study was for anxiety to decrease by one year. Martha's sense of self continued to be below average. Clearly Martha's emotional adjustment at one year was not what it had been when she was expecting her second child. The year had been somewhat more stressful for her than for some of our other families at least partly because of the baby's illness and difficult temperament and Martha's emotional resources were strained. Martha's lower level of adaptation is reminiscent of Shereshefsky and Yarrow's (1973) finding that some women mature during the process of childbearing while a small proportion regress psychologically.

Grete, a thirty-two-year-old upper-middle-class woman for whom this child was her first, sounded very much in control at one year. She had made room for things she liked to do and tried to change things she felt bad about. For Grete, too, her physical appearance was very important as part of her sense of self.

Interviewer: How are you doing?
Grete: I've been doing fine, my mood is good. I'm still not down to my original weight and my self-image is very much affected by feeling fat and ugly. I recently got my hair cut and I've started to diet.
Interviewer: Do you find you have enough time for yourself?
Grete: [Laughs.] I suppose there's never enough time. I go to garage sales every Saturday morning and I taught one course this year. I might like to work more, part-time. I try to read while he naps. I feel a very strong need to relax.

Grete struck us throughout as someone who knew what she wanted and then went about getting it. Her scores in the first contact reflected anxiety and depression in the average range, and her general psychological functioning was high. At one year, her anxiety and depression scores were low, and her feelings about herself very positive. The only wrinkle for Grete came during the labor and delivery period, when she had unexpected complications and was thrown off her stride. Her need to be organized and in control was temporarily upset by the events of the childbirth, but she quickly regained her equilibrium. Barring severe stress, Grete and her family should continue to do well.

To summarize, for the women in our study, psychological adaptation at one year postpartum was related to the relatively enduring personality characteristics of being fairly free from emotional conflict and depression. It was also related to higher socioeconomic standing, absence of stressful life changes, and marital satisfaction. For first-time mothers only, pregnancy-related factors such as strong motivation for the child and a smooth adaptation to the pregnancy period were also very important.

The Marriage at One Year Postpartum

Our evaluation of a woman's marriage one year after the baby's birth was based on a repeated administration of paper-and-pencil measures of marital satisfaction and sexual functioning and on an interview with her about how successfully she and her husband were dealing with parenthood as a couple and how satisfied she was with the current division of labor.

At two months postpartum, marital satisfaction was higher among women who were less anxious and depressed at the initial contact, who were of higher socioeconomic status, who described themselves as more feminine, and who had reported more satisfying marriages early in the pregnancy. However, the quality of the marriage was much more important to the overall adaptation of first-time mothers than to those who already had one or more children.

The best predictor of the state of the marriage at one year postpartum was the state of marriage at previous contacts. A woman's marital adjustment during the first trimester of pregnancy and at two months postpartum was a very strong predictor of overall marital adjustment at one year (see Table 6, "Marital Adjustment"). Psychological factors also predicted strongly. Women who were more anxious and depressed earlier had sub-

Table 6. Women's Marital Adjustment at One Year Postpartum

	Marital Adjustment			Adaptation to Spouse			Sexual Activity and Satisfaction		
	All Mothers[a]	First-Time Mothers[b]	Experienced Mothers[c]	All Mothers[a]	First-Time Mothers[b]	Experienced Mothers[c]	All Mothers[a]	First-Time Mothers[b]	Experienced Mothers[c]
First trimester									
Psychological dimension									
Life adaptation	.22	.08	.37[a]	.18	.16	.22	.10	-.30	.38[a]
Anxiety	-.45[c]	-.26	-.61[c]	-.10	-.24	-.01	.01	.02	.06
Depression	-.42[c]	-.17	-.65[c]	-.25[a]	-.20	-.37[a]	.08	.13	.09
Conscious motivation	.28[a]	.38[a]	.15	.21	.23	.17	-.03	.11	-.07
Femininity	.16	.06	.26	-.18	-.27	-.04	.26[a]	.06	.38[a]
Adaptation to pregnancy	.21	.23	.19	.29[a]	.32	.26	.17	-.03	.31
Identification with mother	-.09	-.16	-.02	.01	.15	-.13	-.04	.19	-.22
Physiological dimension									
Premenstrual tension	-.30[a]	-.08	-.46[b]	-.22	-.13	-.26	-.03	.25	-.22
Medical risk	-.42[c]	-.39[a]	-.46[b]	-.04	-.34[a]	.16	-.18	-.02	-.12
Sociocultural dimension									
Socioeconomic status	-.36[a]	-.29	-.43[b]	-.16	-.17	-.17	.11	.24	.01
Life change	-.20	-.08	-.27	-.07	-.15	.02	-.17	.17	-.38[a]
Marital dimension									
Marital adjustment	.55[c]	.69[c]	.49[b]	.23	.34[b]	.15	.00	.04	.01
Sexual activity and satisfaction	.03	-.23	-.30	-.18	-.29	-.01	.57[c]	.58[b]	.52[b]

Marital style	-.03	.18	-.10	.25[a]	.29	.31[a]	-.04	-.20	.12
Years married	.03	-.03	-.02	.16	-.01	.34[a]	-.12	-.46[b]	-.20
Eighth month of pregnancy									
Anxiety	-.37[b]	-.24	-.54[b]	-.05	-.25	.10	.25	.24	.31
Symptoms	-.36[b]	-.32	-.44[b]	-.21	-.24	-.18	.30[a]	.45[a]	.23
Life change	-.32[a]	-.29	-.33[a]	-.09	.09	-.39[a]	-.02	-.05	.02
Conscious motivation	.44[c]	.57[c]	.37[a]	.33[b]	.52[b]	.16	.11	.24	.08
Labor and delivery									
Adaptation to labor and delivery	.32[a]	.39	.28	-.02	.05	-.08	-.21	.15	-.40[a]
Two months postpartum									
Psychological adaptation									
Emotional well-being	.22	.32	.12	.38[b]	.39[a]	.35[a]	.19	.13	.29
Anxiety	-.47[c]	-.44[a]	-.54[b]	-.29[a]	-.31	-.29	.00	-.15	.10
Depression	-.45[c]	-.38[a]	-.50[b]	-.34[b]	-.27	-.41[a]	-.13	-.42[a]	-.01
Marital dimension									
Marital adjustment	.59[c]	.61[c]	.54[b]	.37	.50[b]	.19	.00	.00	.00
Adaptation to spouse	.19	.13	.29	.42[c]	.48[b]	.37[a]	.34[a]	.39	.36[a]

Note: These correlations are based on the following samples: For first-time mothers, N ranges from 18 to 32; for experienced mothers, N ranges from 23 to 30; for all mothers, N ranges from 50 to 62.

[a] $p \leq .05$, two-tailed

[b] $p \leq .01$, two-tailed

[c] $p \leq .001$, two-tailed

stantially more negative views of their marriages at one year. This relationship between marital adjustment and the women's emotional adjustment has shown up repeatedly in this study. Women who were more strongly motivated for this pregnancy were more satisfied with their marriages at one year. As we have seen at previous contacts, social class was related to marital adjustment with women of lower socioeconomic status reporting themselves less satisfied with their marriages.

Sexual activity and satisfaction did not seem to be a primary criterion for the women in the overall evaluation of their marriages. At one year postpartum the best predictor of a woman's rating of her level of sexual interest and satisfaction was her rating of this dimension early in pregnancy (see Table 6, "Sexual Activity and Satisfaction"). Self-described sexual activity and satisfaction was relatively stable over time, as assessed by our measure. The relative independence of the level of sexual satisfaction and overall marital satisfaction was consistent from early pregnancy to one year postpartum for the women in this study. This finding is consistent with other researchers' findings that for women sexual satisfaction is relatively independent of positive emotional adjustment (for example, Fisher, 1973; Lowenthal, Thurnher, Chiriboga and Associates, 1975). There were some differences between first-time and experienced mothers in their sexual adaptation. For first-time mothers, the longer they had been married, the higher was their rating of sexual interest and satisfaction. In addition, a period of postpartum depression had a negative effect on their sexual adjustment at one year. The two factors that seemed to enhance the sexual adaptation of multiparous women were better general psychological functioning and higher femininity scores. Those women who were more successful at reestablishing the marital dyad by two months postpartum reported themselves more sexually interested and satisfied at one year. Overall, then, there were some minor differences between primiparous and multiparous women in the factors that related to a good sexual relationship. More interesting, perhaps, is the finding of the peripheral nature of sexual issues in these women's lives, especially as it contrasts with the relative importance of sexual functioning to their husbands.

The interview measure of the marriage elicited more immediate and practical information than did the paper-and-pencil scale about how the couple was managing as a couple with a one-year-old in the house. We asked the couple if they spent enjoyable time together, how they divided labor in the household and how satisfied were they with their arrangement, and whether they were aware of and trying to meet one another's needs. To a much larger extent than was true for the more general rating of marital adjustment, the fact of parenthood had a substantial impact on scores for this measure of adaptation to spouse. For example, both the motivation for and adaptation to pregnancy was relevant here (see Table 6, "Adaptation to Spouse"). Those women who had wanted their babies more, particularly as assessed at the eighth month contact, and those who did better and felt better early in the pregnancy seemed more satisfied with their husbands at one year. The early parenting experience was even more strongly predictive. Women who felt better about themselves as mothers at two months postpartum and those who were less anxious and depressed had better relationships with their husbands at one year. Not surprisingly, women who were satisfied with their marriages and who were judged to have successfully resolved parenting issues with their husbands at two months postpartum were also doing well in the marriage at one year. There were no substantial differences between first-time and experienced mothers in these relationships.

Interestingly, marital satisfaction at one year was predicted by marital style ranked on a scale from traditional to egalitarian. This measure of marital style, which reflects the division of labor of household tasks, predicted marital satisfaction at one year, such that for the primiparous women in our study, a very traditional marriage was associated with increased anxiety at one year. Among the multiparous mothers, those with the more egalitarian marriages had better relationships with their husbands at this one-year postpartum contact. These findings are consistent with several reported earlier, that primiparous women from more egalitarian marriages had fewer pregnancy-related symptoms at eight months and more reciprocal relationships with their infants at two months postpartum, but are in contrast to our findings that experienced mothers from more traditional marriages had a higher level of observed maternal adaptation at two months postpartum. It seems that the more egalitarian marital style has positive effects on a woman's experience of her pregnancy and on her view of her marriage, but the implications for her mothering are complex and may well vary with the age of the child, as well as with the standards used to judge maternal care. At one year, perhaps women in more traditional marriages experience anxiety because they are unable to fulfill the traditional expectation that a new mother should be able to manage her child and her home with little help from her husband.

We also sought to determine which aspects of the husband's experiences and functioning related significantly to his wife's experience of the marriage at one year. The men's assessment of their marriages both in the first trimester and at two months postpartum were significantly predictive, as one would expect. Just as the women's evaluation of the couple's success in reestablishing a good relationship at two months predicted to her marital adjustment and to the couple's adjustment to parenthood, so also did the husband's evaluation at two months. These relationships were stronger and more consistent for first-time parents, a continuation of the pattern seen earlier.

Once again the degree of the man's identification with his own mother was significantly related to his wife's satisfaction. Men who had positive perceptions of their mothers and identified strongly with them had wives who were significantly more satisfied with their marriages. This relationship was very strong for the experienced fathers, and not particularly strong for first-time fathers. At one year, as at two months, the women's assessment of the marriage was very strongly related to their husbands' anxiety level.

It seems, then, that the best predictors of a wife's feelings about how she and her husband are coping with their one-year-old are their overall marital situation, the man's anxiety level, their adjustments to pregnancy, and finally and perhaps most importantly, their abilities as very new parents, struggling and coping with the stressful demands of their new baby.

On the relationship between children and marital satisfaction, the literature is somewhat inconclusive. Several studies report that parenthood has a negative effect on marital adjustment (Bernard, 1972; Hicks and Platt, 1970; Jordan, 1976; Laws, 1971). These studies report an increase in the woman's sense of alienation, a decrease in her decision-making power and options in the marriage, and a decrease in the husband's involvement in household tasks—a constellation of changes that researchers have termed the *disenchantment phenomenon*. Others, however, have suggested that the research to date does not warrant any conclusions about the relation between parenthood and marital success (Christenson, 1972; Luckey and Bain, 1970).

Almost every woman in our study reported that having children produced negative effects on the marital relationship. For example, Katherine said, "We try to get out one evening a week, but it often doesn't work. The relationship has changed. We're very wrapped up in the kids and sometimes lose sight of our own needs." Yet Katherine and her husband received among the highest scores on the marital dimension at one year. While they acknowledged that after the birth of their third child, more of their energy was directed toward their children than toward each other, they seemed to be comfortable with this temporary decrease in the time they had for themselves.

Grete and her husband were also rated very highly on their marital satisfaction, and yet they clearly felt that their relationship as a couple had suffered. Grete reported that "Most of the time the relationship is very good, very solid. We feel the stress when we're tired and we have to do something for the baby. Family life is more limited. We should have had baby-sitters earlier."

For some couples, the arrival of their new baby had a major negative effect on their marriage. Susan and Jim had been married for only a year when their first child was born. Throughout the study their scores on marital satisfaction were above average, but they had difficulties late in the baby's first year, which Susan described for us: "When the baby was about nine months old we had a period of problems. Jim would go out with the guys, and I felt that he had more independence than

I did. I was losing my independence and didn't want to. I just wanted to go out, so I'd go out by myself and have a drink. We got that together, but it was a big adjustment. Now we go out together once a week. There are times for all of us, for the two of us, and I go to work every day and play basketball two nights a week. We socialize more with families now. It gives you more energy, the more you do." After their period of disequilibrium, Susan and Jim seemed to have formulated a pattern that works for them as a couple. However, we wonder how this style, which takes her out of her home so much, will affect her relationship with her baby.

Despite the stresses and strains of having a new baby, many couples expressed strong feelings during the interviews about the compensations and rewards. Although their personal freedom was somewhat restricted, most felt that having a child more than compensated for any restrictions. Although not all couples verbalized their feelings, we saw the delight and brightening when a woman said something like "she's just blossomed all of a sudden" or "we take such great pleasure in observing him." Couples shared a new sense of family and a sense of relief and accomplishment at having successfully coped with the first year of their child's life. Although dissatisfaction with the marital relationship itself seemed to increase for many of our couples, overall life satisfaction, including the joys of parenthood, seemed to increase as well.

Maternal Adaptation

In order to evaluate the women specifically as mothers, we interviewed them to assess how they were feeling about their child and about their competence and confidence as a mother. We also observed each mother in a sustained interaction with her child. The observational ratings represent a clinical judgment of the woman's relationship with her child and supplement the woman's interview account of herself as a mother. We defined a good mother as one who was emotionally involved in a loving way with her infant, was sensitive to her child's physical and emotional needs and skilled in meeting them, encouraged her child's development, and had a comfortable sense of her own competence. The group as a whole was doing very well at mothering, as reflected in above average mean scores on both the interview and observational assessments. Overall these women seemed to be feeling good about themselves as mothers and to be responding warmly and appropriately to the children.

First-time mothers scored significantly higher on our observational measure of mothering than experienced mothers, who were somewhat less sensitive and responsive. Considering that the experienced mother must attend to a more complicated family situation, and that each new developmental step may not seem quite as wonderful the second or third time around, this finding is not surprising. Whether in fact the greater attentiveness represents better mothering is hard to say. That the difference has consequences for the children is amply attested to by the substantial differences between first-born and later-born children on a variety of dimensions later on in life (Schachter, 1959).

Information gathered from the interviews with the women and from our observations of them correlated very highly. There also seemed to be some consistency through time, as women who were better adapted as mothers at two months postpartum continued to do well at one year (see Table 7). This latter relationship was not very strong, however, and it seems likely that some mothers had not yet become comfortable with their infants at two months, that some were still recovering from a difficult delivery, and that some had infants who were particularly difficult in the early period. Thus, although maternal adaptation at two months postpartum is a predictor of adaptation at one year, some women whose adaptation at two months was poor improved significantly by one year.

At two months postpartum, the women who were assessed by us as doing better at mothering tasks were those who had been less anxious late in pregnancy, those who had had an easier time and adapted better to the labor and delivery, and those whose babies had been larger and more alert at birth. For first-time mothers, older women, those who were free from depression early in pregnancy, and those in a highly satisfying

Table 7. Women's Maternal Adaptation at One Year Postpartum

	Observed Adaptation			Interview Measure of Adaptation		
	All Mothers[a]	First-Time Mothers[b]	Experienced Mothers[c]	All Mothers[a]	First-Time Mothers[b]	Experienced Mothers[c]
First trimester						
Psychological dimension						
Life adaptation	.15	.03	.19	.25[a]	.31[b]	.21
Anxiety	-.26	-.49	-.24	-.29[a]	-.51[b]	-.20
Depression	-.09	-.12	-.11	-.31[a]	-.34[a]	-.34[a]
Femininity	-.07	-.55	.08	-.06	-.39[a]	.21
Adaptation to pregnancy	.18	.35	.17	.25[a]	.23	.30
Physiological dimension						
Medical risk factors	.21	.50	.15	.19	-.14	.32[a]
Premenstrual tension	-.13	.15	-.33	-.20	.00	-.33[a]
Sociocultural dimension						
Socioeconomic status	-.06	.16	-.05	-.11	.14	-.18
Social supports	-.42[a]	-.32	-.52[a]	-.09	-.09	-.09
Life change	-.48[a]	-.07	-.63[b]	-.03	-.08	.01
Marital dimension						
Marital adjustment	-.05	.20	-.27	.29[a]	.22	.32[a]
Sexual activity and satisfaction	-.15	-.14	-.14	.00	-.33	.32[a]
Years married	-.05	-.81[c]	.40	.08	.00	.33[a]
Eighth month of pregnancy						
Anxiety	-.22	-.53	-.13	-.41[c]	-.51[b]	-.38[a]

Symptoms	-.08	-.04	-.12	-.15	-.02	-.27
Adaptation to pregnancy	-.06	-.21	.06	.36[b]	.53[b]	.15
Conscious motivation	-.04	.42	-.28	.11	.29	-.02
Life change	.09	.08	-.17	-.07	.15	-.37
Marital adaptation	-.26	-.46	-.25	.18	.12	.24
Couple preparedness	-.11	-.03	-.07	-.06	-.01	-.05
Labor and delivery						
Complications of labor and delivery	.02			.00	.17	-.23
Caesarean section	-.08			.06	.06	-.06
Adaptation to labor and delivery	.17			.21	.27	.12
Two months postpartum						
Psychological adaptation						
Emotional well-being	.35			.40[b]	.33	.46[b]
Anxiety	-.41[a]			-.40[c]	-.29	-.50[b]
Depression	-.34			-.40[c]	-.51[b]	-.34[a]
Maternal adaptation						
Observed maternal adaptation	.47[a]			.07	.26	-.01
Interview measure of maternal adaptation	.45[a]			.24	.31	.23

Note: These correlations are based on the following samples: For first-time mothers, N ranges from 22 to 34; for experienced mothers, N ranges from 24 to 32; for all mothers, N ranges from 48 to 66, except for the two-month postpartum observation, where N ranges from 14 to 26.

[a] $p \leq .05$, two-tailed
[b] $p \leq .01$, two-tailed
[c] $p \leq .001$, two-tailed

marriage were judged as better at mothering in this early postpartum period.

As we saw at two months, very few variables predicted to
the observed quality of mothering at one year. However, wom-
en who were doing well with their infants were continuing to do
well with their one-year-olds. In addition, women who had been
less anxious at two months were doing better as mothers of one-
year-olds. Another interesting finding is that for first-time
mothers only, maternal adaptation was poorer for women who
had been married longer. Perhaps couples who have been married longer have greater difficulty integrating a new member
into their dyadic system.

A great many more factors were significantly related to
the women's self-assessment of maternal adaptation than to our
observational ratings (see Table 7). The strongest predictors
were in the sphere of the woman's psychological health at each
of our contacts. Women who were more anxious and depressed,
particularly late in pregnancy and at two months postpartum,
and who felt less comfortable with themselves at two months
postpartum, appeared from the interview to be having more difficulty with mothering. In addition, those women who had adjusted better to the pregnancy itself—that is, those who had felt
more positive and accepting of the physical and psychological
changes and who had felt emotionally more prepared for motherhood—seemed better adapted as mothers of one-year-olds.

Looking at predictors from the marital dimension, we
found that women who rated their marriages as better early in
pregnancy were rated more highly on mothering from the interview but not from the observations. For first-time mothers, the
longer they had been married the worse their observed mothering, to an enormous degree.

Finally, there was a strong relationship between babies
who were better adjusted at two months postpartum and good
mothering at one year. It remains to be seen whether good
babies facilitate good mothering or whether good mothering
fosters good babies. Most likely the complex mutual interaction
between mother and child accounts for this correlation. In any
case, it looks very much as if good mothering is facilitated most

importantly by a woman's own psychological integration, though a satisfying relationship with her husband and a well-adjusted baby are also important.

There were few important differences between first-time and experienced mothers in these findings. Perhaps by one year all mothers are experienced in the sense that first-time mothers have by then resolved the issues of identity and role change, and so the two groups are fairly similar in their psychological adaptation.

One interesting finding for the first-time mothers, however, is that those rated higher on a femininity scale were not doing as well at mothering at one year. There is at least some support in the literature for this finding. Bem (1976) reported that feminine women did not distinguish themselves in a study of nurturing behaviors towards infants and speculates that successful nurturing of an infant actually involves some masculine behaviors, such as taking initiative and improvising. The more feminine women in her study tended to take fewer risks. Bem feels that adrogynous women, those with both masculine and feminine traits, are most successful at mothering because they are both emotionally responsive and effective in performance. Our data provide partial support for her speculation.

At two months postpartum, the woman's treatment of her new infant was substantially linked to aspects of her husband's functioning. His anxiety level, age, and marital satisfaction related to her skills and warmth in handling the baby, as assessed by both observation and interview measures. For first-time mothers, the husband's anxiety continued to have what appeared to be a substantial negative effect on the quality of their mothering at one year. First-time mothers with more anxious husbands were judged by us to be noticeably less adept. Men who were both very anxious and whose sense of self was poor at two months postpartum had wives whose mothering was observed to be significantly impaired at one year. The only other relationship between the men's scores and the quality of the women's mothering at one year was that the wives of men who had more positive views of marriages in the first trimester were doing better with their babies.

As we noted in earlier discussions of the interview material, Katherine continually showed psychological strength, and her marriage was good. When we asked Katherine how confident she felt as a mother, she replied, "Ninety percent confident and ten percent guilt-ridden. Sometimes I feel like a nag, shrewish, too caught up in getting the house picked up, but then I think I'm as adequate as most mothers." Although she recognized areas of difficulty, Katherine presented herself as basically comfortable with the quality of her mothering. She is as "adequate as most mothers" and that is acceptable to her. In fact, Katherine's modesty prevented her from talking about her very real sense of pride in her excellent mothering. In our observation of Katherine and her child, she was among the few given the highest possible score.

Martha, in contrast, was rated as below average and her response to the question, "How competent do you feel as a mother?" was peppered with comments like "I feel bad about not paying attention to Marty," "I've made mistakes," and "I have to change."

Susan seemed to gain a sense of confidence as a mother by watching Josh grow, change, and respond. He seemed to be doing well, so she felt that she must be a good mother. The mutually reinforcing aspect of good adaptation is particularly clear in her remarks: "I feel really confident. Everything is going easily now. I feel like I'm giving him the right kind of environment. He really responds to you, comes up and gives you a big hug." Our observation was less glowing, but we felt that Susan was doing an adequate job of mothering a one-year-old.

As we have seen, there were several factors related to good mothering at one year, including the woman's psychological health and good adaptation to the pregnancy and to the early postpartum period. First-time mothers were rated more highly in general. In contrast to the cultural stereotype, women who identified themselves as highly feminine were less likely to be very good mothers. The quality of mothering, the baby's health and condition, and the quality of the marital relationship were highly interdependent factors in the family picture at one year.

Working Mothers

Investigations of working mothers repeatedly report that there are no striking differences between their children and the children of mothers who stay at home (Clark-Stewart, 1977). With the exception of the finding that working women tend to have smaller families, the only other consistent differences in families with working mothers are that the husbands respond more favorably to their wives' working and that the marital relationships are structured in a more egalitarian way (Siegel and Haas, 1963). The women themselves, however, almost always feel a conflict in their roles and strain (Epstein, 1974). Professional women, in particular, are likely to see employment and parenthood as involving incompatible and competing roles (Beckman, 1978).

Among the sixty-four women remaining in our sample when their children were one year of age, roughly one third, or twenty-two, had resumed their employment or schooling; ten were working, or going to school, full-time and the remaining twelve, part-time. Forty-two mothers were at home full-time. The most important difference between those who worked or resumed schooling and those who did not was the style of the marriage. The more egalitarian the marital style when we first saw the couple, the more likely it was for the woman to resume work or school at some point during the child's first year. This was most true when the husband's motivation for having a child had been very high. In addition, women whose incomes were higher and those for whom this child was the first were more likely to return to work.

There were no correlations between the employment of the woman and her psychological health at one year. Employed women were not more or less anxious and depressed, felt no more or less comfortable with themselves, nor were they doing any better or worse with their children or their husbands than mothers who stayed at home. In addition, the one-year-olds of working women did not appear different on our measures of intellectual and emotional adaptation. Our data do not support the contention that working mothers are less capable than mothers who stay home, nor do they support the contention that mothers who do not work feel dissatisfied and incomplete.

Summary

By the time a baby is one year of age, families have settled into fairly stable patterns and routines. The period of major upheaval has passed; families have by this time adjusted to the shifting patterns of needs and relationships and integrated the new child into the family system. By one year postpartum, first-time mothers have adjusted their sense of identity to now include motherhood as an aspect of that identity. The developmental crisis has passed, and many women have attained a new level of emotional maturity. Others, however, find the task of motherhood too great for their emotional resources; they seem less stable, less able to cope well with their life situations than before the pregnancy. Not surprisingly, a very complex intertwining of factors determines the kind of adaptation that a woman makes: her psychological health, her husband's psychological health, their marital adjustment, and their sociocultural assets and liabilities—all these interact to influence the mother's adaptation. Particular factors affect first-time and experienced mothers in different ways, as we have seen repeatedly throughout this study. Whereas experienced mothers are more influenced by issues and events in the external environment, first-time mothers are more affected by intrapsychic dimensions and issues more closely related to the pregnancy itself.

As the children grow older, change, and develop, their changing needs will interact in a complex manner with the psychosocial assets and liabilities of their parents. The success with which these families will navigate new issues can be predicted to some extent by how well they have done in the past. To an important degree, however, new issues represent new opportunities for enriched relationships and family experience.

7

Experience of Fathering

Today, many fathers are very much involved in the daily care and nurturing of their young children. Although most fathers work outside the home, no longer do economic realities and social role expectations exclude the father from this kind of participation within the family. As families have increasing leisure, and as more mothers are employed outside the home, more possibilities exist for men to become more involved in their families. Concomitantly, as the nuclear family becomes increasingly isolated from close geographic proximity to extended kin, and as the world of work becomes more bureaucratized and impersonal, the family has become the haven and last resort for closeness, emotional warmth, and relatedness.

As recently as the 1950s, the cultural view of the role of fathers was that their responsibilities were to provide emotional support for their wives and economic security for their families. They were not expected to be directly involved in childcare (Burlingham, 1973; Nash, 1965; Rapoport, Rapoport, and Strelitz, 1977). However, cultural practices often change before cultural expectations do, and there is evidence that for a number of years men have been increasingly involved in childcare. Although Gardner (1943) found that a large sample of fathers reported themselves as having little involvement in childcare activities, by 1952, Tasch reported that the fathers he interviewed saw themselves as actively involved in childcare, and greatly valued the companionship of their children.

Gavron (1966) studied London working class and middle-class families with at least one child. Of the fathers, 44 percent were willing to do anything required in the care of their infant or child, 21 percent would do all but one or two particular things (changing diapers or feeding), and 35 percent were not performing any childcare activities, for one reason or another. Virtually all these men were more involved in housework and childcare than either their fathers or fathers-in-law had been. In the sample of 120 couples described by Entwisle (1977; also Doering, Entwisle, and Quinlan, 1978), 65 percent of the fathers had diapered their newborn infant before it was a week old, and when the baby was two to three weeks old, the fathers were holding the baby an average of one-and-a-half hours a day. Finally, Lamb (1976, 1977c) has convincingly concluded that modern-day American babies know their fathers, develop strong attachments to them, and for some activities, even prefer them to their mothers (see also Kotelchuck, 1976; Lewis and Weinraub, 1976).

Although it is now recognized that the experiences of fatherhood are central to the sense of wholeness and creativity of many American men, the new cultural expectations of fathers have created a number of problems. In most of the roles required of them in the past, men were viewed as primarily instrumental (Benson, 1967; Rapoport, Rapoport, and Strelitz, 1977). Now the wife looks increasingly to her husband for companionship (Burgess, Locke and Thomas, 1965; Young and Willmott, 1973), a role that requires him to be more emotionally expressive and less restrained, rational, and objective. Caring for children also requires emotional availability and warmth. As husbands and fathers, men are moving away from the instrumental model toward an expressive one, but without any clear guidelines about their new and appropriate role in the family (Green, 1976; Knox and Kupferer, 1971). For example, both professionals and fathers are uncertain about the appropriate amount of authority a father should command and demand in a modern family (Benson, 1967; Bronfenbrenner, 1973). Studying another area of confusion, Wenner and others (1969) found that many expectant fathers who were not providing adequately had the potential to be much more helpful but they did not know what they should or could do, because they felt their role to be vaguely defined. Finally, Miller (1971), a self-described "confused middle-class husband," plaintively and clearly discusses how difficult it is to forge a new role without adequate models or supports.

This confusion about role models is further aggravated by the fact that, until very recently, boys in our culture have not been prepared to accept many aspects of their new role. To cite several examples, most boys are given little experience or education in dealing with infants or young children, unlike girls, who often babysit or are in other ways expected to be interested in children. Further, with some exceptions, we continue as a culture to encourage boys to be aggressive, powerful, independent, and ambitious—characteristics which interfere with interpersonal sensitivity (Coleman and Coleman, 1971; Fasteau, 1974; Knox and Kupferer, 1971).

The role of father as breadwinner and stabilizer of the family is yielding to a new model, father as companion and caretaker of his children and companion to his wife. Social scientists are just beginning to study these changes. We know remarkably little about what modern fathers do with their children, how they feel about parenting, and how various patterns and styles of fathering affect the family members (Green, 1976; Nash, 1965).

Most of the studies of the experiences of first-time fathers have focused on the degree to which fatherhood is—or is not—traumatic. LeMasters (1957) interviewed couples within five years of the birth of the first child and reported that 83 percent of these middle-class couples were clinically judged to have experienced extensive and severe crisis: "Listening to them describe their experiences, it seemed that one could compare these young parents to veterans of military service—they had been through rough experiences but it was worth it" (p. 355). He attributes their degree of crisis to the lack of realistic preparation for parenthood.

Dyer (1963), studying thirty-two couples within two years of their child's birth, found 28 percent of the couples to have experienced extensive crisis, and 25 percent severe crisis, on the basis of a checklist of complaints. The fathers' complaints included loss of sleep (50 percent of the fathers), difficulty adjusting to new responsibilities and demands (50 percent), discomfort over upset schedules and daily routines (37 percent), incredulity over the amount of time and work the baby required, and increased financial worries and adjustments. Less crisis was reported by those men who were more satisfied with their marriages after the birth of the baby, those who had taken a course preparing them for marriage, and those who had been married a longer period of time.

Hobbs (1963, 1968), using a different measurement technique, was not able to replicate Dyer's or LeMasters' findings. None of his couples was judged to have had an extensive or severe crisis. The only two issues that a majority of the fathers checked as being somewhat or very bothersome were the interruption of their routine habits (75 percent) and increased financial problems (60 percent). The only variable in his data that related to the degree of crisis was the father's income: fathers earning more money reported less crisis. In his 1968 study, he did find a relationship between marital adjustment and degree of crisis. Hobbs concluded that the measurement techniques probably account for the differences in his data and those from the earlier studies. Also, Hobbs studied couples during the infants' first year, when the families were still undergoing the stress and consequently have more need to deny just how difficult a time it is. LeMasters and Dyer talked to parents several years after childbirth, when in retrospect they might well be freer to recognize and report their earlier discomfort.

Several clinical studies have also reported the negative aspects of the experience of becoming a father (Freeman, 1951; Reitterstol, 1968; Wainwright, 1966; Zilboorg, 1931; all reviewed by Lacoursiere, 1972). These studies focused on men who had developed serious psychological problems, in most instances a psychosis, subsequent to the birth of their first child. Lacoursiere concludes that becoming a father is a stressful experience and emphasizes issues around dependency that get stirred up during the wife's pregnancy and the first weeks postpartum. Dependency needs are aroused in part because the husband often receives less of his wife's attention while she deals with her own physical and psychological needs. If the husband has a history of unresolved issues around dependency, he might become depressed by the change in his wife's ability to nurture him. The potential sources of difficulty during this time, Lacoursiere feels, are concerns about masculinity and "pregnancy envy"—a phenomenon which Coleman and Coleman (1971), from their review of the literature, describe as ubiquitous. Overall, Lacoursiere views fatherhood as a period requiring the recapitulation and new resolution of earlier developmental conflicts. If issues from these earlier phases have been inadequately resolved, then the successful adapatation to pregnancy, birth, and early parenting will also be in jeopardy. Wainwright's (1966) discussion of men hospitalized after the birth of their first child acknowledges the importance of reality factors which add to the new father's stresses. For example, the mother's work is often interrupted by the birth of the new child, removing a source of income to the family and placing additional financial pressures on her husband.

Although these articles discuss men who responded pathologically to fatherhood, they also represent a way of thinking about the experience of new fathers that has been developed more generally into a theory about early fatherhood. This view, the psychoanalytic, is perhaps best represented by Benedek (1970a). She struggles with the question of whether there is any biological need for fatherhood, or whether the only pure instinct in the male is for sexual release. However, she is impressed with the importance of fatherhood for men, and cites evidence of men during the war happy to be leaving their wives pregnant, even if they might never see their offspring, or similarly, men's letters from the war describing their fantasies about their children and the importance to them of their children's survival. She feels the tie created by the child gave the men a "sense of obligation and by this, an aspiration to life" (p. 171). She believes the biological root of fatherhood is the drive for survival, and the birth of a son allows immediate identification by the father, who projects his aspirations onto the boy infant. Fatherhood also allows a man the opportunity to master his own regressive-dependent tendencies and to successfully compete with his own father. He thereby conquers his own fear of competing, becomes a link in the chain between his father and his child, and thus furthers his psychosexual maturity.

Although Benedek believes that a man's early experiences with his own mother and father influence his fatherliness, she concludes that only if he had a tender loving father can he accept his own loving feelings. A harsh punitive father forces him to repress his own tenderness and prevents him from developing a warm and loving relationship with his child.

In her view, a central factor that potentially disrupts good fatherliness is an excessive aspiration to be a good provider, an ambition that often takes the father away from his family and makes him unavailable. Benedek also discusses the real gratifications a father receives when all is doing well. The sense of being a good father and of obtaining real pleasure from interactions with the baby, the enhanced sense of personal identity, and the deepened sense of meaning in the marriage—all are genuine and important satisfactions to be gained in successful fatherhood.

McCorkle (described in Jessner, Weigert, and Foy, 1970) identified three kinds of orientations in prospective fathers. *Romantic fathers* had a casual approach to parenthood. They were awed at the thought of supporting their wives and infants and felt the pregnancy to be a maturational experience that forced them to assume adult responsibilities. *Career oriented fathers* saw prospective parenthood as a burden that would interfere with their pursuit of their careers. *Family oriented fathers* accepted their new responsibilities easily and felt fulfilled at the idea of having a family. They saw the pregnancy as a gift and felt closer to their wives as a result of it. They felt they had been changing before the pregnancy, but now the process was intensified. Some of the men felt threatened by the extent to which the pregnancy and birth appealed to their more feminine characteristics, while others felt enriched by allowing these traits to be developed and expressed. McCorkle's discussion is valuable because he suggests that there is no one adequate style of adapting to fatherhood but a variety of possible modes.

Deutscher (1970) concludes that both men and women have two psychological tasks during the first trimester: to distinguish between illness and pregnancy, and to shift patterns of dependence and nurturance. He reports that prospective fathers described their fears of annihilation, or of being abandoned by their wives for the child. Deutscher observed that the spouses behaved in a parental way towards each other. Couples with good relationships formed strong alliances with each other to work on these issues. With quickening, there was a stronger sense of a triadic form. The third trimester was most difficult for most couples.

This literature reflects some of the changes that have taken place as men have become more involved in the childrearing process and as men and women, in at least some sectors of our culture, have expectations that men should be active participants in childrearing. We will conclude our review of the literature on fatherhood by discussing several recent studies which are particularly relevant to our research.

Trehowan (1965) compared men whose wives had recently delivered with men whose wives had not been pregnant during the previous nine months. Significantly more of the expectant fathers reported having suffered physical symptoms than the other men did. The highest incidence of these symptoms, which included loss of appetite, toothaches, and nausea or sickness, came during the third month of the wives' pregnancy. There were no differences between first-time fathers and experienced fathers; men reporting more symptoms, however, tended to be more anxious. Coleman and Coleman (1971) emphasize how common these so-called couvade symptoms are in our culture. Liebenberg (1969) suggests these symptoms represent pregnancy envy; the more traditional view of couvade interprets these symptoms as the man's way of participating in the pregnancy and birth (Coleman and Coleman, 1971).

Liebenberg (1969) interviewed middle-class white husbands during their wives' pregnancy and at one, three, and six months postpartum. Most of the men said they remembered being pleased about the pregnancy, but were worried about the emotional and financial responsibilities of having a child. From the interview material, Liebenberg concluded that many men felt a heightened sense of dependency during the pregnancy, yet found their wives less ready than usual to take care of and nurture them. Many of the men seemed envious of the pregnancy and also very anxious. None of the fathers was present during the delivery, and most of the men described themselves as feeling abandoned and deserted. After the birth of the baby, most helped with housework and childcare during the early postpartum weeks but had stopped by three months; none of the wives worked outside the home after the birth of the child. On the basis of the interviews, Liebenberg hypothesizes that a major influence on a father's feelings toward his new child is his feeling about his own father and siblings. Liebenberg's findings that men had a relatively negative experience during the labor and delivery—from which they were at least partially excluded—and that they underwent considerable stress in the postpartum period, are consistent with data from other studies.

Two studies contribute to our understanding of the contemporary father's experiences and are in marked contrast to the rather negative views presented by earlier researchers. Greenberg and Morris (1974) studied whether a father's having contact with his baby in the delivery affected his involvement with his newborn. They found few differences between those who had delivery room contact and those who did not. What is striking about their findings is the intensity of all the fathers' feelings towards their children, a set of feelings Greenberg and Morris term *engrossment*. The new fathers were totally captured by their newborns to a degree beyond what most of them had thought possible (see also Shapiro, 1980).

Fein (1974) studied middle-class couples four weeks before and six weeks after the birth of their first child. Most of his sample of men were with their wives during the labor and delivery, and most described it as a very positive experience. He concluded that the crisis for these men was just before or at the birth of the baby, and it subsided quickly. Four weeks before, many appeared anxious and dependent; by six weeks postpartum they appeared substantially more comfortable. His findings were independent of the amount of time men were spending in childcare activities. Fein concluded that men's adjustment to postpartum life is dependent on their having defined for themselves a role that meets their needs and those of their family: the particulars of the role they adopt do not seem to matter. The father's process of defining his role is significantly easier when a man and his wife are in agreement about the appropriate roles for the father.

With these previous findings providing the background, we now want to describe the men in our study and relate their experiences.

The Men in Our Study

Seventy-one men participated in our study, thirty-five first-time fathers and thirty-six men with one or more children. Their ages ranged from twenty-four to forty-six. The average first-time father was twenty-eight years old and had been married about three years; the average experienced father was thirty-two years old and had been married almost seven years. About one third of the men had occupations in the upper-middle-class range, forty-five percent in the middle-class, twelve in what could be termed blue collar, and one lower class. Their annual earned incomes ranged from $2,000 to $40,000, with the average a little above $16,000.

The men varied enormously in the interpersonal resources available to them from friends and family, as reflected in their responses to a questionnaire asking about supports, and also varied in the number and magnitude of life changes they, with their wives, had experienced in the past year.

In the first meeting with the couple, when both the men and women were interviewed individually and privately, we asked the men about their reactions to the pregnancy as well as about their lives in general. In addition, the men were asked to fill out a number of paper-and-pencil tests. Our first goal was to learn about their experience of early pregnancy. Beyond that, we were interested in looking at aspects of their personalities and life situations that would predict adaptation to pregnancy, birth, and early parenting. In general, and in the context of the theoretical literature, we thought that the same general dimensions of the men's lives would predict their adaptation as would predict the women's adaptations. Therefore, we obtained measures of the men's psychological health, sociocultural context, and marital situation.

First Trimester

A man's adaptation to early pregnancy was judged on similar grounds as that of his wife. A man was considered to be doing well if he was primarily pleased about the pregnancy, described his first reactions as positive, was dealing well with whatever physical symptoms his wife was having, and was not yet anxious about the labor and delivery.

As with the women, we were aware that the men were giving us somewhat sanitized versions of their experiences and deemphasizing their negative, fearful, and ambivalent feelings. We suspected this tendency was stronger because all the interviewers were females. Nonetheless, there were marked individual differences in the degree of ambivalence and anxiety the men described. We also assessed their conscious motivation for the pregnancy with a paper-and-pencil scale.

In general, the men were pleased about the pregnancy. Nearly all indicated they wanted the baby and most said the pregnancy was planned. First-time fathers were more eager than experienced fathers; for first-time fathers only, the lower their socioeconomic status, the less pleased they were with the pregnancy and the coming birth. This relationship between responses to pregnancy and socioeconomic status has been described by Duvall (1967) and Kohn (1963).

The men did express some concerns about the upcoming labor and delivery, about the health of the new baby, and about some stress in the marital relationship. In general, they were judged as moderately well adapted to the pregnancy at this early contact, and there were no differences between first-time and experienced fathers in the judged quality of their adaptation.

In studying factors that might predict adaptation at this early point in the pregnancy, we obtained several measures of the men's psychological health. The men's life adaptation was assessed by numerous independent ratings of the interview material. We rated each man on how well he was coping with the major tasks of adulthood (including his work and his marriage), his relationship to his own parents, and the degree to which he was hampered by serious physical or mental symptoms. Most were functioning well, and only four men received scores reflecting marked impairment in general adaptation. Men with lower socioeconomic ratings were doing less well overall in their lives. Experienced anxiety was measured by a paper-and-pencil scale. According to this scale, the men reported quite low levels of anxiety. We also assessed the extent to which the men described themselves as having stereotypically feminine and masculine characteristics, on a paper-and-pencil scale, in part because some recent literature suggests that androgynous men are more comfortable with aspects of parenting (Bem, 1974).

Finally, on the basis of literature suggesting that a man's capacity to be nurturant may depend on his having been well nurtured as an infant and child (Benedek, 1970a), we looked at the extent to which the men felt their mothers had been good mothers, the extent to which they were like their mothers in some important respects, and the extent to which they were comfortable with that degree of identification. Most men perceived their mothers as nurturant and identified strongly with them. They attributed most of their warmth and positive feelings about the nurturing they had received to their mothers; most had little good to say about their fathers in this respect and did not feel they were like their fathers.

On a paper-and-pencil measure of marital satisfaction and freedom from conflict, the men described their marital adjustment as very good, with the men anticipating their first child indicating significantly more marital satisfaction than those with one or more children. On a questionnaire about the frequency, importance, and amount of satisfaction derived from sexual life, the men indicated that their sexual relationships with their wives were of substantial importance to them and a major source of satisfaction.

Of the factors we measured, few significantly predicted the men's adaptation to the pregnancy at this very early point, in contrast to our findings for the women. It appears as if during the first trimester, the pregnancy is not yet having a major effect on the men, possibly because the men have not yet fully realized the reality of the pregnancy. Consequently the men's psychosocial strengths and liabilities are not yet relevant to their adaptation.

One intriguing set of findings did appear. Men judged as more comfortable about the pregnancy and more pleased about it tended to be more masculine and less feminine than were men who were not doing as well. This finding is particularly interesting in that it raises the possibility, as Lacoursiere (1972) and McCorkle (in Jessner, Weigert, and Foy, 1970) have suggested, that the wife's pregnancy arouses issues of sexual identity in the husband. Wishes to be female or to be pregnant, or identification with the protected and passive fetus, could cause some anxiety at this point in men who have fewer stereotypically masculine characteristics. Levinson (1978) suggests that the psychological issues that arise in starting a family include a man's coming to recognize and accept the feminine in himself, as well as in others. There is some evidence that men who have primarily stereotypically masculine characteristics cut themselves off from potentially enriching aspects of their inner lives. Consequently, these men might well sound—and genuinely feel—comfortable with their coping, but at a cost of emotional awareness.

Following are fairly extensive excerpts from interviews with expectant fathers, selected as representatives of markedly different levels and styles of coping. The first excerpt is from the initial interview with a middle-class man whom we considered to be coping well with the pregnancy and whose level of anxiety was relatively low. This pregnancy was his wife's first; they had been married almost three years at the time of the interview.

Interviewer: What's it like being an expectant father?
Bob: Not too different so far. I don't know if I feel outrageously expectant or anything like that.

I look at Marian more, more as becoming a mother now, rather than solely as my wife, as becoming the mother of my child. I think I've thought for a while about the responsibility. I don't think anything has changed drastically since the day we found out she's pregnant.

Interviewer: So were you pleased when you found out she was pregnant?

Bob: Well, I was a little surprised it happened so fast. She had gone off the pill. But it surprised me that it happened within a matter of weeks.

Interviewer: But you were planning the baby?

Bob: Oh yes, but I just assumed it would take three or four months. [He elaborated on why he thought that.] But I'm pleased.

Interviewer: How do you think this part of the pregnancy has been for her?

Bob: I think it's had its difficulties. She's fairly stoic in most cases, so I don't think she lets on, much as it might be bothering her. I try to understand what she's going through. Although I know I don't fully understand, because it's not really happening to me, it's something I've never experienced. She's getting nauseous occasionally. I'm not consciously aware twenty-four hours a day, but when I sit back and notice, I become aware maybe she's not feeling as chipper. I like to think I try to bend over a bit to help. [He explains that he tries to help around the house, to do "his share." He does not feel she is asking for more help around the house or emotional help.]

Interviewer: What do you think it will be like to have a new baby?

Bob: [Laughs.] Boy, that's a broad question! I tend to think of it, at least initially, as feeling that I'm more responsible now. I was used to being by myself when I was single. We got married, and I felt there was somebody else I had to think after besides myself. I look forward to

raising a child in what I think is the right way.
I hope to do the right thing, to correct things
that I notice that are wrong. I want to give my
child every break in life, to make sure he or she
has the best opportunities. [He tells us he imagines things like taking the child to a baseball
game or circus, more than he thinks about
a baby.]

Interviewer: Do you think at all about the labor and delivery?

Bob: I haven't given that too much thought.

Interviewer: Do you worry about it?

Bob: No.

Interviewer: What role do you want to play, do you want to
be there?

Bob: Oh yes, I want to be there. I want to be there
the minute she starts going into labor. I want
to always be by her side, experiencing as much
as I can experience.

He was hoping for a boy, but added, "I'll take whatever
comes." He and his wife had talked about names, at length. He
was definitely planning to participate in a childbirth education
class with his wife.

We judged Bob to be positive about the pregnancy—despite his initial surprise—supportive of his wife and somewhat
aware of her needs at this stage in the process, not anxious
about the labor and delivery, and looking forward to the effect
of a baby on their lives. Using McCorkle's classifications, described earlier, we could label Bob as family oriented, eagerly
anticipating the experience of childrearing and committed to
sharing as much of it as possible with his wife. He was also
high in masculinity and low in femininity, and he illustrates
how adaptive that style can be. His support and empathy for
his wife did not lead him to overidentify and hence take on her
anxieties.

Ben, a man with similar scores—high adaptation to the
pregnancy and low anxiety—was expecting his second child. He
gave similar responses, except for the strong emphasis on having

experienced this before, and consequently feeling more accustomed to it.

Interviewer: What is it like for you to be an expectant father?

Ben: Well, right now it's not any different from before when I was an expectant father. Before Barry was born, I think I had some trepidation of what was to come, how much adjustment I was going to have to go through. But now, having adjusted to him, I don't anticipate it will be terribly different with a second child. So, I'm not thinking about it much.

Interviewer: What was your reaction when you found out Linda was pregnant again?

Ben: Well, I didn't have any very strong reaction. I was kind of glad because we wanted another one. I figured out if there was anything to do or plan for, I'll worry about it later. [Laughs.]

In response to a question about whether he thinks about what it will be like to have a new baby around the house, he reminisced about how hectic things were for the first three months with their first child, and talked without much anxiety about how they would "ease the pain" for Barry when the baby comes.

Ben: I anticipate getting up in the middle of the night and the complications, of you know, Barry's being asleep when the baby's awake. It'll be a little more hectic. I guess those are my images, I haven't yet come to think of the new baby as a person, as somebody who has positive and negative attributes. That's my primary image of Barry, as a neat little guy who's fun to have around. And I'm sure it'll get to be that way, but that's not the picture I have in my mind.

Interviewer: Do you think much yet about labor and delivery?

Ben: No. I expect that we'll do what we did before,

which was a modified Lamaze program. I'll be with her during labor and delivery. It went pretty well the first time, and generally second births are easier than the first.

Interviewer: Do you have any preferences for the sex of the baby?

Ben: No, I don't. The first one, I actually preferred a girl. But now that Barry's here, and he's a boy, he's so much fun, it would be hard to imagine a girl could have been as much fun as he was, or for that matter, how another boy could be as much fun. You know my feelings are sort of directed towards him as a person. But this time, I can see advantages on both sides.

Ben, as an experienced father, was much more aware of the difficulties involved in caring for a baby but was also more confident about his capacity to be a good father. As Coleman and Coleman (1971) suggest, the confidence experience instills can greatly enhance a man's freedom to take pleasure and satisfaction in a subsequent pregnancy. Ben's response about his preference for a boy or girl reflects what actually happens in generally well-functioning families: the strong tie parents develop to a healthy and responding infant by and large overcomes any initial disappointment about the sex of the child.

In contrast, Ralph, an accountant, was given a relatively low score on adaptation to pregnancy, and he was quite anxious. He and his wife had been married three years, and were expecting their first child.

Interviewer: What's it like for you to be an expectant father?

Ralph: I'm very excited about it. It's our first child, both of us are very excited. My second reaction was that I felt responsible for more than two parties.

Interviewer: How did that make you feel?

Ralph: Nervous, anxious. You know, it's a mixture of

the two. I feel anxious and excited at the same time. I'm not sure either one of us has felt the impact of this baby yet.

Ralph had felt the pregnancy had gone well for his wife. She had felt tired, but had not been nauseous, according to him. She had not asked him to do more around the house, but he had felt inclined to do more: "If she asks me to do something, I'm a little more inclined to do it than I would before." He said he found extra meaning in his life at the moment, since his wife was carrying a baby. He felt she did not need any more emotional support lately. He knew when she was upset because she cried.

Interviewer: What do you do when she does that?
Ralph: I respond. It generally means I haven't been paying attention to her or listening to exactly what she wants to say to me. And once I see it, I understand it's gone a little bit too far and she needs me. So I sit down and talk to her and hold her and we talk it out. But that hasn't occurred since the pregnancy started.

He said they had read about husbands who had emotional reactions to a pregnancy, who felt excluded. He had thought about it and they had talked about it, but he was not feeling that way. They had talked about it only once or twice, but when they did, they reassured each other it would never be that way.

Interviewer: Do you think of what it will be like to have a new baby?
Ralph: No.
Interviewer: Not at all?
Ralph: Well, a little bit. [Ralph then talked of how much he liked children, and he felt he relates well to them.] Personally, having my own child, I don't think it's really hit me.

Interviewer: Have you thought about what it will be like to have a baby around?

Ralph: Yes, we've thought about it, that our freedom will be a little less; we're not going to be able to run off whenever we want to. But I've also thought in terms of it's no longer myself and my wife I have things to do for, but another person. These are just the beginnings of thoughts.

Interviewer: Do you think at all about the labor and delivery?

Ralph: Yes. My wife wants me to be in the delivery room and I'm a very squeamish person at heart. But my wife has explained to me, in fact, just the other day, that part of the reason she wants me to be there is because she's afraid of the delivery herself. [He told us that friends and relatives had described delivery to them.]

Interviewer: How do you imagine it will be for you and your wife?

Ralph: I have images in my mind. The image my wife has, and therefore, I have, is that she's going to be in a lot of pain. [Laughs uncomfortably.] And she's going to need me to stand there and hold her hand and tell her it's all right, and to help her through whatever happens. I view my role during her labor as support.

Interviewer: Do you worry about it at all?

Ralph: I haven't worried about it, but I will. I'm not sure I will. I may get so caught up in it that I won't worry about it. But I tend to be a worrier, anyway.

Ralph had had some experiences with his brother's infant. He worried about the baby's fragility but also enjoyed the baby. He said he had no preference for the sex of the baby. They had talked about names, but had not decided. They had not yet talked about a bedroom.

When further pressed, he said his concern was that he have a healthy baby, and "that my wife come through as well."

He again emphasized his anxiety about his increased responsibility and about the baby's health. He mentioned that he knew people whose babies were "mongoloid or something like that." His wife was born with a minor abnormality, and she was also anxious about the baby's health.

Ralph was judged as being positive about the pregnancy, relatively in touch with his wife's needs and relatively supportive of her, but notably anxious about the labor and delivery and health of the infant. When he said that neither one of them had felt the reality of the baby yet, his feelings were representative of most men in this study, who were not, at this first interview, very much aware of the baby, although they were often aware of their wife and her physical and emotional experiences. McCorkle (in Jessner, Weigert, and Foy, 1970) also describes the vagueness of the expectant father's image of the baby in the early stages of pregnancy. Ralph's expressed anxiety about the labor and delivery and the health of the infant at this early stage in the pregnancy is in marked contrast to most of the men, who typically had not yet thought about it; even in the eighth-month interview, when they had thought about it, most men did not report much anxiety. Some men were able to be aware of, and willing to share with us, their worries and mixed feelings without being acutely discomfited, as Ralph appeared to be.

The Eighth Month

When we saw the couples in the eighth month of the pregnancy, we interviewed them together and gave them more forms to fill out.

From the tape of the interview, we evaluated the husband's adaptation to the pregnancy on three dimensions: his acceptance of the pregnancy, his sense of having grown or changed during the course of the pregnancy, and his emotional preparedness for fatherhood. On the average, the expectant fathers were doing moderately well, showing some expected ambivalence toward the pregnancy, some limited sense of maturation, and some readiness for growth and change. As at the first contact, there was no difference in the quality of adaptation between the first-time expectant fathers and experienced fathers. We also reassessed the level of each man's anxiety at this contact. Not surprisingly, the more anxious the expectant father was at the time of the first contact, the more anxious he was at eight months.

Two aspects of the men's previous behavior predicted to better pregnancy adaptation at eight months. Men who perceived their mother as nurturant and identified more strongly with her and those who were satisfied with their sexual life (early in the pregnancy) were adapting better to the pregnancy. These data are consistent with Benedek's (1970a) and Kestenberg's (1975) findings about the importance of a man's identification with his mother and Lowenthal, Thurnher, and Chiriboga's (1975) findings about sexual satisfaction.

These factors—identification with mother and sexual activity and satisfaction—predicted much more strongly for first-time fathers than for experienced fathers. For first-time fathers only, general life adaptation predicted their comfort with the pregnancy. Although the data are not conclusive, this correlation suggests that becoming a father is more stressful the first time and that a man's general adaptive capacity is challenged to a greater extent during a first pregnancy. For the experienced fathers, only their self-described masculinity predicted their adaptation to the pregnancy. This correlation between masculinity and adaptation again suggests that men with a clear masculine identification are better able to cope with the potentially feminine aspects of their responses to their wife's pregnancy. A few brief excerpts illuminate these empirical findings.

Bob was expecting his first child. In the first trimester, we described him as adapting well to the pregnancy, low in anxiety, and high in sexual activity and satisfaction. At the eighth-month contact, he was again judged as adapting well, and he had a moderate anxiety score.

Interviewer: What's the pregnancy been like for you?
Bob: It hasn't affected my life one way or another.
Marian: You've been excited.
Bob: Yes, I'm excited. But there are times when I wish

	the baby were already here. It hasn't affected my everyday life. I am probably more consciously aware of what Marian is up to, when we're out doing something, something like that. Otherwise, I don't think it's affected my life.
Interviewer:	Have you noticed any changes in yourself?
Bob:	Possibly more protective. Certainly more than I would have expected. I think that we entered into this pregnancy thinking we didn't want to really affect the things that we did or didn't do, like babying Marian because she was pregnant. I think that it's fine for you to say that in the first one or two months, but especially in the last couple of months, I realize I am being more protective of Marian, concerned with how she's feeling every minute. I notice that she gets tired more easily, she can't stay up as late. Around the house she's probably not doing as much as she usually does, I can see that she's struggling to keep up the normal routine, but she's tired. [Marian was still working full-time.]

Marian noted that she found herself paying more attention to herself and less to him than she ordinarily did. She felt that Bob responded by calling attention to himself in ways he ordinarily did not, for example, complaining more about a sore throat than he would otherwise: "He might go to sleep or take a nap, and then I feel I need to do something for him, so I'll cook dinner for him and bring it up, where ordinarily I wouldn't have done it. I think he feels a little neglected even though I don't think he's conscious of it." Bob replied that he wasn't conscious or aware of behaving that way. He said that he didn't feel neglected, but perhaps he was appearing to be feeling neglected.

The interviewer asked what they thought the baby was like. After Marian talked at some length about how active the baby was inside her, Bob responded: "I'm aware he's very active. When we're just lying in bed, I'll put my hand on him, he'll kick and punch, or whatever he's doing. If I had my druthers, I'd want an active kid. I like the fact that he's showing signs of being a real scrapper, I guess." When asked about sexual activity, they both laughed and Bob explained, "That's a dead issue, for the last several weeks." They both said how humerous it was to try to have sex with her being so pregnant. The interviewer asked Bob if that was hard for him, and Bob answered: "No. It's really only been in the last, well, the frequency has been falling off, now it's down to zero. But I recognize that as something that was going to happen, and this is the time. I don't feel any bad feelings. It's an understandable thing." They both said their relationship hadn't been affected by the pregnancy, other than their sexual activity.

Bob then talked of how surprised they were going to be if the baby were a girl. He said that they assumed that Mutt—their pet name for the baby—was a boy, and they would be really shocked if they had a girl. When asked, Bob said he imagines the baby when he is two or three years old, adding, "Maybe I'm subconsciously blocking out the first year or so, because I know that's the toughest."

The couple were asked if they ever talk to the baby. Bob said, "I knock on the stomach and say, 'Hello down there! Come on out!' or 'Knock twice if you can feel this,'" and then he puts his hand down to feel and "I yell into her belly button."

When asked about their thoughts on the labor and delivery, Marian talked about her anxieties and current concerns about whether she was prepared to tolerate the pain of an unmedicated delivery, and Bob said: "I think I probably suppress the feelings that Marian's talking about, that I'm going to pass out or that I'm going to get really hyper, run around and tell the doctor: 'doctor, doctor, do something, my wife's in pain.' I sort of can see myself right now as being very calm, take it easy, relax, stuff like that. And I think there is a very great chance I will scream and yell at the doctor that he's not doing his job because my wife is in a lot of pain. [General laughter.] I think that my thoughts at that particular point are going to be with Marian, the fact that she is in a certain amount of discomfort, or whatever. But I'm not scared of it. I recognize that a certain amount of pain or discomfort is going to happen, for the child to be born. I don't worry that she's not going to, you know, survive; it's for a relatively short amount of time." After a pause, he added: "I'm still going to pass out. I don't like to see my friends in pain, especially my wife."

Coleman and Coleman (1971) suggest that men's fear of childbirth, and particularly their reluctance to witness it, comes not simply from the culture's reluctance to allow men to participate. Rather, they maintain that the fear comes from the unease of men in witnessing the "ultimate female secret"; indeed, some cultures believe that a man will die if he observes childbirth. However, although this anxiety may well be present, albeit usually unconscious, it seems that most men in our culture today are far more comfortable participating in the birth than being forced to rely on their imagination and not being allowed to play a role.

Interviewer: You will be going to the classes?
Bob: As long as it doesn't interfere with softball.
Marian: You'd better watch it!
Interviewer: Do you have any plans for when you go to the hospital?
Bob: Yes, it had better be at work, because work is a lot closer to the hospital than here.
Marian: Yes, I was thinking that too. [General laughter.] So I'll say "ready!"
Bob: You'll see papers flying out of my office, running down the hall.
Marian: I think the look on his face is going to be absolutely priceless.

Their plans were for Bob to take a four-day vacation when Marian comes home. They wanted to be without anyone else for the first few days; then her mother would come. They both described the preparations they had made: they had clothes and a crib and had painted the room but not furnished it yet.

Interviewer: Is there anything else I haven't covered that I should know about?

Bob: We're getting a divorce! [Much shared laughter.]
                          We're putting the kid up for adoption, or for sale!

We judged Bob to be accepting the pregnancy, to have some sense of change or growth—for example, his acknowledgment that they had to make accommodations to the pregnancy—and to have made preparations for fatherhood. Bob and Marian's interview illustrates the tone of many of the well-functioning couples at this eighth-month interview; some of the best adapted couples had this quality of giddiness, of shared anxiety and excitement. Their naming the baby and their shared play with the baby are similar to the play described by Deutscher (1970). Further, their joking about the labor and delivery, the divorce, and the sale of the baby allow them to release genuine concerns in a way they can share and can accept, without increasing their anxiety. Marian's awareness that she is less available to nurture him, and her efforts to do so, are consistent with the views of Lacoursiere (1972) and Deutscher (1970) about the role of dependency in a man's response to pregnancy. Coleman and Coleman (1971), in discussing the risk of the father's feeling left out and isolated as his wife turns increasingly inward, suggest that one task of a couple during pregnancy is to develop a new alliance that emphasizes their interrelatedness in dealing with the pregnancy.

The change in Bob and Marian's sexual interests and activities is striking, given the importance of sexual activity in their relationship. However, a marked reduction in sexual activity is not atypical in late pregnancy. They appear to have kept it from becoming too destructive a change in their relationship by being able to talk—and joke—about it. They described this change as a shared experience rather than as an injury or limitation one member of the couple inflicted on the other.

Ralph, described earlier as quite anxious about the labor and delivery and the baby's health and as low on sexual activity and satisfaction, again received a low score on adaptation to the pregnancy at eight months. Indeed, his wife alone, and the two as a couple received low scores on all aspects of their adaptation to the pregnancy. His wife was becoming irritable in response to her anxiety, and Ralph was tending to respond angrily, although he was trying to restrain his anger because he knew that her irritation was caused by the pregnancy. Ralph was still very concerned about the delivery, but he was also beginning to worry now about the time after the delivery, "when you end up with the kid at home." They were having difficulty doing the things they felt needed to be done in preparation for the baby, such as getting the room ready, buying clothes, and the like. Even though they thought they were working to prepare, they felt there was much more to do, and the work was not getting done. During the interview, they felt the need to explain that their difficulty doing these things did not seem to them to be related to unpreparedness for the baby but to anxieties about the pregnancy itself.

This couple did not express the pleasure and fun that Bob and Marian had. Nor had they worked out together a way of dealing with their anxieties that strengthened their relationship. Instead they felt more alone and unrelated as they attempted to adjust to the stresses of the pregnancy and impending labor and delivery. They seem to illustrate a finding of Meyerowitz (1970) that wives accept their pregnancy well when they feel it brings them closer to their husbands.

This last excerpt is from our interview with Ron, who was judged to be coping well with the pregnancy; as before, his anxiety score was high. Ron was able to articulate some of the more subtle maturational changes that fatherhood effected.

When asked how things were going, both he and his wife said they felt more relaxed than they had at the time of the first interview. After Jessica elaborated on her perspective, Ron commented, "The first time I feel I was getting used to the pregnancy. When you were here, I was anxious about it. Now I'm used to being pregnant. [All laugh.] I know something's going to happen, but it hasn't happened yet. I feel fairly comfortable with what's happening now."

When asked about whether the pregnancy had caused any changes in himself, Ron responded: "I guess you realize you're no longer a child yourself. I feel that in subtle ways, in regard to my work. I'm going to have a child who will look to me the way

I looked to my father; that is an interesting experience. I feel more responsible in my job, more concerned about making enough money from it. I guess I feel good about it."

When asked how the pregnancy had changed their relationship, Ron agreed with Jessica that things had changed, and that the changes had to do with dependency and intimacy. He explained that for him, feeling the first kick and going to the prepared childbirth classes gave him another way of understanding and being involved in the pregnancy. Those activities made it easier for him than it had been at the beginning, when he had only the idea of her being pregnant.

When asked about their thoughts and feelings about labor and delivery, Jessica talked about her growing anxieties when she heard from the class and from friends about the experience. Ron said: "I feel a lot of excitement about it. I wonder if I'm going to be able to remember all those instructions they give in class, or if I'm going to be just totally flustered. [Laughs.] I do see it as this very intimate time that's a lot of fun, that you can enjoy. It could be frightening, I guess, but I somehow feel we're not going to have those problems, that we'll be able to deal with it. And I feel real excited about it."

When asked if there was anything else they wanted to add about any aspect of the experience, Ron volunteered: "I think some of the fun should be stressed. The talking, planning, joking about whatever—that's been pretty good."

Jessica talked about the broader issues raised for her by the pregnancy, and a sense of growth, of new life beginning, and of broad religious questions about life. Ron added, "I guess I see that this fetus will come to be a child, this child will come to be an adult. The fact that this child's coming into life is pushing me to realize many more things about life and about adulthood. You don't want to give up a few things from your childhood that you have to give up, in one way; in another way, there's lots of big issues and big things to do that are a challenge, and I guess I feel that happening to myself. I guess I feel that when the child arrives, I'm not going to have arrived at adulthood, to have everything figured out. There's the whole issue of how do you bring up a child. I think it requires that I sort out who I am. I think there's just lots to do."

Ron's comments touch upon aspects of the psychological work of pregnancy that are central to adaptation: the necessity of making some changes in the relationship, the feeling of finally relinquishing some old issues from childhood, and the accepting of one's status as an adult. Even though Ron was very anxious, we sensed that he was able to support his wife and reduce her anxiety, for example, by his comments about the labor and delivery. His strong sense of continued growth and his awareness that parenthood will require both intrapsychic work and change are, we sense, feelings experienced by many of the men and women who were doing well with the pregnancy.

Labor and Delivery

Unfortunately, we did not talk with all the fathers at the time of labor and delivery. Those who were present when we interviewed their wives were very excited and told us how much it had meant to them to be present at the labor and delivery, a finding consistent with that of Shapiro (1980). With few exceptions, these men were much taken with their new infants.

The interviews with these couples in the hospital provide anecdotal support for the hypothesis that greater involvement in the labor and delivery facilitates the husband's positive evaluation of the process and his early involvement with the infant (see Bradley, 1962; Deutscher, 1970; Greenberg and Morris, 1974; Shapiro, 1980; Strassberg, 1978). This observation contrasts sharply with the responses reported by Liebenberg (1969) and Pedersen and Robson (1969); on the basis of interviews with the wives about their husbands' reactions, the latter noted the enormous variability in the men's responses and in their wish to be involved.

Summary

During the clinical interviews with the men early in their wives' pregnancies, the men seemed excited about the prospect of having a new baby and also somewhat concerned about how that new baby would affect their own lives. They were already expressing some fears, either about the health of the baby or about their ability to earn enough money to support their expanding families. We also had the impression that many men had not yet fully understood that this event was happening and the fact that it had not registered was reflected in the quantitative findings: very few characteristics of their personalities or their life situations predicted their adaptation to the pregnancy at this early point.

At eight months, the men were much more involved with the pregnancy, usually more protective of their wives, and certainly more worried than they had been earlier about the labor and delivery. Most had recognized the need to change their relationships and life patterns, but some—particularly first-time expectant fathers—were still resisting such changes.

One finding that appears here for the first time and reappears throughout the study is the importance of a man's feeling he was well nurtured by his mother and his sense of being in some ways like her. The men's capacity to respond enthusiastically and without undue anxiety to their wives' pregnancies seemed to rest, in part, on this earlier experience of being nurtured and loved. That this finding was irrespective of the men's overall life adaptation strengthens our view of its importance.

In contrast to recent suggestions that more androgynous men cope better with life experiences that require warmth and expressiveness, in our study men who described themselves as more masculine and less feminine—that is, men who fit the cultural stereotype—seemed more comfortable with their wives' pregnancies. Possibly, feeling that they were in synchrony with the cultural ideal gave them a sense of confidence and self-esteem that was more important than possessing any of the specific characteristics considered masculine or feminine. Possibly also their security in their manliness afforded them a comfortable sense of differentiation from their pregnant wives and their as yet unborn babies.

Finally, as we observed when discussing the women, for men, a first pregnancy seems to have substantially more psychological impact than do later pregnancies and calls on more of their adaptive capacities to cope well with the stresses it brings.

Fathers and the First Year of Infancy

During the first year of his infant's life, a father has a number of psychological tasks to accomplish. If he is a first-time father, he needs to come to see himself as a father and to feel adequate and comfortable with the view of himself in that role. He must work out a balance between devoting time to his family—to meet their needs and his needs for them—and having time for himself. He must be involved in, and yet maintain some sense of perspective on, the intense and anxiety-rousing period of his child's infancy. While these changes in self-image and allocation of time and energy are much more striking for the first-time fathers, they are required of the experienced father, as well. He has the enormous task of being the father of more than one child, with the responsibilities that entails; he must make time for the infant and maintain his ties to his other children, while still having time enough for his wife, himself, and his job.

Another of the father's major tasks during the first year is to support his wife, to help minimize her anxieties and pre-

vent her from becoming excessively consumed by the early
mother-infant bond. In addition, in the face of the pressures of
parenting on a marriage, he must continue to work together
with his wife on their relationship to keep it satisfying and reasonably comfortable.

Finally, a father has to develop a relationship with his
new infant. He has to come to know his infant, to be able to
respond warmly and without undue anxiety. He needs to accept
the qualities of the baby: its sex, appearance, temperament and
the like, whether or not these characteristics match his previous
fantasies and expectations. In sum, the father has a great deal of
psychological work to do during the first year of his infant's life,
and there is some reason to believe some of the tasks are larger
and more difficult for first-time fathers.

We again talked to the men in our study at two months
postpartum. At this point, there were sixty-three men in the
study, thirty-three first-time fathers and thirty experienced
fathers. We had selected two months as a time to visit because
we thought it would be a time when families were beginning to
reorganize after the chaos of the early weeks with the new baby,
yet were not so far away from the stresses and strains of that
period that they had forgotten them entirely.

At this meeting, the man was interviewed separately. We
asked about how things were going in the family and about his
relationship to his wife and to the new baby. He was asked to
fill out some paper-and-pencil forms, and whenever possible,
we observed him interacting with the infant.

We examined three areas of the man's adaptation at this
point in his adult development: his psychological health, his relationship with his wife, and his relationship to the new baby.
Although his relationship with his other children is also a measure of his adaptation, we decided that such information was
beyond the scope of this study.

Psychological Health at Two Months Postpartum

The interview measure of the man's psychological health
included judgments about the extent of his anxiety about the

infant, his awareness and acceptance of his own needs as well as of the needs of his two-month-old, his general physical condition and energy level, and his recent mood. In addition, a repeat of the paper-and-pencil measure of anxiety was used to evaluate the man's current psychological comfort.

Implicit in these measures is our conception of good adaptation for a man in this early postpartum period. Our position—and we must emphasize that there are no substantiated findings and little speculation about such a definition in the literature—is that in our culture, a man who is doing well for himself and his family is maintaining his work status; is involved, psychologically and otherwise, in efforts to reestablish and stabilize his family's functioning with the new infant as a family member; and yet he also has enough separateness from the process to bring some perspective to it. (Rapoport, Rapoport, and Strelitz, 1977, in contrast, define the central task of both the mother and the father at all stages of parenting as negotiating the balance between self and family.) We discovered from the interviews with the women that most of them were still virtually consumed by the experience and process at two months postpartum, and most were potentially extremely anxious. One important function of the man, who has been less engulfed from the beginning, is to use his separateness to help his wife gain some distance from her total involvement with the newborn and to reduce her inevitable anxieties about the vulnerabilities of the new infant and, for first-time mothers, of herself as a mother. Burlingham (1973), Deutscher (1970), and others use the term *rescue function* to describe the husband's helping his wife extract herself from complete absorption in the mother-infant tie. However, a man too distant from the experiences of his wife and infant will not have the necessary ties at that point in time to serve as a life line for her. Such an uninvolved stance also deprives a man of the richness of experiencing his own nurturant empathic qualities and can, at times, initiate his long-term alienation from his family.

In general, the men in this study were doing quite well on these dimensions of adaptation. They were not unduly anxious in general or about the infant. They were somewhat aware of their own needs, as well as aware of the demands the infants were making on the family, and were beginning to achieve a delicate balance between doing some things for the family at this time of great stress and maintaining the rest of their lives. The stress they experienced was, by and large, the stress on the family system. At two months postpartum, the fathers' division of their time was closer to what it had been prior to the birth than the mothers' routines were. The bond between father and infant was not as close as that between mother and infant, and fatherly duties were less time-consuming than maternal ones. Too, as workers, the fathers' absence from the house for many hours of each week protected them from experiencing some of the daily disruption of household routine caused by the infant. Some men had resumed leisure activities, playing tennis or bowling, although perhaps only once a week instead of three times as they had previously. Most of the men reported feeling pretty good; they were no longer overly tired and were generally quite pleased with their lives.

Of the measurements made at the first contact, the strongest predictor of a man's psychological health at two months postpartum was his anxiety level and his life adaptation, that is, his general ability to cope with the tasks of adulthood (see Table 8, "Emotional Well-Being"). Men who were doing well in their lives early in their wives' pregnancies and who were not unduly anxious then, were also not excessively anxious at two months postpartum and were judged to be making progress in coming to terms with themselves as fathers of new infants.

Another strong predictor of a man's psychological health at two months was his description during the first-trimester contact of how active and satisfying his sex life was. Since both in this study, as well as in other research, men's sexuality and general ego strength or adaptation are found to be highly related to one another, this finding is essentially a restatement of the first. It is remarkable only as it contrasts with the findings of the women, for whom sexual activity and enjoyment have little to do with general life adaptation and, at times, appear to adversely affect their postpartum adjustment.

We also found that men who more strongly identified with a nurturantly perceived mother were feeling more comfortable about themselves and their roles. This relationship is consistent with our earlier findings that men with stronger maternal identifications tended to be better adapted to the pregnancy in the first trimester and were more strongly so at eight months. Similarly, Pressman's (1979) data showed such men to be more involved with their young children and more committed to family life.

One last variable from the psychological dimension predicted to better psychological health at two months postpartum. Men who described themselves as having more characteristically feminine traits tended to be more comfortable with themselves early in the postpartum period. This appears puzzling, since at previous contacts there had been some evidence that high masculinity and low femininity related to good adaptation to aspects of the pregnancy. It is possible that men having more feminine traits are somewhat more nurturant and flourish when given the opportunity to care for an infant.

Finally, one variable from the sociocultural dimension predicted to the men's psychological health at this time. Men, who with their wives experienced more major life changes during the previous six months, were doing less well, and this was particularly true for experienced fathers. This finding is similar to that which showed the effect of external events on the adaptation of experienced mothers at two months, and in contrast to the minimal role such external circumstances seemed to play for primiparous women.

While there were some other differences in the patterns of relationships for first-time and experienced fathers, the role of anxiety and life adaptation is similar in both groups.

One measure from the wife's adaptation predicted strongly to her husband's anxiety level at two months, and is worth noting. Men whose wives had more psychological difficulties near the time of labor and delivery were themselves more anxious at two months postpartum. This relationship holds even when the wife's anxiety and her marital adjustment are statisti-

Table 8. Men's Adaptation at Two Months Postpartum

	Emotional Well-Being			Anxiety			Marital Adjustment		
	All Fathers[a]	First-Time Fathers[b]	Experienced Fathers[c]	All Fathers[a]	First-Time Fathers[b]	Experienced Fathers[c]	All Fathers[a]	First-Time Fathers[b]	Experienced Fathers[c]
Psychological dimension									
Life adaptation	.39[b]	.36	.41[a]	-.31[a]	-.42[a]	-.17	.47[c]	.27	.68[c]
Anxiety	-.28[a]	-.32[d]	-.18	.49[c]	.71[c]	.22	-.35[b]	-.42[a]	-.03
Masculinity	.04	-.02	.28	.09	.15	-.08	.11	-.04	-.10
Femininity	.26[a]	.24	.28	.04	-.01	.12	.24	.05	.46[b]
Identification with mother	.42[b]	.48[a]	.34[a]	-.13	-.11	-.11	.15	-.16	.37[a]
Sociocultural dimension									
Socioeconomic status	-.20	-.14	-.26	.16	.15	.15	.04	-.04	.00
Life change	-.25[a]	-.07	-.41[a]	-.01	-.07	.05	.11	.01	-.27
Age	-.12	.11	-.24	.09	-.05	.13	.15	-.13	.04
Marital dimension									
Marital adjustment	.21	.13	.26	-.19	-.23	-.09	.52[c]	.67[c]	.12
Sexual activity and satisfaction	.45[c]	.43[a]	.46[b]	.10	.12	.13	.02	.06	-.10
Marital style	.10	-.19	.33	-.22	-.15	-.22	.01	-.23	.08
Multiparity	-.08	–	–	.14	–	–	.19	–	–
Years married	.01	.20	.01	-.06	.03	-.40[a]	.21	-.31	-.08

Eighth month of wife's pregnancy									
Adaptation to pregnancy	.23			-.01			.01		
Anxiety	-.19			.43[b]			-.38[b]		
Labor and delivery									
Complications	.18	.05	.32	.04	-.03	.26	.06	.06	-.16
Caesarean section	.23	.32	.11	-.14	-.17	.04	.02	-.12[b]	-.01
Maternal adaptation	.03	.05	-.05	-.36[b]	-.32	-.39	.44[c]	.61[b]	.28

Table 8 continued

	Adaptation to Spouse			Interview Measure of Paternal Adaptation			Observed Paternal Adaptation
	All Fathers[a]	First-Time Fathers[b]	Experienced Fathers[c]	All Fathers[a]	First-Time Fathers[b]	Experienced Fathers[c]	All Fathers[a]
Psychological dimension							
Life adaptation	.33[a]	.30	.33	.26	.26	.20	.14
Anxiety	-.16	.12	-.11	-.18	-.03	-.22	-.18
Masculinity	-.16	-.31	.09	-.05	-.03	.28	.01
Femininity	.05	-.04	.11	.10	.26	-.03	.16
Identification with mother	.10	.17	.05	.26	.54[b]	.10	.31
Sociocultural dimension							
Socioeconomic status	-.28[a]	-.51[b]	-.14	-.28[a]	-.28	-.28	.02
Life change	-.27[a]	-.19	-.33	-.21	-.11	-.32	.17[b]
Age	-.22	.12	-.36	-.40[b]	-.25	-.20	-.45[b]
Marital dimension							
Marital adjustment	.27[a]	.31	.14	.36[b]	.41[a]	.19	.17
Sexual activity and satisfaction	.24	.04	.33	.28[a]	.33	.12	.01
Marital style	.27[a]	.10	.31	.26	-.10	.20	.12
Multiparity	-.11	—	—	-.43[c]	—	—	-.40[a]
Years married	-.03	.25	-.03	-.24	.37[a]	-.05	-.09

Eighth month of wife's pregnancy							
Adaptation to pregnancy	.33[a]			.51[b]			.14
Anxiety	-.21			-.01			.04
Labor and delivery							
Complications	.33[b]	.27	.41[a]	.46[c]	.37[a]	.38[a]	.35[a]
Caesarean section	.10	.21	-.02	.24	.26	-.07	.10
Maternal adaptation	-.01	.09	-.17	-.08	-.06	-.21	.09

Note: These correlations are based on the following samples: For first-time fathers, N ranges from 27 to 33; for experienced fathers, N ranges from 26 to 30; for all fathers, N ranges from 55 to 61.

[a] $p \leqslant .05$, two-tailed
[b] $p \leqslant .01$, two-tailed
[c] $p \leqslant .001$, two-tailed
[d] The multiple r, when men's first trimester anxiety and their life adaptation scores are used together to predict their sense of self is .45 (F=4.8, $p \leqslant .05$) and when used to predict their two-month anxiety score is .56 (F=2.8, NS)

cally controlled. Since a woman's psychological experience of labor and delivery was not related to the degree of actual complications in the delivery, we cannot describe the husband's anxiety as a response to actual threatening situations. Does the wife's uneasiness cause her husband's anxiety, or does his anxiety cause her uneasiness? Our best guess is that more anxious men are less able to support and comfort their wives through the process of childbirth, and these men continue to be more anxious in the postpartum period.

Thus, a man's emotional well-being at two months postpartum, is best predicted by four factors: how well he was doing in his life early in the pregnancy, how anxious he was then, whether he strongly identifies with a nurturantly perceived mother, and, to a lesser degree, whether he has a number of prototypically feminine characteristics.

The Marriage at Two Months Postpartum

We assessed the marriage by an interview measure of how comfortable the man felt with the division of labor he and his wife had evolved since the birth of the baby and how well he felt he and his wife had succeeded in reestablishing their marital dyad. We also repeated the paper-and-pencil marital adjustment scale.

By both measures, the men were quite satisfied with their marriages at two months postpartum. They considered their marriages strong, were mostly pleased with the arrangements for sharing the jobs and responsibilities in the household, and felt they were making progress in restabilizing the marital relationship. Most were quite aware of some stresses on the marriage, the most common and obvious one being how little time they and their wives had alone together. In some cases, this was a source of dissatisfaction equally shared by wife and husband, and for these couples some changes in scheduling and some patience would lead to a solution. In other instances, this decrease in time together was a source of conflict between husbands and wives; most often in these cases, the husband complained that his wife spent more time with the baby then he appreciated. As had occurred in the first contact, first-time fathers described their marriages as more satisfying and less discordant than experienced fathers.

The best predictors of the men's marital satisfaction at two months from the first contact were their life adaptation, their anxiety level, and their earlier marital satisfaction (see Table 8, "Marital Adjustment"). Also men of higher socioeconomic status and those who experienced less recent major life change were judged by us as having reestablished better relationships with their wives.

Shereshefsky and Yarrow (1973) found that a greater number of external stresses—including anxieties about financial security, job dissatisfaction, and the like—related to poorer adaptation to the marriage by the husband and wife during a first pregnancy and the early postpartum period and also to less responsiveness of the husband to his wife during the pregnancy. Since, in general, men of lower socioeconomic status have less satisfactory jobs, these men are also more apt to be experiencing these external stresses.

Just as their wives' adaptation to labor and delivery predicted to—but most likely did not cause—men's anxiety level at two months, so too did it predict men's marital adjustment at this period. Men whose wives had a more difficult psychological experience of labor and delivery were themselves less satisfied with their marriages at two months postpartum. Again, we do not attribute his lack of adjustment to her experience of labor and delivery, rather we argue that the woman's reactions to childbirth are a reflection and magnification of the couple's history of interaction and behavior. Therefore, it is not surprising that this measure relates strongly to a variety of aspects of postpartum adjustment.

Most interestingly, the man's relationship to his wife concerning parenting issues was better if there were *more* complications of labor and delivery. Apparently men become more involved and more responsive to their wives, as well as to their infants, when their wives are less able to cope, as women often are after a complicated delivery. (This point is discussed in further detail later.)

Despite these latter relationships, it is noteworthy how few of the measures related to the experience of pregnancy predicted the man's postpartum adaptation to the marriage or his psychological health. Indeed, the psychological reactions to pregnancy and birth, so consuming at the time in their psychological and physical manifestation, were by two months postpartum no longer so engrossing or overwhelming.

Fathers and Their Two-Month-Olds

Finally, we assessed the man's adaptation to his infant on the basis of an interview. This assessment comprised fourteen dimensions, including the father's acceptance of the infant and specific characteristics of the infant (sex, apparent temperament, and appearance), his apparent responsiveness and sensitivity to the infant, and his degree of expressed affection. Most men received high scores on this dimension, indicating at least from the interview a high level of warmth and psychological involvement with the baby.

In some but not all instances, we were able to observe the father's interaction with his baby, and then were able to rate his fathering on the basis of the quality of physical contact, degree of expressed affection, sensitivity and responsiveness, and acceptance of the infant.

We did not formally measure the men's involvement in childcare activities. In the typical family, we estimate the woman did between 75 percent and 85 percent of the childcare tasks, with the husband enthusiastically doing the rest. Many of the couples said that when the man was not at work, he did about half of the diapering, feeding, and the like. Our sample did include families at both extremes: in one couple, the man stayed home and his wife worked during the infant's first year; in other families, the father played no direct role in childcare during the child's infancy.

First-time fathers appeared to fulfill the fathering role substantially better than experienced fathers, possibly because the latter were busy taking care of the older child at this early stage. Also, younger men and men of higher socioeconomic status were doing substantially better (see Table 8). For first-time fathers only, the longer they had been married, the better they were doing. The quality of the marriage and the man's sexual activity and satisfaction both predicted how well he was doing with the infant, and this was more true for first-time than experienced fathers. Finally, first-time fathers who identified more strongly with a nurturantly perceived mother were seen by us as doing better with their infants.

It is interesting to consider why age is a factor in these findings. Possibly younger men simply have more energy to devote to their babies. An alternative explanation proposes the influence of the period when these younger men were growing up. The younger men, those in their twenties, were teenagers in the 1960s, when strictly codified male and female roles were beginning to break down under the stress of demands for change and increased authenticity. During these men's adolescence, our culture was questioning its sex role stereotypes. In contrast, the older men in the study reached maturity at a time before major changes in marital styles and childrearing approaches occurred. Hence, these data concerning age and adapatation to the infant may reflect the cohort these men grew up in rather than the actual impact of age on a man's capacity to nurture and respond to an infant.

Men from lower socioeconomic classes have previously been observed as less involved in the rearing of their children (Benson, 1967; Handel, 1970), as less positive about the pregnancies, labor and deliveries of their wives, and as less interested in their own young infants (Duvall, 1967; Kohn, 1963). However, Parke and Sawin (1976) described the lower-class men they observed as absorbed by their infants in the hospital and skillful at handling them; Gavron (1966) found working-class men in London more involved in the daily care of their young children than a sample of middle-class London men. Possibly what researchers usually see of lower-class fathers is distorted by context, or other demands on their time and energy. The relationship between the quality of the marriage and the man's adaptation to the infant is consistent with Benson's (1967) conclusion from the admittedly scanty literature that marital adjustment is important to the father's adaptation to his parental role and Westley and Epstein's data (1969) on the relationship between the parents' marital and sexual satisfaction and their offspring's well-being.

Although the men's adaptation to the pregnancy in the first trimester did not predict to their relationship to the infant, the ways fathers responded to late pregnancy did. As was noted before, in the first trimester, before there are external and palpable signs available to the father, it is hard for him to participate in the pregnancy or even believe in it entirely, and his lack of responsiveness then is not predictive of later difficulty. However, if by late pregnancy, when there are numerous tangible signs of the pregnancy, a man has not become involved with the process, that bodes ill for his responsiveness to his newborn early in the postpartum period.

With the birth of the infant, new factors arise which may influence the man's later adaptation. One intriguing finding, that appears clinically sound as well as quantitatively substantial, is that a man's involvement with his infant—as with his wife—is significantly better if there were *more* complications of labor and delivery. When a woman has had a caesarean section or other complications, she has less psychological and physical energy available for the new baby in the early postpartum period. Her husband then has both the opportunity and need to develop a closer relationship to his baby than he might were his wife healthier.

Although the literature is replete with data indicating marked differences in the ways fathers respond to boy and girl infants (Aberle and Naegele, 1952; Kotelchuck, 1976; Lamb, 1976, 1977a, 1977b, 1977c; Pedersen and Robson, 1969; Rubin, Provonzano, and Luria, 1976), we found no sex differences in our data. Possibly our relatively global measures account for the lack of consistency with other studies.

In terms of their emotional well-being, their marriages, and their relationships with their infants, these men were, by and large, doing well and were beginning to enjoy themselves and their families by two months postpartum, although they were most aware of stresses in the marriage. Our data suggest that the period of crisis surrounding childbirth is substantially shorter and less intense for men than for women. Only late in pregnancy do men begin to experience the substantial impact and involvement that women have felt since the first trimester. By the same token, at two months postpartum, the men genuinely seemed out of the crisis, whereas in our judgment women were still feeling substantially disrupted. This is consistent with Fein's (1974) impression that most men in his sample seemed to have settled into a reasonably satisfying style of relating to their families by six weeks postpartum (see also Hobbs, 1963). Fein's data, and ours, differ from the earlier findings of LeMasters (1957) and Dyer (1963), who found marked crises in their families. The measures LeMasters and Dyer used were different from Fein's or ours, however, and they asked parents for retrospective reports of the first year.

Excerpts from the interviews illustrate aspects of the men's experiences. Bob had received high scores on adaptation to the pregnancy at the first trimester and at eight months, and a high score on adaptation to the infant at two months.

Interviewer: How's it going? What's it like being a father?

Bob: It's pretty neat. I guess I'm a little anxious for him to do a lot of other stuff, really smile a lot, you know. But he's really growing on me, no question about it.

Interviewer: What are the nice parts about it?

Bob: I don't know, I guess it's having something that's really your own. He gives me a lot of joy, like when you do get him to smile.

Interviewer: What are the unpleasant parts of it?

Bob: If I have a tough day at the office or something like that, and I come home, and I just want to sit down and get myself lost in something. He's usually fussy when I come home. His fussy time is seven to ten o'clock, something like that. And it's aggravating at times.

Interviewer: Do you think things are getting back to normal?

Bob: They are as much back to normal as I would ever

expect them to be with a child. It's not normal
in the sense of the way it was before he came,
but we're in a pretty set routine.

Bob said that both he and his wife were around the house
more, and both of them were doing more work in the house
than previously. He hadn't changed his work schedule since the
baby was born.

When asked how he juggled his responsibilities as a father
and husband, he said he did not consider himself to be juggling.
When he was home, he preferred to do things for the baby such
as change diapers or feed him since he did not get a chance to
do that when he was at work. Generally he felt he had enough
time with Marian and the baby, although occasionally he wished
he and Marian had more time just to talk. He had continued
going out for sports once a week; he did not know what he
would do when the season changed to one when he was usually
more involved in sports. He said he did not need much time on
his own to do his own things, but he had whatever he needed.
He did not feel increased financial stress or work stress, and he
did not worry about the baby.

Interviewer: What's Marian like as a mother?
Bob: She's super. I think this is what she wanted to
                 do. And I think she's doing a great job. I never
                 was sure she could really handle a kid and the
                 house and all that, and really do everything well,
                 but she has far exceeded my expectations.
Interviewer: What's it like for you to have to share her with
                 the baby?
Bob: Well, there are some times when we wish we
                 could just sit down and talk or just do something
                 ourselves, and we can't, because of Joshua. But
                 I think I recognized that those situations were
                 going to happen well before he was around. So
                 I guess it's maybe something you just put up
                 with. It's part of the price.
Interviewer: What's it like for the two of you as a couple
                 now?

Bob: I think we're a lot closer. I look forward to it
                 more, when I'm at work, to getting home and
                 doing nothing, being with Marian and Joshua.
                 I don't have to go out and go to a movie and be
                 entertained. Maybe that's changed a little bit.
                 Maybe outwardly I show more affection towards
                 Marian. I don't know that it's really changed in-
                 wardly. We haven't been alone, except out with
                 friends occasionally.

Interviewer: What's Joshua like?

Bob: I think he's fairly easy. You feed him, change his
                 diapers, and then he's sleeping most of the time.
                 I'm looking forward to when he can really do
                 stuff, when you can really pal around with him.
                 I try to get him to really smile a lot; when I come
                 home, I usually put him in my lap and try to get
                 him to smile. And it's not always easy to get
                 a smile from him. [Throughout this part of the
                 interview, the baby is fussing and "talking" in
                 the background.] He sleeps through the night
                 now.

Bob said they both wanted a boy, and he was pleased although he had worked during the last month to get them prepared to accept a girl. "I knew, bingo, as soon as he came out,
before the doctor said, that he was a boy!"

When asked about the baby's temperament, he struggled
with his feeling that when he sees the baby, he is often fussy,
but said his wife reassures him that he just sees him most during
the week at his fussy time. When asked about how the baby was
doing, he knew quite a lot about what the baby was eating,
when he slept, what was effective in getting him to sleep, and
other such details.

He fed the baby, changed him, played with him, but never
made the formula, and had bathed him just once, the first bath
he ever had. When asked if that amount of involvement was
what he preferred, he said he thought it was all right but he felt
there were areas of the baby's functioning and life he knew
nothing about, and as Joshua got older, he would like to be more

involved. He had taken care of him alone for several hours at
a time, but his wife prepared everything for him when he did
that.

In general, we felt Bob was maintaining his emotional
well-being, continuing his strong ties with his wife, and now
finding pleasure and enjoyment in his new baby.

Ralph, who received low scores on adaptation to the
pregnancy at both first-trimester and eighth-month interviews,
and seemed to have particular difficulty in managing his anxiety
in a way that did not disrupt the relationship between him and
his wife, was doing all right with the baby at two months and
received reasonably high scores on his psychological health and
his relationship to his wife. His anxiety score continued to be
very high as was his self-described femininity. His wife had an
uncomplicated labor and delivery, even though her scores were
not particularly high on adaptation to that experience, and the
baby was doing well. Ralph seemed to be enjoying the baby
quite a lot, and felt things were beginning to settle down. What
he had minded most was when the baby had cried a lot in the
first several weeks and they did not know why the baby was
crying or what to do about it.

One characteristic that distinguished Ralph from Bob was
the amount of anxiety he experienced about the baby. When
asked if he worried about the baby, Ralph said, "Oh yes, all the
time," and he elaborated on all the things he worried about:
whether the baby was healthy, what little breathing noises meant,
if he was eating enough, and the like. Secondly, when asked
about his marital relationship, Ralph felt they were doing fine
because they were focusing all their interests and energies on
the baby. They had not spent time together yet, but he felt
that was a mutual decision: they were enjoying the baby and
that was creating a bond.

They both had felt they wanted a girl, but now were really
pleased with their son, Alan. About taking care of the baby's
physical needs, Ralph said, "I wouldn't say it's a pleasant experience, but I don't mind it. I do it."

Possibly a reason Ralph was doing all right at this point
despite his anxieties and some difficulties between him and his

wife during the pregnancy was his capacity for nurturance, reflected in his high femininity score. He enjoyed caring for the baby and did that well. These nurturing skills are substantially different from those required of a man during pregnancy, when providing support for his wife and reducing her anxiety seem most important. However, this couple's earlier difficulty during the pregnancy and the woman's relatively poor adaptation to labor and delivery suggest we might well see marital difficulties later on.

Ron and Jessica were particularly interesting at this two-month interview because he was better able and willing to verbalize the discomfort than most other fathers. Many couples told us at the one year visit: "Things were awful when you were here before, but now they're much better." Listening to their interviews, however, one might never have known how awful they had felt their situation to be. Ron and Jessica were more open and articulate about their doubts and discomforts.

Ron was judged as doing very well with the baby and his wife, and quite well in his emotional well-being. As before, his anxiety score remained high.

Interviewer: What's it like being a father?
Ron: What's it like being a father? It's different from not being a father. . . . It's too new to crystalize. There are parts of it that are a lot of fun; there are other parts of it that are not so much fun.

To him, the joys included the baby's responsiveness and playfulness and the sense that it was right for him and his wife to have had a baby now—the time was right, and it was what they wanted to do in their lives. The not-so-nice times were when the baby cried and they could not make her comfortable or satisfied. He was also feeling economic pressures, wondering if he would be able to provide for his family. Ron clearly thought that things were not yet back to normal: "I don't feel comfortable with the routine we've worked out, and I'd like to improve it." What troubled him the most is that he and his wife did not have much time together anymore. Ron talked with

some amazement at how much work was involved in being responsible for the baby: "If you get to brush your teeth, you've
accomplished something!" He hoped that would change as their
daughter gets older.

When asked if he worried about the baby, he said, "Not
really. She seems to be doing all right. She's growing. Sometimes
I have a little bit of a fantasy perhaps. . . . She's so cute now,
and yet if she ever just stayed at this stage, it would be such an
incredible blow. Really just sort of a vague thought; I don't really
worry about it."

Things were a bit strained between himself and Jessica.
They did not spend as much time together as they had previously; they did not communicate as much as they used to. When
we asked him how he felt about Jenny's being a girl, he said,
"I think I wanted a boy because I lost my father several years
ago, and I liked the idea of a boy who would have his name. So
if you ask me how I feel about having a boy or a girl, I think
I wanted a boy. How do I feel about Jenny, my daughter! I feel
terrific. I don't want anybody else other than her; she's great.
So if the question is boy or girl, there's one answer; if the question is boy or Jenny, I want Jenny."

As one might predict, this man knew in great detail about
the eating habits, sleeping patterns, and problems of his daughter.
In terms of his direct involvement in childcare, he changed her
diapers and fed her about half the time when he was around. He
did not bathe her and he did not usually get up at night.

Several important aspects of family functioning are illustrated by Ron's comments. At two months postpartum, things
are at best just beginning to settle down for many families, and
much remains to be worked out, although many of the men feel
their own lives are more settled. Ron's marked discomfort about
the times when the baby was unhappy and he did not know how
to comfort her epitomizes one of the most commonly expressed
distresses about early parenting: it is hard to know what the
baby is wanting or feeling, and very hard to tolerate sustained
distress. Ron is somewhat atypical in our sample in the extent
to which he was involved in the psychological events of childbearing. Consequently, he was more distressed still at two

months than many other men, as well as being unusually able to discuss this.

The stresses on the marriage described by this couple, who emphasized so much the importance of their relatedness to each other, echoes the complaints from the couples Fein (1974) interviewed that they had too little time alone together in the early postpartum period. Finally, Ron illustrates another general process in his reactions to his infant being a girl, when he had hoped for a boy. Although he was aware of, and willing to voice, his earlier preference for a boy, that did not appear to interfere in the least with his genuine attachment to, and fascination with, his child who happened to be a girl. Our impression was that this was the case for nearly all of these at least moderately well-functioning couples. The positive feelings elicited by a healthy baby overcame, at least during this early period, any marked dissatisfaction that the baby was not of the sex one had preferred.

Summary

In sum, looking at these men at two months postpartum, the men were beginning to feel comfortable about themselves, their relationships with their wives, and their ties to the new babies. The men's psychological health, reflected in their anxiety and their life adaptation measured at the first contact, were the strongest predictors of their psychological health at two months postpartum. Men who were earlier more active and satisfied with their sexual lives, those who were more strongly identified with a nurturantly perceived mother, and those who were more characteristically feminine, were also experiencing better psychological health. Greater recent life change related to less comfortable personal adaptation at two months, particularly for experienced fathers.

Men whose earlier life adaptation was better, those who had been positive about their marriages early in pregnancy, and those who were less anxious were more satisfied with their marriages at two months. Men of higher socioeconomic status and those who had experienced less recent life stress appeared to us to have been more successful at reestablishing their marital tie after the disruption caused by the birth of the baby. When their wives had had more complications during labor and delivery—and most often, in this sample, that meant a caesarean birth—the men were more satisfied with the way they and their wives were managing things together.

Few men in this sample assumed a major proportion of childcare responsibility. Most seemed involved with the babies and were enjoying playing with them, and many made a substantial effort to participate in childcare activities when they were home. First-time fathers, younger men, and men of higher socioeconomic status had better relationships with their infants. The quality of the marriage early in pregnancy as well as the man's earlier sexual activity and satisfaction predicted his adaptation to the infant, and particularly so for experienced fathers. First-time fathers who had been married longer and those who more strongly identified with a nurturantly perceived mother were assessed as better at fathering.

Although the man's adaptation to the pregnancy in the first trimester did not predict how he would be with the infant in the early postpartum days, his response to late pregnancy did predict the quality of his relationship with his infant at two months. Also, when the baby had arrived after a complicated birth, the man was more involved with, and related to, the infant than were fathers of babies delivered without complications.

The One-Year Postpartum Visit

When we approached our one year data for the fathers, we were particularly interested in following some of the earlier results to see if the same factors continued to play a role. Were his feelings about himself and his marriage changed or influenced by his experience of parenthood? Would earlier scores predict how he would be doing with his baby, and in particular would his age or social class make a difference as it had before? We wondered if the sense of newness and excitement and anxiety that were still very much part of the father's experience at two months postpartum would be important when the family had had a year to become accustomed to the new baby, and also if the father would have much involvement with the one-year old. Finally, we continued to be interested in the role the man's sense of his masculinity or femininity and his identification with his mother played in his experience of early fatherhood and in his relationship with his baby. With these questions, and others, we approached the data from the fifty-three men remaining in the study at one year.

At the one-year visit, each father was interviewed alone about how the year had gone for him. We asked him questions about the baby: its temperament, schedule, preferences, and the like. In addition, he was asked to fill out another set of forms. As at the two-month visit, we evaluated the men's functioning in three areas—their psychological health, the marital adjustment, and their relationship with the baby.

Psychological Health at One Year Postpartum

We measured the men's internal psychological state in two ways. We assessed his current anxiety level from a repeat of the pencil-and-paper anxiety scale and his emotional well-being from the interview with him. This interview measure reflected our assessment of his current mood, his comfort with the role he had currently within the family, the extent to which he was aware of his own needs as well as the needs of his family, and his attempts to achieve a workable balance in meeting those needs.

In general, the men's anxiety scores remained low, and their sense of emotional well-being was high at this visit. As we found at eight months and at two months postpartum, the best predictor of a man's anxiety level was his previous anxiety level (see Table 9). Thus it does not look as if the level of a man's anxiety is influenced by the experience of his wife's pregnancy, childbirth, or the subsequent first year of his child's life; in fact, men's average anxiety levels did not appreciably change over the eighteen months of the study.

A man's sense of emotional well-being as having integrated fatherhood into the rest of his life was related only to his anxiety level. It is possibly of significance that, for the first-time father, how well things were going for his wife at the eighth

Table 9. Selected Correlations Predicting to Men's Psychological Adaptation at One Year Postpartum

	Anxiety			Emotional Well-Being		
	All Fathers[a]	First-Time Fathers[b]	Experienced Fathers[c]	All Fathers[a]	First-Time Fathers[b]	Experienced Fathers[c]
First trimester (men's scores)						
Psychological dimension						
Life adaptation	-.32[a]	-.49[b]	-.15	.14	.15	.14
Anxiety	.58[c]	.73[c]	.41[a]	-.38[b]	-.19	-.63[c]
Conscious motivation	.00	-.31	.32	.25	.11	.36[a]
Adaptation to pregnancy	-.24	-.30	-.22	.14	.32	-.01
Masculinity	.15	.26	-.12	-.03	-.02	-.03
Femininity	.01	.02	.00	-.03	.20	-.29
Sociocultural dimension						
Socioeconomic status	.09	.08	.11	-.02	-.05	.01
Age	.01	-.11	.16	-.08	-.16	.02
Marital dimension						
Marital adjustment	-.30[a]	-.33	-.30	.16	.06	.25
Sexual satisfaction and activity	-.10	.05	-.31	-.10	.08	-.28
Eighth month of wife's pregnancy (men's scores)						
Adaptation to pregnancy	.09	.13	.02	.12	.25	-.18
Anxiety	.60[c]	.58[b]	.64[b]	-.20	-.21	-.20

Two months postpartum
(men's scores)

Emotional well-being	-.23	-.26	-.22	.18	.38	-.17
Anxiety	.70[c]	.66[c]	.79[c]	-.30[a]	-.20	-.44[a]
Marital adjustment	-.40[b]	-.46[a]	-.25	.09	.04	-.02
Adaptation to spouse	-.16	-.21	-.13	.04	.10	.14
Paternal adaptation	-.01	.01	-.09	.15	.27	.01

Note: Only those correlations that are statistically or conceptually significant are presented. These correlations are based upon the following samples: For first-time fathers, N ranges from 24 to 27; for experienced fathers, N ranges from 18 to 21; for all fathers, N ranges from 36 to 51.

[a] $p \leqslant .05$, two-tailed

[b] $p \leqslant .01$, two-tailed

[c] $p \leqslant .001$, two-tailed

month and how prepared the two of them were for the impending birth was predictive of the man's sense of comfort with himself and his situation at one year postpartum. Husbands whose wives at eight months were more positive about the pregnancy, were adjusting better to it, and who together as a couple were better prepared for the birth were feeling significantly better about themselves as individuals and in their new roles at one year.

Thus, there is some evidence that for men who are new to parenthood, how well they negotiate the crisis of pregnancy with their wives might bear upon how well they will do when the tumult and excitement are over—that is, how they will adapt to their spouse. Perhaps, then, clinical intervention with prospective new parents during the pregnancy could have consequences for how both men and women will function in the family later on. Shereshefsky and Yarrow (1973) did find such counseling helpful for couples' adaptation to early parenthood.

For experienced fathers, measure of their adaptation to the pregnancy predicted little about their emotional well-being. Experienced fathers who were more anxious in the first trimester and at two months postpartum, those who had more depressed wives in the first trimester, and those who themselves were less positive about this pregnancy originally, had less positive feelings about themselves at one year.

In sum, the best predictor of a father's anxiety at the time of his child's first birthday is his earlier level of anxiety. For new parents, the couple's preparedness for childbirth predicts the husband's integration of the fatherly role into his life; for experienced fathers, reliable predictors include his general anxiety level and his wife's level of depression early in the pregnancy.

In the interview, we asked the fathers to describe what their lives have been like since they had the baby. The following comments represent their overall impressions of the experience:

"It's been a much fuller life. I don't think of it as fun but as the thing to do, I guess."

"It's been actually a lot of fun. When I'm with her, I'm elated. She's so bright, and everything she does, she works so hard. She's always using all her energy."

"It's been a teeny bit more expensive."

"She's a pleasant kid, a cute kid. That's what it's been like."

"It's been a lot of fun, to watch him grow, to watch him learn things. At the same time, it's a lot of responsibility. When he was a little baby, it was easy. Like this Saturday, I baby-sat all day, and I was a nervous wreck by the end of the day."

"I just didn't have any idea what being a father was like. Now I'm really attached to him, I find myself thinking about him when I'm at work. Every day he learns something new, and you want to see it. At the beginning, we went through a lot of changes. We bought a house, my wife went back to work. I was really depressed. It was so much responsibility, it was really overwhelming. We had a terrible summer because of that. Now I'm coming out of it. I really feel good."

"It's been a tough year. Enjoyable, but hard doing all the things we've had to do taking care of the baby also." [He explained that he had taken a new job that was very demanding and his wife had gone to work part-time.]

It was not uncommon for a couple to make one or several other major life changes simultaneously with the new baby's arrival, inadvertently creating additional stresses for them to cope with. If these couples had known more about the realities of having a new baby, they might well have chosen not to make so many other changes in their life during the first postpartum months. It is painfully obvious how unprepared some young couples are for the reality of early parenting.

We asked the fathers if they had enough time for themselves now that the baby was a year old. Their answers ranged from an emphatic no to an equally certain yes. No one set of variables from our material predicted, or determined, which fathers felt they did have enough time and which did not.

Still exploring the changes in their lives, we asked if they had noticed changes in themselves since the baby was born. We were interested in the question of adult development, whether the fathers experienced their fatherhood as promoting significant change and growth. None of the experienced fathers described changes related to the second child. A sizeable number of the new fathers did describe a feeling of growth in themselves:

"I have a greater appreciation of people, especially people with small children. I know they're really doing something that matters."

"It's caused me to reassess my actual responsibility. It's someone else's turn to be the baby, essentially, a solidifying of the family priority."

"I think I feel better about myself, more complete, more in the place I want to be, at least in retrospect."

It would be interesting to explore further how the feeling of personal growth resulting from fatherhood related to other aspects of the family functioning, such as how involved the men were in the day-to-day care of the baby. Our data, however, do not permit us to say more about this area.

The Marriage at One Year Postpartum

The measures of the marriage included the man's marital adjustment score on a paper-and-pencil scale, the questionnaire on his sexual activity and satisfaction, and our rating of his adaptation to his spouse, based on the interview. This last rating was similar to the two-months postpartum measure, and included a judgment of how well the couple had recemented the marital dyad after the birth of the baby and how comfortable the spouse was with the division of household labor.

Overall, the marriages were going quite well at one year, as reflected in these scores. The couples' sexual lives were almost— but not quite—as they had been before the baby was born. The best predictor of the man's marital adjustment at one year was his earlier evaluation of his marriage (see Table 10). His marital adjustment in the first trimester of pregnancy predicted strongly to his view of the marriage at one year and his assessment of the marriage at two months postpartum predicted even more strongly to one year. To a very limited extent, his anxiety at eight months predicted to his martial adjustment, although at earlier contacts, the tie between anxiety and marital adjustment was quite strong for the men. (In fact, the man's marital adjustment at one year postpartum is predicted very strongly by looking together at his marital adjustment at two months, his anxiety level at that time, and his adaptation to his wife regarding parenting issues.)

We continue to find the disenchantment phenomenon described earlier: the longer the men were married, and for experienced fathers, the more children they had, the less satisfied they were with their marriages. Not surprisingly, the man's assessment of his marriage at one year was similar to his wife's assessment.

Considering the man's reported sexual interest and activity, at least in part, as a reflection of his experience in the marriage, the only strong predictors for the sample as a whole were his and his wife's earlier responses to that same measure, as well as his wife's response to that questionnaire at one year (see Table 10, "Sexual Activity and Satisfaction"). Men who described themselves as sexually active and interested, and whose wives in the past and at one year described themselves in the same way, described themselves that way at one year postpartum. For first-time fathers, their marital adjustment during the first trimester also related to their reported sexual interest and activity at one year postpartum.

Thus, those aspects of a man's functioning in his marriage that are not directly tied to his and his wife's life with a baby seem entirely unaffected by the experience of pregnancy and early parenthood. In contrast, a man's relationship to his wife concerning parenting issues and the way the couple managed the pregnancy were more relevant to their adaptation to spouse at one year. For the sample as a whole, and even more strongly for first-time fathers, the way the husband and wife dealt with the pregnancy at eight months was strongly predictive of how they were coping with parenthood at one year postpartum (see Table 10, "Adaptation to Spouse"). To a lesser extent, but consistent with this finding, men and their wives who had more positive feelings about themselves in their roles as parents at two months postpartum and who had better relationships with their infants were, from the father's perspective, doing better together as parents at one year. Thus, the new father's behavior during pregnancy and early parenthood is highly predictive of his behavior as the parent of a one-year-old.

Table 10. Selected Correlations Predicting to Men's Marital Adaptation at One Year Postpartum

	Marital Adjustment			Adaptation to Spouse			Sexual Activity and Satisfaction		
	All Fathers[a]	First-Time Fathers[b]	Experienced Fathers[c]	All Fathers[a]	First-Time Fathers[b]	Experienced Fathers[c]	All Fathers[a]	First-Time Fathers[b]	Experienced Fathers[c]
First trimester									
Psychological dimension									
Life adaptation	.04	-.32	.29	.13	.40[a]	-.05	.05	.06	.10
Anxiety	-.21	-.20	-.19	-.27	-.24	-.39[a]	.02	-.20	.27
Masculinity	-.31[a]	-.21	-.48[b]	.03	-.07	.15	-.01	-.10	.18
Femininity	.24	.02	.40[a]	-.14	-.09	-.15	-.08	-.08	-.08
Adaptation to pregnancy	-.13	.08	-.27	-.05	.14	-.34	.01	.01	.00
Identification with mother	-.06	-.22	-.22	.30[a]	.34	.34	.07	.14	.14
Sociocultural dimension									
Socioeconomic status	.07	.00	.15	.11	-.22	.38[a]	-.07	.10	-.27
Age	.06	-.15	.42[a]	-.09	-.13	-.33	-.17	-.20	-.22
Marital dimension									
Marital adjustment	.40[b]	.72[c]	.17	.09	.08	.23	.33[a]	.68[b]	.08
Sexual activity and satisfaction	.00	.14	-.15	-.09	.05	-.18	.56[c]	.71[c]	.46[a]
Years married	-.20	-.53[b]	.12	.25	.07	.34[a]	-.19	-.42	-.20
Number of children	-.23	—	-.37[a]	.26	—	.35[a]	-.02	—	-.09

Eighth month of wife's pregnancy (men's scores)									
Anxiety	-.33[a]	-.39	-.26	-.14	-.20	.04	-.11	-.37	.19
Adaptation to pregnancy	-.18	.11	-.62[b]	.43[b]	.50[b]	.30	.05	.04	.07
Two months postpartum (men's scores)									
Emotional well-being	.05	.02	.04	.29[a]	.47[a]	.07	.32[a]	.24	.45[a]
Anxiety	-.09	-.16[c]	.03	-.35[a]	-.33	-.41[a]	.12	.05	.26
Marital adjustment	.63[c]	.70[c]	.56[b]	.18	.23	.20	.24	.36	.08[b]
Adaptation to spouse	-.13	.00	-.25	.27	.30	.32	.33[a]	.14	.54[b]
Paternal adaptation	-.06	.14	-.30	.18	.44[a]	.16	.13	.07	.24

Note: These correlations are based on the following samples: For first-time fathers, *N* ranges from 22 to 26; for experienced fathers, *N* ranges from 17 to 24; for all fathers, *N* ranges from 44 to 48.

[a] $p \leq .05$, two-tailed
[b] $p \leq .01$, two-tailed
[c] $p \leq .001$, two-tailed

These factors were not predictive for experienced fathers. Experienced fathers who were less anxious, those who had been married longer, those who had more children, and those who were of lower socioeconomic status were judged by us as adapting better to their spouse at one year (see Table 10, "Adaptation to Spouse"). On the face of it, this finding conflicts with the other data supporting the disenchantment phenomenon. Our impression from the interviews is that these older, more experienced fathers were simply accustomed to the role of parenting a baby, and had worked out a style with their wives of sharing the care of the children that was reasonably comfortable to them. Why fathers of lower socioeconomic status seemed to be doing better in this area is not entirely clear, although of course socioeconomic status did not correlate with the number of children. Possibly these couples had clearer ideas about the appropriate roles of mothers and fathers, thus providing the father with more structure for his role and consequently bolstering his comfort with it. Not surprisingly, the man's adaptation to his spouse at one year related to his wife's adaptation to him at one year, and also her sense of comfort with her role as mother.

The differences between first-time and experienced fathers were as marked in the interview as in the quantitative findings. When asked in the interview how family life had changed since the baby was born, first-time fathers all commented on some changes, in their feelings, their routines, and often their sense of being more of a family.

"There have been minor, mechanical changes, like having to get out of bed early in the morning."

"My life has gotten a lot more regular. I don't work late as often. I'm always at home in time to help with the baby's bath. And I get up early. I'm home more than I would be."

"I feel like we're more of a family."

"We don't go out as much. It's really hard to get baby sitters. Our social life has really changed a lot. We used to go out maybe three or four times a week. It's changed my whole life. When you decide to have a baby, you don't think your whole life is going to change. It's different, but it's fun."

In contrast, fathers who already had at least one other child said the new baby had not made much difference in their lives and that all the major changes had happened after the first child was born.

Finally, we asked if there had been noticeable changes in the marriage itself since the baby's birth. Few men described any changes. Those who did mentioned increased stress caused by disagreements about parenting issues or closer emotional ties with their wives because of their shared involvement with the baby. Listening to the tapes of the interviews, we sensed that there were often subtle changes the men were not aware of or were not choosing to share with us. Most of these changes were increases in stress and strain in the marriage, and these changes were reflected in the lower marital adjustment scores described above. Typical comments include the following:

"We don't go out nearly as often as we once did, but then we don't have as much money as we once did either."

"Emotionally, as a couple, it's been really good. Sexually —with the baby sleeping in the alcove nearby—we haven't made love as often as before."

"It hasn't changed things."

"Life is changed a lot. There are more strains, more disagreements, and we're also more of a family now. We used to talk at supper, that was the main time we'd talk together. Now one of us is feeding her, she's dropping things on the floor, banging, you can't talk. We've had problems, like whose turn it is to get up at night."

Overall our couples seemed to feel that in general the baby had enhanced their marital relationship, even though it created more stresses on it, a view similar to that of the primiparous couples studied by Meyerowitz and Feldman (1966).

In sum, those aspects of the marriage not directly related to shared parenting seemed, for these men, unaffected by any aspect of pregnancy and early parenthood. (Not surprisingly, this was substantially less true for their wives.) The first-time fathers' evaluation of how successfully the couple shared parenthood was strongly predicted by how well they handled the pregnancy and parenthood up to two months postpartum. For experienced fathers, enduring personality and situational factors were often more predictive of the couple's adaptation to parenting.

Fathers and Their One-Year-Olds

We measured the father's relationship to his baby at one year from the interview, rating fathers on a number of different dimensions, including acceptance of the child, feelings of competence with the child, expressed warmth, and the like. In general, the fathers received scores indicating high levels of judged competence and relatedness with their toddlers. There were no significant differences between experienced and first-time fathers.

A comparison of the scores fathers received on this measure and our clinical impressions based on simply listening to the interviews did not generate much confidence in this particular score. Fathers did not discuss the less socially acceptable aspects of their feelings and reactions towards their babies, and the interview material did not allow us to differentiate very clearly between higher- and lower-quality fathering. Despite that, we found several interesting and apparently meaningful relationships.

The best predictor of how the father was relating to his baby at one year was how he was relating to his infant at two months (see Table 11). Men who were doing well at two months and those who were not anxious at two months were doing exceptionally well relating to their babies at one year. As we have seen consistently before, for first-time fathers, many earlier measures predicted strongly and significantly to their adaptation. First-time fathers with stronger positive identifications with their mothers, those who were older, those who with their wives were better prepared for the baby during late pregnancy, those who themselves were better adapted to the pregnancy then, those who had a more positive sense of themselves, and those who were relating better to their infants at two months were doing better with their babies at one year. Finally, fathers whose infants received higher Brazelton alertness scores shortly after birth were also doing better with their one-year-olds.

For experienced fathers, in contrast, few scores predicted to their relationship with their one-year-olds. Men who were more anxious, those who were of lower socioeconomic status,

Table 11. Selected Correlations Predicting to Men's Paternal
Adaptation at One Year Postpartum

	Paternal Adaptation		
	All Fathers[a]	First-Time Fathers[b]	Experienced Fathers[c]
First trimester			
Psychological dimension			
Life adaptation	.03	.10	-.07
Anxiety	-.12	-.05	-.22
Masculinity	.11	.06	.27
Femininity	.00	.35	-.38[a]
Adaptation to pregnancy	.20	.34	.10
Identification with mother	.30[a]	.57[b]	.57[b]
Sociocultural dimension			
Socioeconomic status	-.08	.14	-.26
Age	-.29[a]	-.55[b]	-.04
Marital dimension			
Marital adjustment	.30[a]	.28	.33
Sexual activity and satisfaction	.00	.12	-.13
Years married	.09	.08	.30
Number of children	.05	—	.29
Eighth month of wife's pregnancy (men's scores)			
Anxiety	-.05	-.05	-.10
Adaptation to pregnancy	.37[a]	.51[b]	.07
Two months postpartum (men's scores)			
Emotional well-being	.36[b]	.48[b]	.17
Anxiety	-.36[b]	-.18	-.62[b]
Marital adjustment	.16	.21	.07
Adaptation to spouse	.18	.17	.19
Paternal adaptation	.44[b]	.71[c]	.29

Note: Only those correlations that are statistically or conceptually significant are presented. These correlations are based on the following samples: For first-time fathers, N ranges from 24 to 29; for experienced fathers, N ranges from 19 to 23; for all fathers, N ranges from 40 to 53.

[a] $p \leqslant .05$, two-tailed

[b] $p \leqslant .01$, two-tailed

[c] $p \leqslant .001$, two-tailed

and those who described themselves as less masculine were judged by us as relating less well to the baby. Men whose infants had lower Apgar scores at birth—these newborns were frequently the product of more complicated deliveries—were doing better with their one-year-olds. As has been noted before, mothers who had a more difficult delivery needed more help with parenting during the first weeks and thus their husbands played a more active, nurturant role with the baby.

It is important to note that we did not find a relationship between the marital adjustment of the couple and the father's relationship to his baby at one year. Previous researchers have puzzled over the question of whether a good marriage is necessary for good parenting (for a review of this literature, see Benson, 1967). However, other data from our study suggest that babies of strong marriages in fact are doing better at one year, consistent with Westley and Epstein's (1969) data on older children.

In these data, there were no differences in how fathers related to boy and girl babies, which is similar to Kotelchuck's (1976) finding, although Aberle and Naegele (1952), for example, document the existence of such differences. When we asked fathers how they felt about the sex of their child, most said they felt fine; only one father openly said he wished his daughter were a second son instead. Given the consistency of the findings indicating that the sex of the baby does make a difference to parents (for example, Lewis and Weinraub, 1976; Radin, 1976) as well as the widely shared view in our culture that parents feel and respond differently to boys and girls, we did not fully believe that these fathers did not have feelings about the sex of their child. Rather, we were impressed with the extent to which they censored their comments to the interviewer, presenting what they felt to be a socially appropriate, nonsexist attitude. To some extent, as well, they hid from themselves their feelings about an issue as relatively significant as the sex of their child. Our impression is that parents are not consciously aware of some of the differences in the ways they respond to sons and daughters, and thus they could not describe these differences even if they felt comfortable enough to try. Other differences, we feel, they may be aware of, but they are reluctant to acknowledge.

In the interview, we asked the men whether they thought they were the same kind of father to their child or children that their own father had been to them and whether they felt more like their father, since becoming a father. The responses were interesting and suggest that these questions merit further consideration and research:

"Definitely not." [He then explained how opposed he was to his father's style of fathering.]

"No. I feel less like him, more conscious of the threat of being like him." [He described in detail his struggle not to be like his father, who was alcoholic and generally unavailable to his children.]

"Different. I feel a little closer to him, now. I think maybe I judged him too hard. He did good by me."

"It's hard to answer. I think I am the same. I do at times feel like him, that this is how my father was with me. It feels pretty good."

"I don't know if my father was that great a father. I'd like to be a better father."

"Yes, pretty much. I play with them, spend time with them, the way he did."

"My father died when my mother was pregnant with me. I had a stepfather from when I was between two and three." [Interviewer: "Are you the same kind of father to your son your stepfather was to you?"] "I believe so. I enjoyed participating in activities with my stepfather." [Interviewer: "Feel more like him?"] "No, he's very different phsyically, psychologically from me."

"I don't remember how my father was to me when I was this age. My father was in the service until I was three."

By and large, the men in this study did not feel their own fathers provided them with a strong and acceptable model of fatherhood. They hoped and planned to be better fathers to their children than they felt their fathers had been to them. (Pressman, 1979, received very similar responses from a sample of suburban men.) One wonders what sources and resources these fathers have to draw on to show them how to be a different kind of father. We did not ask, in this interview, if they felt more like their mothers than they had before—most likely they would not have been able to answer that question—but possibly it was the early experience of being nurtured by their mothers that enabled them to nurture their babies. As we have seen, the men described their mothers as having been good mothers and saw themselves as somewhat like their mothers. Further, the score reflecting these descriptions did predict their paternal adaptation, assessed through the interview. Thus, tentatively we surmise that identification with a nurturant parent, either a mother or a father, promotes fatherliness in a man. The last two responses quoted above suggest the importance of a present and available father to a man's sense of having a model or figure with whom he identifies.

We asked if they thought about what life would be like when their child or children were grown, and with few exceptions they said no. We asked the men what they liked to do with their one-year-olds, and some supplied enthusiastic responses that reflected their excitement and pleasure:

"We played football together the entire NFL season." [Interviewer: "What's that like for you to play with him?"] "Not being able to be a child again but being able to experience the childhood feelings."

"Besides the ordinary things [this man shares childcare activities more than equally when he's home evenings and weekends], I took her swimming, took her to the Home Show alone. I carry her around, play with her." [Interviewer: "What do you like most about the things you do with her?"] "I like most when she laughs." [Interviewer: "Least?"] "When she gets mad. I took her out of the dog dish the other day and she scratched me on the face."

"I put her in my lap and give her little kisses. She's only a year old but she puckers up now for a kiss." [Interviewer: "How is that for you?" "I enjoy the time I spend with the kids." [He takes care of them alone several times a week.]

"I play with him. I feed him. Growl, yelp! Hug. I like the most seeing him in the morning, doing things with him. I like the least changing diapers. I don't like it when I'm taking care of him and he's crying uncontrollably and there's nothing you can do about it."

"I really love to make her laugh."

"Play, throw him up in the air. Fool around with him."

"I love to play with his toys. We run around a lot, play a lot, throwing the ball back and forth, everything he seems interested in." [Interviewer: "What do you like most and least?"] "Seeing him laugh and enjoy himself is what I like most. I suppose diapers aren't very much fun, but it doesn't bother me."

We asked them details about their one-year-old's life: when the baby naps and for how long, what the baby does when put down for a nap, favorite and least favorite foods, and similar questions. These fathers knew many details about their children's day-to-day lives. Most knew a lot about the vicissitudes of naps and bedtime, of meals, of their baby's response to changes in usual routine, and the like. Some—probably about a third—seemed extremely knowledgeable. Possibly as many as a third were clearly relatively unaware. One not uncommon example was the father who knew the details that related only to his own life; for example, he knew his son's waking hours as they related to his own coming and going. Only occasionally did a man in this sample say, "You'll have to ask my wife; she knows about those things." The final third knew quite a lot about the baby but clearly not as much as the mother, who was the prime caretaker for the child.

When we asked how the baby responded to the parents' efforts to limit or control his or her behavior, like saying no or slapping the child's hand, and if the parents ever did those things, the response from the fathers was quite standard. They described the baby's typical response, which ranged from looking contemplative for a minute or so and wandering to find something else to play with to defiantly repeating the forbidden act. Some fathers replied that their only method of discipline was to firmly say no or move the child out of the situation; some said they slapped the child's hand to make the point. If any fathers hit the child more substantially, they did not tell us about it. In one or two instances in the study, we had reason to suspect that the child might have been at least occasionally hit a good deal harder. When asked how they felt when they had to set limits on the child's behavior, they said they did not like to see the child sad or cry but knew it was necessary.

While at two months postpartum, men who were doing well in one domain were doing well in the other, by and large at one year this was substantially less true. The only consistent interrelationships concerned issues bearing directly on how the man was integrating the infant into his life: His emotional well-being in his status as a father, his adaptation to his spouse concerning parenting issues, and his relationship to his toddler were highly interrelated. Characteristics of the men not directly related to the baby or to parenthood, such as anxiety or general marital adjustment, had little to do with those areas of functioning related to parenthood. This finding might well reflect men's tendency to separate their family roles from other aspects of their life, such as their careers. In any case, by the time the baby is a year old, he or she is no longer the central focus of the father's life, which has, in many respects, returned to the pattern it had before the baby's birth.

Summary

Men's life experiences at one year postpartum in areas not directly related to their fatherhood, such as anxiety level, general perception of the marriage, or level of sexual interest and activity—all appear largely unrelated to how the couple dealt with the pregnancy, birth, and first year of the child's life. Men who were earlier anxious continued to be anxious; men who valued their marriages tended to continue to value their marriages; men who were sexually active before continued to be so.

The man's emotional well-being and his adaptation to his wife concerning parenting issues—behaviors more directly related to the new demands placed on the family—were predicted by how the man and his wife coped with the pregnancy at eight months; this relationship held for the sample as a whole and more strongly for couples who had no other children. Men who were in couples better adapted at eight months had a more positive sense of themselves in the fathering role at one year, and had reestablished—or maintained—better relationships with their wives at one year. The inexperienced father's adaptation to parenthood at one year was also predicted by the couple's marital satisfaction and adaptation to parenting at two months postpartum. For experienced fathers, other factors seemed more important: those men who were less anxious and whose wives were less depressed were feeling more comfortable at one year.

Finally, the best predictor for the sample overall of how well the man would be relating to his baby at one year was how well he had related to his infant at two months. Less anxious fathers also continued to do better. Beyond that, inexperienced fathers were doing well at one year if they had done well with the pregnancy and early childbearing. For experienced fathers, such earlier measures did not seem to matter. They were doing better with their baby at one year if they were not too anxious and if the infant was the product of a difficult delivery.

✄ 9 ✄ ✄ ✄ ✄ ✄ ✄ ✄ ✄ ✄

The Infant

Much of the literature of infancy emphasizes the influence of the mother's parenting on the baby's development. Researchers have postulated complex interactions between the mother and her infant (for example, Bowlby, 1969; Spitz, 1965), and a number of empirical studies provide at least some support for the cultural notion that mothers are of central importance to the health and well-being of their offspring (Westley and Epstein, 1969; Blank, 1976, reviews the relevant literature). Aspects of mothers' behaviors have been found to affect their infants' general development (Brody and Axelrod, 1970; Stern and others, 1969), the frequency of infant crying (Bell and Ainsworth, 1972), and the infant's comfort with brief separations (Ainsworth and Bell, 1969; Stayton and Ainsworth, 1973). Relationships between the sex of the infant and the mother's behavior include the frequency with which the infant looks at the mother's face (Moss and Robson, 1968) and how often the infant looks at and responds socially to a stranger (Robson, Pedersen, and Moss, 1969). Although recent researchers are beginning to call into question previously accepted beliefs concerning the

210

absolute centrality of the mother to the infant, and particularly the relationship's long-term effects (Rutter, 1979), support does exist for the view that mothers have a major influence on their infants.

Recent researchers have studied the effects of fathers on their infants and shown the strength of the tie between infants and fathers (for example, Ban and Lewis, 1974; Kotelchuck, 1976; Lamb, 1977a, 1977b, 1977c; Spelke and others, 1973). Few researchers, however, have focused on the effect of this relationship on the functioning of the infant (Earls, 1976, and Lynn, 1974, review these studies). There are data which relate the father's presence or absence to later characteristics of his older children, and Biller (1974) found that infants he considered to be well fathered were more secure and trustful, had more advanced motor development, and showed less separation anxiety than poorly fathered infants. While it seems obvious that when fathers have significant and substantial relationships with their infants, those relationships must affect the infants, data about such effects has not yet been gathered.

The third individual contributor to the development of the infant is, of course, the infant itself. Beginning with Shirley (1933), Bergman and Escalona (1947–1948), and Fries and Woolf (1953), we find the hypothesis that the infant is born with, or develops extremely early, a characteristic style that substantially influences his or her eventual personality. More recent studies of this phenomenon include Thomas and others (1963), Thomas, Chess, and Birch (1968), Carey (1970), and Bennett (1976).

One major problem for researchers interested in studying infants' contribution to their own long-term development is the lack of apparent continuities in infants' behaviors from one time period to the next. In its extreme form, this problem is stated by Bell, Weller, and Waldrop (1971), who recorded frequencies of a number of specific behaviors in newborns. When they looked at these same babies eight hours later, they found very few behaviors that reflected consistent individual differences in the infants. However, Birns (1965), Birns, Blank, and

Bridger (1966), Brazelton (1973), and others using Brazelton's Neonatal Behavioral Assessment Scale (Bakow, 1974; Bakow and others, 1973; Horowitz and others, 1971) have found some behaviors that appear stable over at least relatively short periods of time, or that relate consistently and sensibly to other behaviors at other times. Yang and Moss (1978), for example, found continuity between the newborn dimensions of maturity and a tonic-active dimension at ninety days for boys only. Blank (1976), however, concludes that it has not yet been demonstrated that the infant's given characteristics at birth interact in any predictable way with environmental factors to allow predictions to later functioning. Researchers have developed a number of promising measures of infant behavior, but have reached few conclusions about the infant's contribution to later parent-child interaction or to later infant and toddler adaptation.

Finally, in a dramatic demonstration of the subtlety and complexity of the interactional process between infant and care-taker, Stern's (1971) films of mothers and their three-and-a-half-month-old infants *en face* showed that reciprocal initiation of facing behavior—that is, getting the other to make eye contact—occurred within half-second intervals. Similar demonstrations of the mutual interdependency of mothers' and infants' behaviors have been highlighted by Brazelton, Koslowski, and Main (1974) and Brazelton and others (1975).

One major point that emerges from a review of the literature is that the evaluation of infant-parent relationships and of the adaptation of the infant cannot be understood by focusing solely on the mother, or for that matter, solely on the infant. The mother and infant together must be considered, and it is very likely that in families where the father develops a strong and early tie with the baby, the father's role and relationship towards both his wife and the infant are also centrally involved. The difficulties in designing a study that allows one to look at the wholeness of the infant's life as embedded in his or her physical self and socioemotional and interpersonal worlds are obviously many. While this study is not designed to provide such an analysis, nonetheless it illuminates some interesting and important facts and relationships about infant adaptation.

The Infants in Our Sample

The families in our study had a total of eighty-nine infants: Of the eighty-seven who survived, forty-three were first-borns and forty-four second or later children. There were two sets of twins. (In all analyses, only one twin from each family is considered.) We obtained from the medical records the newborns' Apgar scores, reflecting their health and neurological functioning five minutes after birth, and their birth weight. In addition the Brazelton Neonatal Behavioral Assessment Scale was administered within the first days of birth by an examiner trained in Brazelton. The scale yielded three factor scores reflecting the newborns' alertness, motor maturity, and irritability. The infants in this study were a healthy, robust lot, on the whole. Their mean Apgar score was 9.7 on a ten-point scale; only three infants scored less than 8. Their average weight was 3.29 kilograms (7 pounds, 4 ounces). Thirty-nine were girls, forty-eight boys. They had relatively high levels of alertness and motor maturity and a relatively low level of irritability.

A very few of them appeared to be in difficulty at birth and shortly after. Three infants, one singleton and one pair of twins, were substantially premature and had a variety of associated medical complications. Two infants died at birth, one, a two-pound baby born very prematurely and the other, an infant born with multiple congenital problems.

Twenty-one infants—or 23.7 percent of our sample—were delivered by caesarean section. In all, eighteen mother-infant pairs were given a high score for complications of labor and delivery, reflecting some substantial threat to the mother or infant, including fetal distress, uterine inertia, and premature birth.

Most of the mothers received some medication during the labor and delivery, most often a regional block and no analgesic.

Interrelationships Among Infant Scores at Birth

Babies delivered by caesarean section tended to be heavier (the pelvic disproportion created by large babies was the most frequent reason given for the surgical delivery) and to have somewhat lower Apgar scores; not surprisingly, their mothers were given more medication during the process of delivery. The only other consistent relationships among the data were among the Brazelton factor scores. More irritable babies were less alert on that set of scores but showed higher levels of motor maturity.

Infants at Two Months

In our two-month evaluations of the infants, we gave them the Bayley Scale of Infant Development, which yields a score reflecting their perceptual and social functioning, the Mental Development Index (MDI), and a score reflecting their motor functioning, the Psychomotor Development Index (PDI). We also observed the infant's general style and behavior during the less structured parts of our two-hour visit with the family. These visits were scheduled at a time when the mother thought the baby was most likely to be alert and responsive, providing some control for such "state" characteristics as level of hunger or degree of fatigue, which greatly influence infant performance, although it is difficult for anyone to predict how a two-month-old will act or feel on any given day. During the interview, we asked the mothers detailed behavioral questions, which were scored on the same dimensions as the observational ratings. The infant adaptation scores from the observation and from the maternal interview were comprised of assessments of the infant's adaptability to change, irritability, vulnerability to stress, ease of recovery from being upset, tension, characteristic mood, and affective stability, based on Shereshefsky and Yarrow's (1973) empirically determined factor which they call *Adjustment*. (We also have Carey Temperament data on the infants at two and six months as well as a modified Chess and Thomas rating of temperament from the mother's interview. The results, for the most part, do not add substantially to the other findings; thus, we have not included them in the discussions or the tables.)

Finally, we obtained a physiological health and maturity score based on the mother's report of the infant's regularity, quality of eating and sleeping, and frequency and severity of health problems since birth.

At this visit, the infants seemed relatively oblivious to the chaos they were creating in the house. Most of their time was devoted to eating, sleeping, eliminating, and complaining. At the same time, they were becoming more obviously responsive to people and things around them, spending increasing amounts of time looking around and smiling at people. Individual differences were very apparent in such behaviors as fussiness, social responsiveness, and activeness. Most had not yet achieved a regular schedule, as illustrated to us by the difficulty the mothers had recommending a time for us to come when the baby would be awake and alert.

At two months, the babies as a group were functioning at about the average range in mental and motor development. (Their mean scores on the MDI and PDI were 101.9 and 105.2 respectively.) They were physiologically mature and in good health. Their overall adaptation, from our observations, was moderately high and from their mothers' reports, even higher.

Infants with higher-level cognitive and social functioning, reflected in higher scores on the Bayley MDI, also showed higher levels of large motor skill (reflected on the Bayley PDI), had more mature and healthy physiological functioning, and looked better to us in our observations. Surprisingly, infants with higher levels of motor skill were not necessarily performing better in other areas. This is the first emergence of a finding that reappears at each time period we studied: early development of more advanced motor skills—walking, reaching for, picking up, throwing, and the like—seems to be unrelated to other areas of functioning, at least in a basically normal and healthy population of infants.

Comparing the measurements of the babies obtained shortly after birth and the babies' behavior at two months postpartum, we found that, for the sample as a whole, only one measure taken at birth predicted to how the babies were doing at two months, a finding which is consistent with the literature that shows so little relationship between early infant characteristics and later functioning. Infants who were delivered with more complications had lower levels of motor skills. For first-born babies only, those born by caesarean section were physiologically less mature and healthy. First-born babies more alert in the neonatal period had better physiological adaptation at two months, while more alert later-born infants looked better to us on our observational measure. In both instances, alertness scores from the Brazelton scale seemed to predict better functioning. Why the higher level of adaptation was expressed differently in the group of first-borns and later-borns is puzzling. Finally, later-borns whose level of motor maturity shortly after birth was lower looked better physiologically at two months.

Infants at One Year

At one year we again arranged to visit the families at a time when the mother thought the baby would be most apt to be playful, rested, and alert. We visited for about two hours, observing the child in a formal testing situation as well as in less structured play and interaction with his or her parents and sometimes with siblings.

We used four scores to describe the baby's functioning at this time. We obtained the Bayley MDI and PDI, a measure of the baby's adaptation from our observation (the average score of raters' judgments of the baby's usual mood, quality of relationships, and curiosity), and a measure of the baby's adaptation based on our judgment of the mother's report during the interview.

At one year, the picture was very different than it had been at two months. The babies were now little people in the family, with clearly defined personalities and styles. Most strikingly, they were on the move, either walking or crawling very fast. They were at a high point in their enjoyment of themselves and their rapidly developing capacities, and, in almost all cases, this sense of pleasure was shared by their families. Their push for independence was visible in all aspects of their day-to-day functioning. By this time, they had developed important and differing relationships with members of the family, including older siblings.

At one year, the babies' development still looked about average overall (mean Bayley MDI of 105.2 and PDI of 107.5).

We rated them very highly when we observed them; they were generally alert, curious, contented, and sociable youngsters. Their mothers continued to see them even more positively. In our clinical judgment, the mothers' slightly rosy vision of their youngsters is an important part of good mothering.

As at two months, babies whose cognitive and social adaptation was high were also doing well on large motor development, that is, the Bayley scores related to each other, and looked good to us in general (see Table 12). A pattern we observed at two months still held true: a baby's advanced motor development did not relate to the observational measure of the baby's adaptation. The more active, well-coordinated one-year-olds were not necessarily observed to be better in general functioning. The mothers' reports of how their babies were doing were similar to our view from the observations, but were not related to the scores obtained from the standardized testing.

At two months, for the sample as a whole, the only score from the neonatal period predicting to the baby's behavior was complications of labor and delivery, with more complications predicting lower levels of cognitive and social functioning as measured by the MDI. The picture is somewhat similar at one year, in that a very few earlier scores predicted the baby's behavior at one year. For the sample as a whole, babies who weighed more at birth had higher MDI scores and were described by their mothers as doing better at one year. (This relationship is somewhat surprising, given the narrow range of variation in birth weight in this sample.)

Babies who had looked better to us from our observations at two months had higher Bayley MDI and PDI scores at one year. For the sample overall, the earlier Bayley scores were not at all predictive of later Bayley scores, although for later-born only, the PDI predicted to itself across that ten-month period. Gerson (1973) also found no relationship between Bayley scores at one, three, or six months, and Blank (1976) reports that same lack of continuity in her review of the infant literature. Rubin and Balow (1979) present data suggesting that extremely low Bayley scores are predictive of later intellectual functioning within the normal range; however, socioeconomic

Table 12. Interrelationships Among Newborn and Later Infant Scores

	Bayley MDI			One Year Scores Bayley PDI		
	All Infants	First-Borns	Later-Borns	All Infants	First-Borns	Later-Borns
Labor and delivery						
Complications	.11	.02	.09	-.02	.04	.01
Caesarean section	.15	.03	.20	.05	.04	.11
Medication	-.20	-.25	-.19	-.24	-.18	-.32[a]
Apgar	.03	-.03	-.03	.13	.23	.01
Birth weight	.25[a]	.33	-.16	.22	.38[a]	.06
Brazelton Alertness	-.02	-.06	-.10	.01	-.31	.46[a]
Brazelton Motor Maturity	-.03	-.06	-.14	.01	.06	-.08
Brazelton Irritability	.12	.14	.08	.06	.17	-.20
Two months postpartum						
Bayley MDI	.03	.06	-.08	.11	-.03	.31
Bayley PDI	-.02	.00	-.13	.23	.08	.51[b]
Physiological adaptation	.16	.25	.08	.23	.26	.18
Observed adaptation	.27[a]	.40[a]	.19	.28[a]	.35	.23
One year postpartum						
Bayley MDI	—	—	—			
Bayley PDI	.38[c]	.34[a]	.45[b]	—	—	—
Observed adaptation	.30[b]	.18	.42[b]	.16	.20	.11
Interview measure of adaptation	.08	.04	.13	.14	.22	.05

	Observed Adaptation			Interview Measure of Adaptation		
	All Infants	First-Borns	Later-Borns	All Infants	First-Borns	Later-Borns
Labor and delivery						
Complications	.07	.16	-.07	.04	.24	-.18
Caesarean section	.04	.09	-.07	.10	.05	.17
Medication	.00	-.16	.14	.39[b]	.21	.52[b]
Apgar	.13	.35[a]	-.08	.10	.09	.12
Birth weight	.19	.22	.16	.36[b]	.19	.52[b]
Brazelton Alertness	.23	.42[a]	.20	.19	.46[a]	-.13
Brazelton Motor Maturity	.09	-.14	.18	-.13	-.28	-.05
Brazelton Irritability	-.09	-.24	.05	-.10	-.13	-.05
Two months postpartum						
Bayley MDI	.19	.15	.22	.03	-.15	.26
Bayley PDI	.01	.03	-.03	-.14	-.20	-.05
Physiological adaptation	.02	.13	-.08	.07	.19	-.04
Observed adaptation	.20	.11	.27	.14	-.17	.34[a]
One year postpartum						
Bayley MDI						
Bayley PDI						
Observed adaptation	—	—	—			
Interview measure of adaptation	.55[c]	.65[c]	—	—		

Note: These correlations are based on the following samples: For first-borns, N ranges from 28 to 35; for later-borns, N ranges from 20 to 34; for all new-borns, N ranges from 47 to 68.

[a] $p \leqslant .05$, two-tailed   [b] $p \leqslant .01$, two-tailed   [c] $p \leqslant .001$, two-tailed

status proved to be a better predictor to a child's IQ at four and seven years.

In sum, for this relatively healthy and well-adjusted group of infants and toddlers, their scores on a variety of measures taken shortly after birth were not strongly predictive of their behavior at two months, and just slightly more so at one year, when birth weight seemed to be a factor. Our observational assessment of the baby at two months and possibly the PDI were somewhat predictive of how the child was doing at one year. In general, we are more impressed with the relative paucity of relationships among the scores than with the fact that some relationships reached statistical significance.

What does predict a baby's functioning at any point in time? Do any characteristics of the baby's mother or father, or the interactions between and among them all, tell more about how the child will behave at two months and one year?

Parents' Scores and Newborns

Unlike the infant scores, which showed little continuity from one time period to the next, there were a number of striking relationships between aspects of parent adaptation and later infant functioning. Of the measures reflecting the woman's status or experience early in pregnancy, a few related to the infant at birth (see Table 13). Strikingly, women who were more anxious early in pregnancy had newborns who were significantly more irritable. These infants also had higher levels of motor maturity. Similarly, women who were more depressed had infants who were less alert and more irritable. So for the sample as a whole, the cultural myth relating a pregnant woman's mood and her baby's health held. Other researchers have recently reported this association between maternal emotional states, especially anxiety, and some characteristics of the newborn (reviewed by Williams, 1977). It is clear that a fetus *in utero* is affected by the pregnant woman's physiological and psychological experiences. Some of the women's first-trimester scores predicted to alertness and motor maturity, but the range in this sample was too small for us to feel confident in discussing these relationships. In this sample, no parent scores predicted to the infant's birth weight.

When we looked separately at first-time and experienced mothers and their babies, more precise findings emerged. For first-time mothers, a number of psychological characteristics, including their general life adaptation, as well as their anxiety and depression predicted to the newborn's irritability at birth; better functioning, less anxious, and less depressed women had infants who were less irritable. In contrast, for multiparous women, no early scores predicted their infants' level of irritability. Rather, a few early (and, we hasten to add, unlikely) scores predicted to their infants' level of motor maturity at birth. That the patterns of relationships are so different for first-time and experienced mothers is consistent with results we have seen throughout the study. The same intense involvement first-time mothers have with themselves and the pregnancy seems to somehow affect the infant *in utero*.

A few of the fathers' characteristics related to the infants' scores (see Table 13). In particular, for the sample overall, younger fathers and those having better marital adjustment had infants with higher alertness at birth. These relationships are quite difficult to understand and may well be fortuitous. However, they are consistent with those of Pedersen and Robson, 1969.

Parents' Scores and Two-Month-Olds

Relatively few background or pregnancy variables of the parents predicted to the newborn characteristics in this sample of relatively healthy families and babies. By two months, it seems intuitively correct that the parents will have had a much greater chance to affect the infant, and one would expect more relationships. Indeed, our data show a number of relationships between the mothers' characteristics and the behavior of their two-month-olds (see Table 14).

For the sample as a whole, and in support of a major interest of the study, mothers who experienced less life change, those who had less premenstrual tension, those who were as-

Table 13. Selected Parents' Scores Predicting to Newborn

	Apgar Score			Brazelton Alertness		
	All Newborns	First-Borns	Later-Borns	All Newborns	First-Borns	Later-Borns
Mothers' scores						
First trimester						
Life adaptation	-.14	-.21	-.05	.07	.06	.01
Anxiety	-.05	.03	-.14	-.17	-.25	-.03
Depression	-.07	.00	-.15	-.29[a]	-.46[b]	-.15
Femininity	.04	.01	.08	.04	.17	-.16
Number of children	.02	—	-.07	-.08	—	.15
Eighth month of pregnancy						
Life change	.00	-.01	.05	-.04	-.03	-.04
Couple preparedness	-.17	.05	-.47[a]	.09	.25	-.12
Fathers' scores						
First trimester						
Anxiety	.23	.06	.40[a]	.14	.14	-.05
Marital adjustment	-.15	.04	-.29	.34[b]	.36[b]	.12
Masculinity	.00	.06[b]	-.11	.07	.45[b]	-.32
Femininity	.16	.42[b]	-.07	.32[b]	.27	.40[a]
Age	-.05	-.19	.01	-.34[b]	-.40[a]	-.11

	Brazelton Motor Maturity			Brazelton Irritability		
	All Newborns	First-Borns	Later-Borns	All Newborns	First-Borns	Later-Borns
Mothers' scores						
First trimester						
Life adaptation	-.11	-.12	-.17	-.22	-.38[a]	.06
Anxiety	.34[b]	.21	.46[a]	.25[a]	.39[a]	.21
Depression	-.22	.07	.33	.31[a]	.53[b]	.04
Femininity	.24	.09	.34	-.09	-.38[a]	.33
Number of children	.32[b]	—	-.51[b]	-.06	—	-.32
Eighth month of pregnancy						
Life change	.14	.40[a]	-.15	-.02	.07	-.03
Couple preparedness	-.27	-.32	-.20	-.32[a]	-.36	-.34
Fathers' scores						
First trimester						
Anxiety	.05	.00	.14	-.02	-.15	.36
Marital adjustment	.01	.01	-.08	-.13	-.26	-.11
Masculinity	-.25	-.32	-.16	-.15	-.34	.24
Femininity	.19	.09	.25	-.17	-.08	-.31
Age	-.03	.14	-.08	.19	.33	.00

Note: All significant correlations are reported. These correlations are based on the following samples: For first-borns, *N* ranges from 27 to 39; for later-borns, *N* ranges from 25 to 40; for all newborns, *N* ranges from 46 to 80.

[a] $p \leq .05$, two-tailed
[b] $p \leq .01$, two-tailed
[c] $p \leq .001$, two-tailed

sessed by us as adapting better to the pregnancy before quickening, and those who were less anxious and less depressed at two months had two-month-olds who scored higher on our observational measure of adaptation. In other words, and consistent with our original hypothesis, selected first-trimester measures of a woman's sociocultural experience and her medical history as well as her current ego functioning predict to a substantial degree not only her adaptation and functioning in the early postpartum period, but also her infant's behavior at two months postpartum. These relationships were even stronger for first-time mothers, and at two months, the importance of the quality of the marriage emerged as well. For first-borns, their physiological adaptation at two months postpartum was better when their mothers had better marriages and were less anxious. In fact, the relationship between the mother's marital satisfaction and her infant's physiological adaptation held up even when her anxiety score was statistically controlled. These findings are consistent with those of Gerson (1973), who found infant functioning at six weeks, three months, and six months were all predicted to some degree by prepartum and postpartum maternal characteristics.

The importance of the marriage to the well-being of the infant is consistent with the findings of Westley and Epstein (1969) who, having studied college students and their families, concluded that the state of their parents' marriage was one of the most important factors influencing the emotional well-being of these students. Their data were particularly striking because they showed that the state of the marriage was more significant than the mental health of the individual parents.

So it is possible to predict, to a certain degree, how a baby will be functioning at two months postpartum by looking at characteristics of the mother early in pregnancy. Few characteristics of the fathers predicted to the two-month-olds' adaptation for the sample as a whole, although there were some statistically significant relationships when first- and later-born samples were examined separately. The nature of these relationships is such that they probably reflect aspects of the mother's functioning as the pattern of scores at two months is unequivocal in emphasizing the saliency of the mothers'—and not the fathers'—direct effect and interrelatedness with the baby at that time.

Both the mother's and father's anxiety late in pregnancy strongly predicted to several aspects of their two-month-old's functioning. Of course, most anxious expectant parents become anxious parents, so while the predictive power of the relationship is clear, whether parent anxiety early in pregnancy or at two months postpartum affects the infant is not clear. It is worthy of mention, but by this point in our discussion not surprising, that the statistical relationships were much stronger and more consistent for first-borns and their mothers than later-borns.

Virtually every aspect of the infant's adaptation at two months—except motor development—was related to the mother's functioning at two months (see Table 14). The strongest ties were between the infant's physiological adequacy and various maternal characteristics. One might be somewhat suspicious of these relationships in that our information about the baby's physiological functioning came from the interview with the mother whose report, naturally, contains her biases and feelings about herself as a mother, as well as information about her baby. However, the physiological score reflects much of what is essential in a two-month-old. The relative smoothness of that functioning is partly a stimulus to the mother and partly a response to her behavior. It is reasonable to assume that their relationship is real rather than artifactual.

The intensity of the tie between mother and baby at two months is further supported by the strong relationship between the mother's anxiety and depression and the infant's adaptation as measured by observation. The absence of any correlations between the mother's functioning at two months and her infant's motor performance might be best explained by the relatively autonomous and automatic nature of motor development.

We found only one relationship between the father's adaptation at two months and his infant's, and that was a weak tie between his marital adjustment concerning parenting issues and the observed adaptation of the baby. This relationship was probably mediated by the mother; that is, the couple's good relationship concerning parenting issues better enabled her to handle the infant competently and comfortably, and thus facilitated good infant adaptation. Thus, despite the recent cultural interest in emphasizing the importance of fathers, the older

Table 14. Selected Mothers' Scores Predicting to Infant at Two Months

	Bayley MDI			Bayley PDI		
	All Infants	First-Borns	Later-Borns	All Infants	First-Borns	Later-Borns
First trimester						
Life adaptation	.03	-.06	.03	-.05	-.05	-.08
Anxiety	-.02	-.11	.10	.02	-.12	.17
Depression	-.06	-.04	-.06	-.07	.07	.07
Adaptation to pregnancy	.09	.05	.20	.36[b]	-.25	.02
Marital adjustment	-.13	-.12	-.23	.03	-.05	.08
Years married	-.25[a]	-.21	-.01	-.02	-.24	.32
Premenstrual tension	.02	.12	-.10	-.25[a]	.31	-.10
Socioeconomic status	.06	.18	-.05	.12	.12	.03
Life change	.13	.18	.11	-.26[a]	.30[a]	.06
Age	-.19	-.10	-.14	-.13	-.37[a]	.16
Multiparity	-.26[a]	—	—	-.10	—	—
Eighth month of pregnancy						
Anxiety	.25	.47[b]	-.06	-.12	-.35[a]	.16
Symptoms	-.03	-.11	.07	.10	.13	.44[a]
Labor and delivery						
Complications	.01	-.22	.08	-.24[a]	-.38[a]	-.18
Caesarean section	.13	-.05	.23	-.21	-.44[b]	.05
Adaptation to labor and delivery	.07	.45[a]	-.26	.23	.30	.15

Two months postpartum						
Emotional well-being	.27[a]	.10	.47[b]	.12	.13	.11
Anxiety	-.32[b]	-.34[a]	-.22	-.17	-.36[a]	.04
Depression	-.25[a]	-.19	-.29	-.02	-.01	-.04
Marital adjustment	.19	-.17	-.10	-.07	-.03	-.10
Adaptation to spouse	.05	.00	.04	.10	.04	.15
Observed maternal adaptation	.09	.07	.30	-.11	-.14	-.03
Interview measure of maternal adaptation	.26[a]	.14	.41[a]	.15	.01	.33

Table 14 continued

	Observed Adaptation			Physiological Adaptation		
	All Infants	First-Borns	Later-Borns	All Infants	First-Borns	Later-Borns
First trimester						
Life adaptation	.10	.06	.14	.02	-.07	.08
Anxiety	-.23	-.45[a]	-.10	-.23	-.39[a]	-.10
Depression	-.22	-.28	-.20	-.16	-.23	-.11
Adaptation to pregnancy	.32[b]	.40[a]	.27	.15	.12	-.19
Marital adjustment	.10	.30	.00	-.01	.45[b]	-.36[a]
Years married	.14	-.11	.32	-.10	-.42[a]	.16
Premenstrual tension	-.24[a]	-.44[b]	-.16	.01	.05	-.07
Socioeconomic status	-.21	.06	-.34	.12	.12	.13
Life change	-.25[a]	-.47[b]	-.14	-.06	.02	-.12
Age	.07	-.14	.23	-.10	-.01	-.16
Multiparity	.02	—	—	-.06	—	—
Eighth month of pregnancy						
Anxiety	-.26[a]	-.50[b]	-.08	-.13	-.25	.02
Symptoms	-.02	-.05	.01	.15	.08	.23
Labor and delivery						
Complications	-.03	-.08	.03	.03	-.12	.21
Caesarean section	-.04	-.03	.00	-.22	-.39[a]	-.04
Adaptation to labor and delivery	.09	.38	-.14	.29[a]	.69[c]	-.13

Two months postpartum

Emotional well-being	.26[a]	.18	.36[a]	.46[c]	.56[c]
Anxiety	-.40[c]	-.60[c]	-.26	-.36[b]	-.06
Depression	-.40[c]	-.45[b]	-.35[a]	-.42[c]	-.25
Marital adjustment	.19	.22	-.12	.18	.15
Adaptation to spouse	.10	.17	.09	.26[a]	.03
Observed maternal adaptation	.29[a]	.26	.32	.15	.11
Interview measure of maternal adaptation	.35[b]	.45[b]	.28	.47[c]	.25

Note: Only those correlations that are statistically or conceptually significant are presented. These correlations are based on the following samples: For first-borns, N ranges from 31 to 36; for later-borns, N ranges from 27 to 35; for all infants, N ranges from 60 to 69.

[a] $p \leq .05$, two-tailed
[b] $p \leq .01$, two-tailed
[c] $p \leq .001$, two-tailed

view that the father is peripheral to the well-being of a very young baby appears to be true, at least for these middle-class married couples.

Parents' Scores and One-Year-Olds

By the time the baby was two-months old, many scores reflecting the mother's functioning related to the infant's own adaptation, and the tie between mothers and infants was much stronger for first-borns than later-borns. Similar relationships were not found between the fathers' behaviors and their babies.

At one year, a baby's "mental" development (Bayley MDI score) was higher if the mother had experienced less life change and was happier with her marriage early in pregnancy and if she was less anxious and depressed in late pregnancy and at two months postpartum (see Table 15). A baby's mental development was also higher when the father was more sexually active and satisfied, liked his marriage more, was doing better in his own life (life adaptation), and had less anxiety in early and late pregnancy (see Table 16). Thus by one year, the baby's cognitive and social functioning was strongly predicted by the psychological health and marital satisfaction of the parents early in the pregnancy. (It is of some interest to note that the baby's behavior was not predicted by such factors as socioeconomic status.) These characteristics of the mothers were most strongly predictive for first-born children. The fathers' characteristics were much more strongly predictive for later-born children.

A number of comments need to be made about these important findings. First, the twin issues of marital satisfaction and adjustment have appeared throughout this study as crucial in predicting how a woman will adapt to pregnancy, birth, and early parenting. A comparison of parents' and infants' behavior shows that these aspects of the parents' experience also affect— directly or indirectly—their infant. Although anxiety and marital adjustment related to each other at each time period, they each individually predicted some of the later infant measures when separated by statistical means.

Second, in virtually all instances, the relationships between the mother's functioning and adaptation and the baby's were much stronger for first-borns, and the relationships between father's functioning and the baby's were much stronger for later-borns. As we have noted before, the mother's intense and somewhat exclusive tie with her first child maximizes the effect of her characteristics on the baby. By the time a second child arrives, the mother does not have the time and energy—and possibly she does not have the need—to develop such an exclusive relationship, and that later-born child has more opportunity to relate to, and be influenced by, fathers and older siblings. Our data—and common sense—do not suggest that one or the other situation is better; they certainly are different.

Finally, the relationship between the father's adaptation and the baby's cognitive functioning, as reflected in the Bayley MDI, is consistent with the literature (for example, Biller, 1974; reviewed by Radin, 1976). For boys, in particular, according to this literature, a close relationship between father and son fosters an analytic cognitive style and greater cognitive competence in the child.

Looking next at the baby's motor development at one year, we see results that follow the pattern observed at two months. Motor development was not essentially related to any of the mother's first-trimester scores. Later scores, from two months and one year, that predicted to motor development were consistently those measures of the woman's relationship with her husband. For the total sample, women who were better adapted to their spouse concerning parenting issues at two months and one year and those who described themselves as more sexually active and satisfied had babies with higher levels of motor skills at one year. The pattern was similar, but stronger, for first-borns examined separately. The situation was the same, only even stronger, for fathers: fathers' marital and sexual satisfaction throughout the study period predicted to the Bayley PDI.

It is intriguing to speculate on the reasons that motor development was so strongly related to marital satisfaction and possibly to sexual issues. One has to wonder whether the psychomotor development score reflects an energy or drive component, possibly genetically transmitted, and is reflected in the parents' sexual energy, which is also somewhat related to marital adjustment.

Table 15. Selected Mothers' Scores Predicting to Infant at One Year

	Bayley MDI			Bayley PDI		
	All Infants	First-Borns	Later-Borns	All Infants	First-Borns	Later-Borns
First trimester						
Life adaptation	.21	.03	.38[b]	.07	-.06	.25
Anxiety	-.15	-.27	-.07	-.08	-.31	.16
Depression	-.12	-.36[a]	.13	.05	-.12	.30
Conscious motivation	-.13	.00	-.21	-.14	-.10	-.21
Masculinity	.16	.14	.13	.07	.02	.15
Femininity	-.05	-.21	.13	-.07	-.09	-.05
Adaptation to pregnancy	-.05	.09	-.19	.04	.33	-.35[a]
Marital adjustment	.24[a]	.22	.22	.18	.27	.10
Socioeconomic status	-.04	-.03	.00	.05	.10	.00
Life change	-.30[b]	-.20	-.40[b]	-.17	-.17	-.19
Age	-.02	.04	.08	.12	.15	.07
Number of children	-.04	—	.23	.02	—	.01
Eighth month of pregnancy						
Anxiety	-.26[a]	-.37[a]	-.14	-.07	-.26	.19
Symptoms	-.11	-.32	.14	.07	-.20	.49[b]
Adaptation to pregnancy	.19	.26	.01	.01	-.03	.15
Conscious motivation	-.06	.20	-.32	.11	.32	-.12
Marital adaptation	.00	.00	-.11	-.07	-.20	.28
Labor and delivery						
Medication	-.20	-.25	-.19	-.24	-.18	-.32[a]
Adaptation to labor and delivery	.10	.06	.14	.13	.25	-.02

Two months postpartum						
Anxiety	-.15	-.32	.04	-.15	-.37^a	.13
Depression	-.25^a	-.48^b	-.04	-.19	-.31	-.04
Marital adjustment	.15	.33	-.10	.13	.37^a	.30
Adaptation to spouse	.13	.24	-.04	.37^b	.50^b	.13
Observed maternal adaptation	.35	.35	.37^a	.17	.29	.02
Reciprocity	.30^b	.29	.30^a	.02	.12	-.12
One year postpartum						
Emotional well-being	.25^a	.42^a	.10	.30^a	.27	.33^a
Anxiety	-.14	-.26	-.05	-.12	-.14	-.11
Depression	-.27^a	-.45^a	-.11	-.20	-.15	-.28
Marital adjustment	.12	.17	.12	.17	.31	.00
Adaptation to spouse	.10	.36^a	-.18	.29^a	.48^b	.02
Sexual activity and satisfaction	.18	.16	.26	.40^b	.43^a	.39^a
Observed maternal adaptation	.39^a	—	—	-.07	—	—
Interview measure of maternal adaptation	.28^a	.35^a	.21	.06	.17	-.05
Life change	-.34^b	-.54^b	-.20	-.22	-.32	-.04

Table 15 continued

	Observed Adaptation			Interview Measure of Adaptation		
	All Infants	First-Borns	Later-Borns	All Infants	First-Borns	Later-Borns
First trimester						
Life adaptation	.20	.32	.06	.19	.13	.27
Anxiety	-.16	-.46[b]	.11	-.28[a]	-.34	-.25
Depression	-.13	-.44[b]	-.02	-.13	-.18	-.07
Conscious motivation	-.23	.05	-.29[a]	-.12	-.06	-.20
Masculinity	.17	.18	.15	.04	.04	.05
Femininity	.02	-.27	.30[a]	-.24	-.37[a]	-.11
Adaptation to pregnancy	.17	.47[b]	-.09	.04	.20	-.12
Marital adjustment	.03	-.05	.07	-.11	-.11	-.12
Socioeconomic status	.06	.07	.07	-.12	.17	-.32[a]
Life change	-.10	-.19	-.05	-.16	-.18	-.15
Age	.00	.00	.17	.28[a]	.09	.50[b]
Number of children	.09	—	.28	.16	—	.36[a]
Eighth month of pregnancy						
Anxiety	-.35[b]	-.51[b]	-.21	-.22	-.18	-.27
Symptoms	-.10	-.25	.05	-.10	-.15	-.04
Adaptation to pregnancy	-.01	-.01	-.06	-.26	-.36	-.07
Conscious motivation	-.13	-.13	-.13	-.04	-.14	.07
Marital adaptation	-.09	-.04	-.23	-.36[b]	-.46[a]	-.35
Labor and delivery						
Medication	.00	-.16	.14	.39[b]	.21	.53[b]
Adaptation to labor and delivery	.05	.02	.09	.17	.28	.08

Two months postpartum					
Anxiety	.11	−.07	.27	.04	.06
Depression	−.12	−.08	−.15	−.11	−.25
Marital adjustment	−.15	−.13	−.17	−.24	−.38[a]
Adaptation to spouse	−.07	−.09	−.06	.09	.15
Observed maternal adaptation	.31[a]	.10	.49[b]	.08	.09
Reciprocity	−.03	.08	−.18	.06	.03
One year postpartum					
Emotional well-being	.32[b]	.37[a]	.28	.30[a]	.26
Anxiety	−.29[a]	−.46[b]	−.14	−.51[c]	−.60[c]
Depression	−.11	−.20	−.02	−.26	−.46
Marital adjustment	.02	.04	.05	.16	.33[a]
Adaptation to spouse	−.01	.12	−.12	.17	.16
Sexual activity and satisfaction	.38[b]	.38[a]	.37[a]	.44[b]	.06
Observed maternal adaptation	−.02	−.10	.04	.08	−.11
Interview measure of maternal adaptation	.60[c]	—	—	—	—
Life change	−.03	.11	−.32[a]	−.19	−.46[b]

Note: Only those correlations that are statistically or conceptually significant are presented. These correlations are based on the following samples: For first-borns, N ranges from 25 to 35; for later-borns, N ranges from 24 to 34; for all infants, N ranges from 49 to 69, except for "Maternal Report of Adaptation," where $N = 26$.

[a] $p \leqslant .05$, two-tailed

[b] $p \leqslant .01$, two-tailed

[c] $p \leqslant .001$, two-tailed

Table 16. Selected Fathers' Scores Predicting to Infant at One Year

	Bayley MDI			Bayley PDI		
	All Infants	First-Borns	Later-Borns	All Infants	First-Borns	Later-Borns
First trimester						
Life adaptation	.26[a]	.03	.44[b]	.15	.05	.25
Anxiety	-.42[c]	-.38[a]	-.44[b]	-.14	-.19	-.06
Identification with mother	.13	-.06	.22	-.04	-.18	.10
Age	-.11	-.04	.01	-.02	-.01	.07[b]
Marital adjustment	.38[b]	.34	.39[a]	.35[b]	.31	.43[b]
Sexual activity and satisfaction	.34[b]	.25	.39[a]	.18	.01	.41[a]
Socioeconomic status	-.04	-.03	.00	.05	.10	.00
Eighth month of wife's pregnancy						
Anxiety	-.34[b]	-.29	-.51[b]	-.16	-.12	-.28
Adaptation to pregnancy	-.07	-.03	-.16	-.18	-.22	-.13
Two months postpartum						
Emotional well-being	.25	-.18	.31	.17	.10	.24
Anxiety	-.17	-.16	-.16	-.12	-.18	.01
Marital adjustment	.28[a]	.30	.21	.31[a]	.37[a]	.16
Adaptation to spouse	.22	.21	.23	.25	.25	.27
Paternal adaptation	.20	.01	.23	.09	.05	.09

One year postpartum						
Emotional well-being	.26	.21	.32	.26	.24	.30
Anxiety	-.10	.00	-.28	-.12	-.20	.07
Marital adjustment	.24	.22	.24	.23	.44[a]	-.03
Adaptation to spouse	.26	.30	.36[a]	.08	.04	.20
Sexual activity and satisfaction	.45[b]	.61[b]	.30	.03	-.16	.28
Paternal adaptation	.00	.00	-.02	.11	.08	.17

Table 16 continued

	Observed Adaptation			Interview Measure of Adaptation		
	All Infants	First-Borns	Later-Borns	All Infants	First-Borns	Later-Borns
First trimester						
Life adaptation	.00	.02	−.04	.19	.04	.30
Anxiety	−.08	−.09	−.07	−.04	−.17	.09
Identification with mother	.19	.13	.21	.29[a]	.01	.49[b]
Age	−.10	−.23	.04	.13	−.15	.42[b]
Marital adjustment	.28[a]	.12	.42[b]	.08	.28	−.12
Sexual activity and satisfaction	.19	−.07	.36[a]	−.23	−.39[a]	−.15
Socioeconomic status	.06	.07	.07	−.12	.17	−.32[a]
Eighth month of wife's pregnancy						
Anxiety	−.08	.03	−.21	−.05	−.02	−.13
Adaptation to pregnancy	−.17	−.02	−.37[a]	−.36[b]	−.40[a]	−.32[a]
Two months postpartum						
Emotional well-being	−.06	−.12	.00	−.02	−.16	.18
Anxiety	−.10	−.04	−.19	−.23	−.16	−.36[a]
Marital adjustment	−.01	−.16	.20	.23	.20	.32
Adaptation to spouse	−.05	.17	−.18	−.01	.09	−.11
Paternal adaptation	−.02	.14	−.14	−.04	−.01	−.08

One year postpartum						
Emotional well-being	.02	.05	-.02	.10	.06	.16
Anxiety	.02	.14	-.12	-.14	-.18	-.11
Marital adjustment	.01	-.07	.05	-.05	-.04	-.11
Adaptation to spouse	.06	.00	.17	.06	-.02	.20
Sexual activity and satisfaction	-.09	-.27	.09	-.20	-.13	-.29
Paternal adaptation	.12	.16	.08	.20	.11	.30

Note: These correlations are based on the following samples: For first-borns, N ranges from 24 to 34; for later-borns, N ranges from 20 to 34; for all infants, N ranges from 39 to 67.

[a] $p \leq .05$, two-tailed
[b] $p \leq .01$, two tailed
[c] $p \leq .001$, two-tailed

Data from our observational measure of the baby's mood, curiosity, and sociability show that, for the sample as a whole, the only strong predictors were from the mother; more anxious women at eight months and those who were rated by us at two months as doing less well with their babies had babies who appeared less well functioning at one year. A number of aspects of the mother's functioning at one year related to this observational score, but the direction of the causal ties is impossible to assess. Undoubtedly, more confident, contented women support good adaptation in their one-year-olds, and cheerful, curious, sociable babies elicit confidence and satisfaction in their mothers.

Looking at first-borns and later-borns separately, we found that, for first-borns, their observed adaptation was strongly predicted by their mother's pregnancy adaptation early in the pregnancy, by her anxiety and depression level at that time, and by her anxiety at eight months. For later-borns, few of their mother's scores predicted. The earliest strong predictors from the mother's data of how these children were doing at one year were the two-month postpartum scores of the mother's marital integration and the observed adaptation to her infant. However, later-born children whose fathers had been more sexually active and maritally satisfied during early pregnancy looked happier and more curious and related more to others at one year. So once again, mothers strongly influence their first-borns, at least up to one year; the fathers' influence is more apparent in second and later children.

Finally, looking at predictors of the mothers' description of their babies' adaptation, we found that older mothers described their babies as doing better, as did less anxious mothers and mothers whose marital adaptation at eight months of pregnancy was better. For first-borns, the couples' marital adaptation at eight months predicted the babies' adaptation. For second and later children, the mothers' report was strongly related to several factors. Older mothers with more children, those of higher socioeconomic status, and those who were less depressed and anxious at two months postpartum described their babies as doing better. Similarly, the babies of older fathers, those who more strongly identified with their own mothers, and those who were themselves less anxious at two months postpartum were reported as doing better by their mothers.

Because this instance is almost the first in which socio-cultural factors play a role in predicting an aspect of infant adaptation, one has to wonder if the mother's description of how well the baby was doing did not reflect most saliently her own sense of comfort and satisfaction at that time. As we have noted before, a mother's adaptation was quite strongly affected by sociocultural dimensions. However, Rubin and Balow (1979) did find a strong relationship between socioeconomic status and intelligence measured at ages four and seven, so perhaps the relationship between socioeconomic status and adaptation is real, but is not discernible until the child is at least a year old.

Summary

Several conclusions emerge from these findings. We found, as others have found before (for example, Blank, 1976) that characteristics of a newborn, within the normal range of functioning, do not predict very well to the baby's behavior two months or twelve months later. Although such characteristics as their irritability level or alertness shortly after birth probably do, in complex ways, influence and interact with their relationships with important adults, and thus play some role in their later adaptation, global clinical measures cannot pinpoint such effects.

In comparing the parents' and infants' scores, the first noteworthy relationship we found was that between maternal anxiety and depression early in pregnancy and infant irritability, alertness, and motor maturity at birth. From conception on, mother and infant form an extremely interdependent physiological system, and the mother's experiences, including the strong emotions she feels, affect the developing fetus. No one has yet been able to describe the process that mediates between maternal emotions and neonatal characteristics (Winickoff, 1976, reviews the speculations about this process), but data that demonstrate this relationship have been presented often enough to provide credible evidence for this hypothesis.

By two months, the infants' physiological adaptation, and our assessment from our observations of their adaptability, were related to a number of aspects of the mothers' enduring characteristics. Mothers who had less premenstrual tension, less anxiety, less depression, and better general life adaptation had infants better adjusted at two months. Few background features of either the mother or father predicted to Bayley scores at that time.

At one year, mothers' and fathers' long-standing characteristics and adaptation predicted substantially to the babies' cognitive and social functioning, as reflected in the Bayley Mental Development Index. Babies who had higher Bayley MDI scores had parents who were more satisfied with their marriages, were less anxious, and had experienced fewer life changes just previous to the pregnancy. The babies were also doing better if their fathers described themselves as sexually more active and satisfied, and if their fathers were individuals whom we considered to be functioning better at the major tasks of adulthood.

In marked contrast, the only predictors of the baby's motor development were aspects of the mother's and father's marital relationships, and their sexual activity and satisfaction. As we have speculated before, it does appear as if the rate of motor development, which is reflected in the Bayley PDI score, is dependent on the infant's activity level, at least in part, and that is somewhat related to the parents' drive level, as reflected in their sexual activity.

At the same one-year contact, the baby's current adaptation, as assessed by our observation, was related not as much to previous life characteristics of the parents but to their current functioning and relationship to their baby. Babies who were alert, curious, related, and happy had parents who were comfortable with their marriage, not unduly anxious or depressed, and comfortable with themselves in their role as parents. Once again marital satisfaction and anxiety were among the strongest predictors.

It is important to summarize what we did not find. Such demographic characteristics as the socioeconomic status of the family and the age of the parents, factors that one might expect to have predictive power, appeared to play a minor role in affecting the child's behavior. Our sample group did not include the extremes of either social class or age, but there was some substantial variation on these dimensions. Yet these demographic factors related to only the mother's description of how well the baby was doing, a description which probably tells us more about the mother's comfort and satisfaction with her life and less about the child's actual development. Also, in contrast to much of the literature, we found virtually no differences in the ways parents treated babies of different sexes. Possibly our measures are not subtle enough to reflect any differences that exist.

A few general comments seem warranted about the difference between first and later children, and the interrelated differences we found between mothers and fathers in their apparent effect on their offspring. In our data, first-born children seemed strongly caught up in their relationships with their mothers. Their functioning at two months and at one year was predicted by a number of characteristics of their mothers early in pregnancy. This is substantially less true of later children. In sharp contrast, by one year, the father's functioning and adaptation related to the adaptation of his later-born child, but not to his first-born in most respects.

One can begin to develop a model, as we have throughout our discussion and interpretation of our findings, of an extremely close tie between mother and first child, lasting at least through the first year of the baby's life (and possibly longer), with the father being somewhat on the periphery, although still very important to his wife and to the family system. With later children, unless special psychological needs come into play, mothers no longer have the time, energy, or possibly cathexis to completely engage and monopolize the relationship with the new baby, and that child is much more open to relationships with, and the influence of, the father and siblings.

❧ 10 ❧❧❧❧❧❧❧❧❧❧❧

Myths of Parenthood Reconsidered

We undertook this study intending to measure various dimensions of women's and men's characteristics and to ascertain how each of these predicted a couple's adaptation to pregnancy, birth, and early parenting. We expected that their psychological health, their sociocultural assets and liabilities, the strength of their marriage, and for the women, the extent to which they were at risk physiologically would be among the most important predictors of parents' ability to cope with the experiences of childbearing. It is of some interest, in conclusion, to look back over the findings and see which of these factors did predict aspects of adaptation and which did not, and to put these findings in the broader longitudinal perspective of the study.

Looking first at those measures which predicted the women's psychological health at various points in this process, we found several aspects of the women's initial level of psychological adaptation to be strongly related to her adjustment in early and late pregnancy, and during the postpartum period.

244

Her early levels of depression and anxiety and, to a lesser extent, her general life adaptation measured during the first-trimester contact strongly predicted how comfortable she would be during the pregnancy and throughout the first year of her baby's life. These psychological factors, however, were not predictive of how she would respond to labor and delivery, and only slightly so to complications of labor and delivery. As we have said, childbirth is more a physiological than psychological event.

In contrast to the strong link between psychological measures from early in pregnancy and those at later points, there was a marked paucity of ties between psychological health measured early in pregnancy and mothering at either two months or one year. Although first-time mothers who were more depressed early in pregnancy were doing less well with their babies at two months, otherwise, within this generally normally functioning sample, the woman's psychological health early in pregnancy predicted her later psychological health, but it did not tell very much about the quality of her relationship with her baby.

From the physiological dimension, women with a history of more severe premenstrual tension were less comfortable with the pregnancy, and first-time mothers with such a history were more anxious and depressed at one year. The complex psychophysiological nature of premenstrual tension precludes our making causal inferences about this finding. The other major measure from this dimension, a medical risk factor, did not predict in this study, possibly because so few women in our sample were at substantial risk for problematic pregnancies. Neither of these physiological factors predicted the quality of a woman's mothering. Because we are not comfortable dismissing physiological factors as influential in a woman's adaptation to these important life events, we must conclude that our sample was limited in range on these variables and possibly that our measures were insufficiently sensitive to the more subtle nuances.

Looking at the sociocultural dimension, we found socioeconomic status to be consistently predictive of how the women were feeling about themselves and the pregnancy. Higher status was associated with fewer symptoms throughout the pregnancy, better pregnancy adaptation late in pregnancy, and less anxiety and depression at two months and one year postpartum. Socioeconomic status did not directly predict the quality of the women's mothering, although there were undoubtedly some interactive effects by way of the marriage, which was influenced by economic factors.

Another major sociocultural measure, reflecting the interpersonal supports an individual had in her life, did not prove to be of significant importance. However, we remain convinced that the availability of interpersonal supports is important to women's adaptation to pregnancy, and suggest that both the conceptualization and measurement of interpersonal support must be refined in order that such relationships may be ascertained.

The extent to which women had experienced a greater number of recent life changes was not related to a woman's psychological adaptation at any point in our study, although more change was predictive of lower quality of mothering at one year postpartum, particularly for multiparous women.

Finally, age, which we considered to be predominantly a sociocultural variable, predicted remarkably little about the women's psychological adaptation, possibly because we did not have extremely old or extremely young women in our sample. Early in the postpartum period, the older women seemed to be better at mothering; but at one year, the younger women were judged as doing better. Further study would help to clarify this relationship.

Lastly, aspects of the marital dimension proved to be among the strongest predictors of the women's psychological adaptation throughout the study. Women who felt more positively about their marriages felt less anxious and depressed in late pregnancy, at two months, and at one year postpartum. They had fewer symptoms during the pregnancy and were substantially better adapted at the time of childbirth than women less pleased with their marriages. In fact, the quality of the marriage emerged as one of the two strongest predictors of the women's psychological adaptation. In contrast, marital adjustment predicted maternal adaptation only slightly, and that only at one year, again evidencing the extent to which a woman's relationship with her baby is not simply a derivative of previously expressed aspects of her personality and life adjustment; this relationship has unique qualities.

Having discussed the marriage as a predictor of later psychological and maternal adaptation, we must also consider that the women's assessment of the quality of their marriages is itself a result of other factors. For most of the women (as well as the men) and particularly for first-time mothers, the marriages appeared to be displaced as a focal source of gratification with the birth of a child. As our data and interview material show, although the marriage remained perhaps the central source of support for the women, it clearly lost its place as the most important issue during the first months of motherhood. By one year, we felt the marriage had regained its place in the women's lives as important, but it never seemed to regain the absolute centrality that it had before the first child was born. Reflecting both the change in emphasis and the strains on the marriage brought by the early period of childrearing, our women experienced some temporary disenchantment with their marriages. The women's satisfaction with their marriages decreased with the birth of their first child. It is of some comfort to note that the birth of a second or later child did not have that same effect, that women did not become more unhappy about their marriages once the couple had survived the first child. Furthermore, the disenchantment phenomenon was accompanied by the positive effects of a new infant—particularly the first—on the marriage; the couples reported feeling a sense of enrichment and enhanced meaning in their relationship. Almost all our couples described that sense with a good deal of satisfaction, even if in the same breath they mourned the effects of the increased stresses and conflicts on their marriage.

A great number of background factors predicted the women's postpartum marital adaptation, another indication that a woman's marriage is a barometer of a variety of aspects of her life: when it is going well, other things are also going well. Women's anxiety, life adaptation, previous marital adjustment, and socioeconomic status—to name some of the most important dimensions—all predicted the health of their marriages at two months and one year postpartum.

An important reminder of the extent to which mother, father, and baby form an interconnected system is the relationship between the men's characteristics and their wives' behavior. Of all our measures, two of the strongest predictors of the women's adaptation to labor and delivery were their husbands' previous anxiety levels and satisfaction with their marriages. The men's anxiety level continued to be strongly related to the women's psychological health at two months postpartum and also to the quality of her relationship with her infant during the early postpartum period. It is clear that women rely enormously on continuing support and reassurance from their husbands for their sustained capacity to deliver and nurture a newborn and respond to its needs without experiencing overwhelming anxiety. By one year postpartum, the lines of interconnectedness in our data between mother and father were inextricably intertwined; nonetheless, we can isolate the men's anxiety level, their degree of identification with a nurturantly perceived mother, and their adaptation to their wives and new infants in the early postpartum period—all strongly interacted with the women's psychological health at one year and the quality of their relationships with their babies.

Regarding the men's experience and adaptation, each of our three major dimensions—psychological, sociocultural, and marital—predicted strongly to men's adaptation to pregnancy and early parenting. From the psychological dimension, anxiety played a powerful role. Men who were more anxious early in their wives' pregnancies were less psychologically healthy at two months and one year postpartum, and were doing less well in their marriages at both these periods. We have said before that wives of more anxious husbands did substantially less well at labor and delivery and continued to do less well with their mothering of their young infants. Thus, anxiety in men greatly interferes with their capacity to enjoy and support their wives in the early phases of establishing a family.

The other major variable from the psychological dimension important to the men's adaptation was their identification with a nurturantly perceived mother. Men who viewed their mothers as nurturant and identified more strongly with them coped better with the pregnancy, felt better about themselves as fathers, and were judged by us to be better fathers at both two months and one year postpartum. These men were also coping better with various aspects of their marriages at both two months and one year. Given the strong clinical evidence in this study of the men's feeling that they had not been well fathered, and their emphatically stated commitment to be better fathers than their own fathers had been to them, it appears that an early relationship with a nurturant parent of either sex allows good fathering to occur.

From the sociocultural dimension, socioeconomic status related to the men's quality of fathering and their marital adjustment but not to their psychological adaptation to parenthood. Men of higher status were generally doing better as parents and as husbands, although at two months postpartum lower socioeconomic status seemed associated with the couple's greater comfort with parenting. In general, it seems that higher socioeconomic status is associated with both the psychological and economic resources that allow more subtle responsiveness in interpersonal relationships. Undoubtedly, men with greater socioeconomic resources find certain aspects of parenthood to be easier.

Regarding other sociocultural variables, our measure of interpersonal supports for the men, as for the women, was not strong enough for us to give it much credence, even though it did occasionally appear in the significant statistical relationships. Age played a complex role for the men in this study: older men scored somewhat higher on some marital measures at one year, but younger men were consistently better in the quality of their fathering.

Finally, considering the marital dimension, the men's satisfaction with their marriages early in the pregnancy was related to their feelings about their marriages throughout the study, of course, and also somewhat associated with the quality of their fathering. Men's sexual activity and satisfaction early in pregnancy was strongly predictive of their adaptation to the pregnancy, their psychological health in the postpartum year, and the quality of their fathering. It is clear, as we have said, that a man's sexual functioning is close to the core of his comfort with himself and is predictive of his adjustment to the early stages of establishing his family.

Just as characteristics of the men were related to aspects of their wives' adjustment, so also women's scores predicted to their husbands' adaptation. Of particular interest was that men were doing better as fathers, and in relation to their wives, if their wives' labor and delivery had been complicated. In response to the extra demands on the family system, these men assumed additional responsibilities for caring for their wives and infants. We speculate that these nurturing activities have lasting effects on the men's relationships to their babies.

From the beginning of the study, we wondered what role the infant would play in the evolving development of the family, and we hoped to be able to tease apart the effects of mother, father, and baby on each other. Our first striking finding was that a woman's anxiety and depression early in pregnancy were related to her newborn's level of irritability shortly after birth. The complex interactions between mother and child, then, begin very early. Secondly, characteristics of the infant shortly after birth had relatively low predictive power for their behavior at two months or one year. To a limited extent, the infant's adjustment and psychomotor maturity at two months was associated with aspects of the baby's functioning at one year, but the absence of relationships was more impressive than the few correlations that did emerge. However, we found we could predict a great deal about the baby's functioning at two months by looking at characteristics of the mother early in pregnancy. The mother's stress from major life change, her usual level of premenstrual tension, her levels of anxiety and depression, and her adaptation to early pregnancy were all related to how well the infant was doing at two months; for first-time mothers, the quality of the marriage emerged as a major predictor variable as well. By eight months, both the mother's and father's anxiety predicted to their two-month-old's adaptation, and at two months postpartum, the mother's and infant's adjustment were so intertwined as to be inseparable. At one year, characteristics of the mother continued to be reflected in the baby's functioning: Substantial life change, marital contentment, and anxiety and depression were again the strongest predictors from the mother's previous characteristics. By one year, however, the father's personality also seemed to come into play. In particular, the baby's mental development—both cognitive and motor—related to the father's sexual activity and satisfaction, marital contentment, life adaptation, and earlier anxiety level. Whereas qualities of the mother predicted most strongly to the functioning of the first-born at one year, those of the father were more strongly predictive of the second and later children. These findings lead us to speculate about the extent to which the mother has an exclusive "option" on the first-born that is usually neither possible nor realized with later children, leaving these later-borns more available for important relationships with their fathers and probably also with their siblings.

Some of our data hinted at the extent to which the infant's characteristics directly influenced the parents' adaptation, but the study design did not allow us to examine these relationships. Questions about the effect of the infant's characteristics on the parents' adaptation require a study specifically designed to study this complex phenomenon.

One of the most consistent and striking sets of findings from this study is the enormous difference in the experience of couples undertaking parenthood for the first time and those who already have other children. Most earlier empirical studies of pregnancy have focused exclusively on first-time parents and therefore have not been able to describe the differences between first and later pregnancies. From our study, we conclude that the occasion of parenthood is considerably different for first-time and experienced parents.

As we have seen at every point in the study, for primiparous women and their husbands, pregnancy and early parenthood are indeed a crisis of considerable proportions wherein many of their resources—psychological, sociocultural, physiological, and marital—are called into play. Those couples with significant problems in any of these areas seem handicapped in their capacity to navigate successfully the enormously complex tasks involved in having a first child. For them, the crisis may indeed have a less than optimal resolution in terms of their feelings about themselves, their marriages, or their relationships to their new baby. For experienced parents, in contrast, aspects of their emotional make-up and of the quality of their marriages are far less important in predicting a successful outcome. For them, a sense of pregnancy and postpartum as a crisis is either totally absent or substantially less than that for first-time parents.

These findings may be a comfort both to parents, who can be reassured that the mastery they attain with their first child will stand them in good stead with later children, as well as to social planners, who can plan educational and preventive programs for inexperienced parents with the knowledge that the help and support offered during the difficult period of the first pregnancy and the early postpartum period will likely have a considerable effect on the parents' chances for success both at this time and throughout their parenting years.

The important role of anxiety in predicting difficulty during the course of pregnancy, childbirth, and the first year of parenthood has been highlighted by the data from this study. Anxiety bears a strong relation to the woman's adaptation during pregnancy and childbirth, to her own psychological comfort during the postpartum period, and to the baby's adjustment throughout infancy. Perhaps the strong physiological component of anxiety is the link relating it so strongly to pregnancy and childbirth. This tie is particularly well illustrated by the relation between anxiety and pregnancy-related symptoms, including obstetrical complications. Throughout the period of this study, more anxious women felt less comfortable with themselves in general, as mothers, and as wives. Further, babies of more anxious mothers were less well adjusted at all points in the study. During infancy, when the emotional and physical connection between mother and infant is at its closest, one might expect to see a stronger relation between maternal emotional states and the baby's behavior than later when other dimensions of the mother's personality and the baby's situation come into play to a greater extent. One aspect that becomes increasingly important as the baby gets older is the father's personality, and particularly his anxiety, which by one year postpartum relates to both mother's and baby's adaptation. Throughout, for the men as well as for the women, the individual's level of anxiety was one of the strongest predictors of his or her health, behavior, and adjustment.

Although all prospective parents experience stress during a pregnancy, there is a good deal of variability in how people perceive, interpret, and deal with that stress by means of psychological defenses; individuals display a very broad range of responses to objectively similar situations. Some people routinely and habitually seem to ignore or deny negative experiences. Other people, within similar circumstances and with what appears to be the same degree of psychological health, seem to revel in their anxiety, or at least deal with it by talking about it and worrying over it. One of the most perplexing questions of this research was to determine whether those who said things were fine were in any real sense doing better than those who were sensitive to and articulate about more negative aspects of their experience.

The feelings of both women and men, as we interviewed them during the first trimester, reflect these different styles of coping as well as their truly different experiences. For example, regarding the various discomforts and symptoms of pregnancy, although almost all women felt a good deal more tired than usual and had at least mild nausea on occasion, their responses to the question "How have you been feeling?" ranged from "perfect" to answers reflecting a good deal of concern. When the woman who said "perfect" was pressed, she reported feeling "exhausted and moody." Her first answer reflected her style of coping with stress, rather than her actual physical condition. Given a certain stressful stimulus, different people not only perceive it differently but employ different coping strategies.

We noted the same stylistic phenomenon in other contexts. Women reported a wide range of feelings about becoming mothers or adding a child to their family. Some primiparous women, for example, felt "totally excited" about the pregnancy and said that the prospect of motherhood was "the best thing that ever happened." At the other extreme, some women spoke of the adjustments to be made now that they were pregnant. They felt uncertain about entering a new phase and felt a conflict between wanting to go forward in a new direction and fearing that something precious of their old life would be lost in the process. Some people adopted an optimistic view of the change, others seemed to have a very acute sensitivity to the conflictual nature of the process.

Our data show that men and women who denied the more negative aspects of their experience had an easier time throughout the period covered by the study. We believe, however, that there is a dimension of richness of experience that is more available to people who are more aware of all aspects of their emotional lives, including their fears, doubts, and conflicts.

Finally, a few words need to be said about what we have come to call the myth of parenthood, our culture's idealized image of pregnancy, childbirth, and parenthood. According to this image, childbearing is undertaken out of the love between husband and wife and their desire to expand and enrich their relationship by having a child to share it with. The myth holds that such a wanted pregnancy is undertaken joyfully, that it unites a couple more strongly during the nine months of gestation which culminates in an uncomplicated delivery. The postpartum period, according to this story, requires a few, and only a very few, moments of adjustment to the new baby and then becomes a time when both parents feel comfortable and natural in their unambiguous roles. Of course, as an ideal image, this is an oversimplification and most parents today do not have such rosy expectations. However, sophisticated as we may be, the myth of parenthood still survives and, to a certain extent, tyrannizes most new parents in their efforts to at least approximate the idealized image.

Our data certainly confirm our sense that pregnancy and early parenthood, while usually full of joy and rich in meaning, also entail major adjustments and inevitable strains. Ours was a very favored group of people. All were married; most were relatively happy and reasonably comfortable; and most had undertaken their pregnancies in a positive and planned manner. And yet, even this group of fortunate individuals found aspects of the undertaking difficult and stressful. Most reported unpleasant physical symptoms during the pregnancy and the majority of the women had some complications of labor and delivery. Most couples experienced strain in their marriages, especially immediately after childbirth. Almost all the parents described the considerable psychological work entailed in adjusting to the new baby and including it in the newly changed family structure. Although many of the couples were able to describe some of these difficulties, we sensed that their reports were self-censored, that the crisis they were experiencing was even more difficult than they were willing to describe, that even these generally privileged couples were at least somewhat tyrannized by the myths of parenthood.

This study was undertaken partly because of our strong belief that the analysis of normative data is essential to a realistic understanding of the experiences involved in pregnancy and early parenting. The idealized image of parenthood only serves to block our vision and to burden us with additional and unnecessary efforts to live up to the ideal. It is only when we come to understand the reality of the experience involved will we be able to teach and prepare our young in a realistic way for the undertakings of adulthood. It is only when the mythical joy is eliminated that a more real sense of richness and satisfaction can emerge in the very important experience of new parenthood.

Variables and Measures

For all scores based on interviews, a set of defined scoring categories was developed prior to the development of the interview. Each variable comprised at least three separate subscores. Some of these scales were modified slightly on the basis of the first several interviews we attempted to score, but the basic structures of the scales did not change. When all of the interviews for any given time period were completed, raters—not aware of other information about the families—were trained to score the tapes. Interscorer reliabilities were not considered adequate unless they reached at least .6. Most scores, and particularly the life adaptation subscales, were scored independently of all other variables; that is, the scorer rated the individual only on that one dimension of life adaptation while listening to the tape.

Note: Copies of previously unpublished measures can be obtained by writing to Frances K. Grossman, Department of Psychology, Boston University, 64 Cummington Street, Boston, Mass. 02215.

First-Trimester Contact: Variables measured for the expectant mother

Psychological Dimension:

1. Life Adaptation: assessed by the Cox Adaptation Scale (Cox, 1970). This score, obtained from ratings made from a semi-structured interview, reflects the extent to which an individual is coping with the major tasks of adulthood. The subscales we used included Adaptation to Work, Marriage, Relation to Own Parents, and Freedom from Symptoms.

Each area of functioning was scored with the rater blind as to other information about the man or woman, and independently of scoring the other areas of adaptation. Interscorer reliabilities for two raters, on a sample of nine tapes was .9 for the total combined score.

The average score for our women was 4.7, of a possible 5, reflecting high levels of functioning.

2. Anxiety: This variable was measured by the State and Trait Anxiety Index (Spielberger, Gorsuch, and Lushene, 1968, 1970). The individual is given two paper-and-pencil-scales that describe twenty anxiety-related experiences; for example, feeling frightened or lacking self-confidence. The individual is asked to rate, on a four-point scale, the relevance of each item to his or her current experience (state) or usual experience (trait). Because the two scales were highly intercorrelated and the State Index was the better overall predictor to our dependent measures, we used the State Index throughout.

The average score for our women was 33.1 on State Anxiety, considerably lower than the means described by Spielberger, Gorsuch, and Luschene for high school students, college students, or psychiatric patients.

3. Depression and Anxiety: This was measured by a twenty-four-item questionnaire designed to reflect depression and anxiety during pregnancy and the puerperium (Pitt, 1968). It yields a maximum score of 48, with high scores indicating pathological levels of depression and anxiety.

The mean score for our sample was 14.6, showing low levels of depression and reflecting their relatively high level of functioning early in their pregnancies.

4. Conscious Motivation for Pregnancy: The scale measuring this variable, developed by Gofseyeff (1977) for this project, is an eight-item questionnaire assessing the conscious wish for the pregnancy and previous contraceptive behavior. The range of scores is from 8 to 40, with high scores reflecting strong conscious motivation for the current pregnancy.

The mean score for our women was 35.36, indicating a high level of conscious motivation.

5. Masculinity and Femininity: These scales for these variables, developed by Bem (1974), assess the degree to which an individual's self-perception is stereotypically masculine or feminine. An individual rates sixty stereotypically masculine, feminine, and neuter adjectives on a seven-point scale, depending on how accurately that adjective describes himself or herself. Each subject receives a Masculinity Score and a Femininity Score, with high scores on each scale reflecting greater perceived amounts of those characteristics.

Bem and Watson (1978) have suggested a way of classifying individuals as *masculine, feminine, androgynous,* or *undifferentiated* depending upon how their scores fall relative to the median score—for men and women combined—of the sample. Thus, *masculine* men and women are individuals whose masculinity score is above the median and whose femininity score is below the median, *androgynous* individuals have both scores above the median, and *undifferentiated* individuals have both below.

The mean scores for our women were 92.65 on Masculinity—or 4.63 on the individual items—and 105.58 on the overall Femininity Scale, for an average of 5.28 on the individual femininity adjectives. Using the Bem and Watson scheme for dividing at the median of the total—male and female—sample, we classified forty-five women as *feminine,* twenty as *androgynous,* six as *masculine,* and thirteen as *undifferentiated.*

6. Modified TAT: This scale is a modification of the TAT developed Lakin (1957). A subject is shown four cards depicting scenes of pregnancy and childcare and is asked to describe the scenes. Lakin's scoring requires raters to judge the affect of each of the stories as positive, negative, or neutral. (Scoring de-

scribed in detail in Gofseyeff, 1977.) The woman's overall score on this measure is the average of the scores for each card, with a score of 5 reflecting entirely positive affect, and a score of 1 reflecting entirely negative affect. The mean score for our women was 2.89, reflecting ambivalence slightly weighted towards the positive.

7. Adaptation to Pregnancy: This score for this variable, developed for this research, is based on our evaluation of the women in five five-point subscales scored from tapes of a semi-structured interview. The interview includes such items as feelings about the current pregnancy, anxiety about the pregnancy or the labor and delivery, and the extent to which the pregnancy seems to be enhancing or disrupting the marital relationship. The assumptions implicit in the scoring are that, early in pregnancy, women who are doing better are much more aware of the positive aspects of the experience and not yet very aware of the anxieties that inevitably develop, or of the (also inevitable) ambivalence associated with childbearing. A woman's score is the average of her scores on subscales; the maximum score is 5. Interscorer reliability was .9 on a sample of ten tapes.

The mean score for the women was 3.59, reflecting a moderate level of judged comfort with, and adaptation to, the current pregnancy.

8. Identification with Mother: This variable reflects several aspects of the women's feeling of identification with their own mothers. The measure is based on Shereshefsky and Yarrow's (1973) data that show relations between such identification and aspects of women's adaptation. Specifically, subjects were asked during the initial interview, "Do you think your own mother was a good mother to you while you were growing up? How much like or unlike her are you? How do you feel about that?" Individuals' responses to these questions were scored on three six-point scales, with higher scores reflecting more positive feelings about the experience of being mothered, greater identification with the mother, and positive feelings about that identification.

The mean score for the women was 4.8, of a possible 6.

Marital Dimension:

1. Marital Adjustment: The Revised Locke-Wallace Marital Adjustment Inventory (Locke and Wallace, 1959; Kimmel and Vanderveen, 1974) is a paper-and-pencil measure of marital satisfaction. It includes self-ratings of level of satisfaction with the marriage in a number of areas, degree of sharing and mutuality, as well as estimates of the frequency and intensity of conflicts between the spouses.

The mean score for the women was 115, of a possible 126, reflecting a high initial level of marital satisfaction.

2. Sexual Activity and Satisfaction: Scores on this variable come from a self-report paper-and-pencil form, developed for this research, that asks for a rating of the frequency, the importance, and the amount of satisfaction derived from marital sex. The maximum score is 20.

The mean score for the women was 13.99, indicating moderately high levels of sexual activity and enjoyment.

3. Marital Style: The score for this variable, developed for this research, was our rating, on a five-point scale, of the section of the taped interview that concerned the extent to which the couple displayed a more traditional division of labor (score 1) or a more egalitarian style (score 5). Ratings were made separately from the men's and women's tapes, and each couple received a final averaged rating.

The average of our couples' ratings was 3.11, reflecting a marital style in which the husbands participated somewhat in childcare and household tasks, but the wives assumed the primary responsibility for these jobs.

Physiological Dimension:

1. Premenstrual Tension: The scale measuring this variable, developed by Shader, DiMascio, and Harmatz (1972), asks subjects to evaluate on a seven-point scale the extent to which premenstrual tension or discomfort interferes with their performance in daily tasks or social situations, how much physical discomfort it causes, and the extent of the overall mood change they experience. The score, with a maximum of 21 indicating

the greatest amount of disruptive premenstrual tension, is the sum of scores on the individual items.

The average score for our sample was 8.05 reflecting a low level of premenstrual distress.

2. Medical Risk: This rating of risk factors, developed by Winickoff (1977), scores medical factors seen by obstetricians as increasing the risk of complicated pregnancy or childbirth (for example, see Friedman and Greenhill, 1974). The factors include such variables as age, parity, and medical and gynecological history. The maximum score, reflecting the greatest possible risk is 28.

The mean score for our women was 6.92; these women were at relatively low risk as a group for complications of pregnancy, labor, and delivery.

Sociocultural Dimension:

1. Socioeconomic Status: This score, from Coleman and Neugarten (1971), places families on a seven-point scale, based on separate ratings of social status of the husband's and wife's education and occupation.

The average rating for our families was 3.1 (see Table 17, Appendix C), reflecting the primarily middle- and upper-middle-class status of the group.

2. Social Supports: This variable was measured by a self-report questionnaire, modified from one developed by Johnston (1971), which assesses the extent to which an individual feels herself to be part of a personally meaningful extended family, community, or subgroup and the extent to which she feels she could turn to members of that group for personal support. The scoring system is open-ended, with an unlimited maximum score.

The mean score for our women was 53.33, reflecting a moderate amount of potential and actual social support in their lives. (There were extremely broad individual differences in our women's responses to this scale.)

3. Life Change: Holmes and Rahe (1967) developed the Social Readjustment Rating Scale, which lists forty-three major

changes that might occur in a person's life. For this first administration, we asked one member of the couple—the husband if he was participating—to fill it out for both himself and his spouse. The score, which multiplies each noted change by weights previously determined by Holmes and Rahe, is for the couple.

The average score for our couples was 272, indicating a moderate level of life change, with enormous variability in the scores.

Control Measures:

1. Social Desirability: We administered the Crowne and Marlowe (1959) scale, designed to measure the tendency of individuals to give socially desirable responses to statements on personality inventories. High scores reflect greater tendencies to give such responses. The maximum score is 33. The mean score for our sample was 15.83.

3. Religiosity: This scale for this variable, developed for this research, is a rating on a five-point scale of the extent to which individuals consider religious belief and observance important in their lives. A high score indicates that the individual places great importance on religion.

The average score was 2.6, reflecting a moderate level of observance and belief.

First-Trimester Contact: Variables measured for the expectant father (the individual measures are all the same as those described earlier).

Psychological Dimension:

1. Life Adaptation: The average score for men was 4.8, reflecting moderately high levels of functioning.

2. Anxiety: The average initial score for men was 33.82 on the State Anxiety scale.

3. Conscious Motivation for Pregnancy: The average score for men was 34.58, indicating high levels of conscious motivation for the current pregnancy.

4. Masculinity and Femininity: On the separate scales, the average score for men was 107.19 on the overall Masculin-

ity Scale, or 5.36 for each stereotypically masculine adjective, and 96.53, or 4.83, on the Femininity Scales. Using median splits, we classified twenty-one men as *androgynous*, thirty-three as *masculine*, six as *feminine*, and thirteen as *undifferentiated.*

5. Adaptation to Pregnancy: The average score for men was 3.92.

6. Identification with Mother: The average score for men was 4.6.

Marital Dimension:

1. Marital Adjustment: The average initial score for men was 111.96, slightly lower than the women's initial score, but still reflecting substantial marital satisfaction.

2. Sexual Activity and Satisfaction: The mean score for men was 15.22, indicating moderately high levels of sexual activity and enjoyment.

Sociocultural Dimension:

1. Socioeconomic Status: The mean rating for our families was 3.1.

2. Social Supports: The average score for men was 51.77.

3. Life Change: The average score for our couples was 272.

Control Measures:

1. Social Desirability: The average score for the men was 14.23.

2. Religiosity: The average score for the men was 2.3.

Eighth-Month Contact: Variables measured for the expectant mother

1. Anxiety (measure described earlier): The average score for the women at this testing was 34.

2. Symptoms: Developed by Erickson (1967), the scale for this variable asks women to rate the frequency with which they experienced thirty physical and emotional symptoms during each of the three trimesters of pregnancy. We administered this scale only in the last trimester and asked the women for their retrospective accounts of the first two trimesters. Scores

for all three trimesters combined ranged from 90 to 360, with higher scores indicating greater difficulty and discomfort.

The average total score, across the three trimesters, was 183.16.

3. Adaptation to Pregnancy: This variable was scored on a measure, developed for this study, rated from tapes of a joint semistructured interview with the couple. This measure is a rating of the woman on three five-point scales: her acceptance of the physical and psychological changes the pregnancy has brought, her sense of growth or stagnation during the pregnancy, and her emotional preparedness for motherhood. Interscorer reliabilities by raters blind as to any other information about the woman was .62, with a sample of twelve tapes.

The average score for expectant mothers was 3.12, of a possible 5.

4. Life Change (same measure as before, but we asked the couple to consider events during the past six months): The mean score of the couples was 158.66.

5. Conscious Motivation for Pregnancy (same measure as above): At this contact, the average score was 36.01.

6. Marital Adaptation: The measure for this variable, developed for this study, was scored from tapes of the joint interview. The score was the average of three subscales: sense of shared and enjoyed experience, sense of comfort—as opposed to unresolved struggle—in the relationship, and sense of having been brought closer by the pregnancy. The interscorer reliability, on twelve tapes, was .72.

The average score for the couples was 3.3, with a maximum possible score of 5.

7. Couple Preparedness: Also developed for this study, the measure represents our rating, from tapes of the joint interview, of the extent to which the couple was emotionally and practically prepared to have a new infant. Interscorer reliability on twelve tapes was .62.

The average score for our couples was 3.49.

Eighth-Month Contact: Variables measured for the expectant father

1. Anxiety (described above): The average score for the men at this testing was 33.68.

2. Adaptation to Pregnancy (similar to measure for women): Interscorer reliability on twelve tapes was .63. The average score was 3.15.

Labor-and-Delivery Contact: Variables measured for the mother

1. Complications: On the basis of medical records, mothers were assigned to one of three groups: uncomplicated (score 1); mild to moderate complications (score 2), including caesarean sections for cephalopelvic disproportion, mid-forceps delivery, tight muchal cord with lowered Apgar, and third or fourth degree lacerations; and serious complications (score 3) including serious fetal distress, uterine inertia, and premature birth (based on Winickoff, 1977, who developed the list from Friedman and Greenhill, 1974). Forty mother-infant pairs had no complications, thirty had mild to moderate complications and nineteen had serious complications.

2. Caesarean Section: This score simply reflected whether the woman delivered by caesarean section or vaginally. Twenty-one infants, or 23.7 percent of the babies, were caesarean deliveries.

3. Medication: The score measuring this variable, developed for this study (with the assistance of S. Wise), ranges from 2 to 8, depending upon the amount and kind of medication the mother had for the labor and delivery. A maximum score reflects the use of both substantial anesthesia (for example, an epidural or a general) and analgesics given at a time when they tend to have maximum impact on the newborn (thirty to sixty minutes prior to the actual delivery).

The women had an average score of 3.92; the typical woman had a mild tranquilizer, regional block, and no analgesic.

4. Maternal Adaptation to Labor and Delivery: This variable, developed for this study, was measured from the interview during the early postpartum period. The average score was 3.58 on a six-point scale. The final score is the average rating of our evaluation of the woman on six dimensions: her subjective reac-

tion to the labor and delivery, her feelings about how she handled that experience, her degree of acceptance of the infant, her
mood, her anxiety about the maternal role, and her satisfaction
with her husband's role during the labor and delivery. Interscorer
reliability, based on nine tapes, was .92.

Labor-and-Delivery Contact: Variables measured for the
infant

1. Apgar: This score, developed by Apgar and others
(1958), is an approximate assessment of the infant's health and
neurological functioning, rated on a ten-point scale by the phy-
sician shortly after birth. The scores we used were from assessments made approximately five minutes after birth.

The average Apgar score for our infants was 9.71.

2. Birth Weight: We recorded the infant's birth weight
from the medical record. The average of the infants' weights
was 7 pounds, 4 ounces (3.29 kilograms).

3. Brazelton Alertness, Motor Maturity, Irritability:
These three scores are obtained from the Brazelton Neonatal
Behavioral Assessment Scale (Brazelton, 1973), usually administered on the third day after birth. The scale, which assesses
various aspects of the newborn's responsibility and state characteristics, has twenty-seven items, each scored on a nine-point
scale. Bakow (1974) performed a factor analysis of data from
the exam and arrived at three major factors: Alertness, Motor
Maturity, and Irritability.

The average score for the infants on Alertness was 63.27;
on Motor Maturity, 51.32; and on Irritability, 45.57.

4. Sex of Infant: Thirty-nine girls and forty-eight boys
were born to the parents in this study.

Two-Months Postpartum Contact: Variables measured for
the mother

Psychological Adaptation:

1. Emotional Well-Being: This variable is measured by
a scale, developed for this research, with four subscale scores—
mother's anxiety about coping with the infant, acceptance of

her own needs, her physical condition, and her mood—rated from tapes of the semistructured interview. The interscorer reliability for twelve tapes was .86.

The mean score for the women was 4.05, of a possible 5.

2. Anxiety (same measure as above): At the two-months postpartum visit, the mean score was 34.34.

3. Depression and Anxiety (same measure as above): The average score at the two-months postpartum visit was 13.36.

Marital Adaptation:

1. Marital Adjustment (same measure as above): The average score for the women was 112.96 at the two-months postpartum visit.

2. Adaptation to Spouse: The measure of this variable was developed for this project and is a mean of two subscales: one evaluates the woman's comfort with the division of labor she and her husband have evolved at this time; the other reflects our judgment of how successfully they are reestablishing the marital dyad after the disruptive effects of the pregnancy and childbirth and the neonatal period. The interscorer reliability for seven tapes was .73.

The average of the women's scores was 4.26, of a possible 5.

Maternal Adaptation:

1. Observed Maternal Adaptation: The measure of this variable is a scale designed to reflect the adequacy of the mother's interactions with her infant, based on observational ratings of four separate dimensions: the quality of physical contact, the degree of expression and of affection, maternal sensitivity and responsiveness, and the mother's acceptance of the infant. The scale was developed for this study on the basis of the work of Shereshefsky and Yarrow (1973). Interscorer reliability of the mean score across the scales for twenty-eight observations was .69.

The average score for the mothers was 16.51 (of a possible 20), reflecting a high quality of observed mothering with their two-month-old infants.

2. Interview Measure of Maternal Adaptation: This variable was measured by a scale designed to reflect the adequacy of the mother's interactions with her infant, based on our judgments from the taped interview of the mother's description of the infant and the relationship between them. Each mother was rated on fourteen dimensions, including those evaluated in the observations (listed above) and others, such as ratings of attachment behavior (from Klaus and others, 1972). The interscorer reliability for the mean score for the mothers or fathers (no distinctions were made in scoring) from twelve tapes was .91.

The average score for the mothers was 4.08, of a possible 5.

3. Reciprocity: This variable is measured by a scale, developed by Price (1975), which reflects the degree of reciprocal relatedness between mother and infant. The score is based on ratings in ten categories of behavior from our observation of a feeding. The categories include such dimensions as spatial distance during feeding, holding style, and maternal expression of affect. Interscorer reliability on the basis of twelve observations was .86.

Our women received an average score of 25.05, of a possible 32.

Two-Months Postpartum Contact: Variables measured for the father

Psychological Adaptation:

1. Emotional Well-Being (same measure as earlier): The mean score for the fathers was 4.13.

2. Anxiety (same measure as earlier): At this visit, the average of the men's scores was 34.68.

Marital Adaptation:

1. Marital Adjustment (same measure as earlier): The average score at this time was 111.70.

2. Adaptation to Spouse (same measure as earlier): The average score for the men was 4.15.

Adaptation to Infant:

1. Interview Measure of Paternal Adaptation (similar to Interview Measure of Maternal Adaptation, above): The average score for the fathers was 4.09.

Two-Months Postpartum Contact: Variables measured for the infant

1. Bayley Scale of Infant Development, Mental Development Index (MDI) and Psychomotor Development Index (PDI): This standardized developmental scale yields standard scores with a mean of 100 and a standard deviation of 15 (Bayley, 1969). The average scores for our infants were 101.93 on the MDI and 105.19 on the PDI.

2. Physiological Adaptation: The scale measuring this variable was developed for this project and patterned after Shereshefsky and Yarrow's (1973) score. From the tape of the mother's responses to the semistructured interview, we evaluated the infant's health in regard to eating (for example, weight gain, digestive ease, hunger cycle), sleeping, and general health. The interscorer reliability was .83 on the basis of twelve tapes.

The average score for the infants was 4.13, of a possible 5.

3. Observed Adaptation: This variable was based on an observational measure developed from the factor analysis of infant scores by Shereshefsky and Yarrow (1973). Our score was based on observational ratings, made during unstructured observations of the infant, on the following seven subscales: adaptability to change, irritability, vulnerability to stress, ease of recovery from being upset, tension, characteristic mood, and affective stability. Each item was rated on a five-point scale. The total possible score was 35. Interscorer reliability on observations of twenty-eight infants was .72.

The average score for the infants was 22.65.

4. Interview Measure of Infant's Adaptation: The measure of this variable, also developed for this project, based on research by Shereshefsky and Yarrow (1973), is the same as the Observed Adaptation measure above, except it is scored from

the mother's report of the infant during the semistructured interview. Mothers described their infants more glowingly than we saw them. The mean score from the interview was 27.78, of a possible 35. Interscorer reliability on the basis of ten tapes was .78.

One-Year Postpartum Contact: Variables measured for the mother

Psychological Adaptation:

1. Emotional Well-Being (same measure as above): At one year postpartum, the average score for mothers was 4.1. Interscorer reliability, on the basis of twenty tapes, was .67.
2. Anxiety (same measure as above): The average score for the mothers at this contact was 32.47.
3. Depression and Anxiety (same measure as above): The average score at this contact was 10.8.

Marital Adaptation:

1. Marital Adjustment: For women, the average score was 112.30. The Dyadic Adjustment Scale given at this contact is a thirty-two-item paper-and-pencil scale developed by Spanier (1976) and is similar to the Locke-Wallace (correlation between the two scales is .93).
2. Adaptation to Spouse (same measure as above): The average score at this contact was 4. Interscorer reliability on the basis of twenty tapes was .62.
3. Sexual Activity and Satisfaction (same measure as above): The average score at this contact was 13.4.

Maternal Adaptation:

1. Observed Maternal Adaptation: This variable reflects the adequacy of the mother's interactions with the baby, based on ratings from unstructured observations of mother-infant interactions. Six dimensions were assessed, including acceptance of aspects of the baby, feelings of competence with the infant,

and awareness of the infant's needs. Interscorer reliability, based on nine observations, was .95.

The average of the mothers' scores was 4.2, of a possible 5.

2. Interview Measure of Maternal Adaptation: The scale for this variable, developed for this project, rates the mother on the same dimensions as Observed Maternal Adaptation above, but on the basis of the tape of the semistructured interview with the mother. Interscorer reliability on the basis of seventeen tapes was .7.

Our mothers received an average score of 4.4.

Other Variables:

1. Maternal Employment: Data were collected about whether the woman was employed and her degree of satisfaction with her employed or unemployed status. Forty-one of the women were not employed at the time of the one-year visit, twelve were working half-time or less, and ten were employed full-time. They described themselves as satisfied with this situation; the average score was 4.3, of a possible 5.

2. Repression-Sensitization Scale: Developed by Byrne (1961), this true-false scale, composed of selected MMPI items, is considered a measure of defense style. Higher scores represent the tendency to repress and deny. The average of the women's scores was 13.34, of a possible 55.

3. Life Change (same measure as above): Couples were asked to complete the scale for events occurring during the past year.

The average of the couples' weighted scores was 161.09.

One-Year Postpartum Contact: Variables measured for the father

Psychological Adaptation:

1. Emotional Well-Being (same measure as above): The average score for the fathers at one year was 4.07.

2. Anxiety (same measure as above): The average score was 34.33.

Marital Adaptation:

1. Marital Adjustment (same measure as above): The average score was 114.

2. Adaptation to Spouse (same measure as above): The mean of the men's scores was 4.28.

3. Sexual Activity and Satisfaction (same measure as above): The average score, at this contact, was 14.78.

Paternal Adaptation:

1. Interview Measure of Paternal Adaptation (same measure as above): The average score was 4.35.

(We were unable to observe enough father-baby interactions to use an observational scale on this dimension.)

Other Variables:

1. Repression-Sensitization (same measure as above): The average score for men was 12.86.

2. Life Change (same measure as for the women): The average score for couples was 161.09.

One-Year Postpartum Contact: Variables measured for the baby

1. Bayley MDI and PDI (same measures as above): The average scores of the one-year-olds on the two scales were 105.2 and 95.8, respectively.

2. Observed Adaptation: The score for this measure, developed for this project, is a mean score of ratings on three subscales: mood, apparent quality of relationships, and curiosity. Interscorer reliability, based on nine observations, was .88. The babies received a mean score of 4.3, of a possible 5.

3. Interview Measure of Baby's Adaptation: This measure, developed for this project, uses the same subscales as Observed Adaptation, but is scored from tapes of the mother's interview. The average score was 4.5.

(Initially we attempted to rate babies on temperament. Neither the Carey Temperament Scale (Carey, 1973) nor a Temperament Scoring Checklist we developed based on categories described by Chess, Thomas, and Birch (1959) related meaningfully to other scores and so were not considered further.)

Statistical Methods

The primary method of statistical analysis was Pearson product-moment correlations. In presenting the results of these analyses, we have taken a conservative stance, that is—except where otherwise noted—we present only those findings that make conceptual or theoretical sense and reach a level of statitistical significance of .05, with a two-tailed test. These criteria are intended to exclude those findings that are statistically significant but random due to the number of variables involved. Thus, differences between first-time and experienced mothers and fathers, and their infants, are presented only when they are statistically significant and conceptually defensible or at least plausible.

In addition, we have used partial correlations and multiple regressions, when such techniques seemed to offer elucidation of the findings. Following Blalock (1961), we carried out partial correlations only when two predictor variables correlated significantly to one outcome variable, and to each other, and when conceptually one could make the argument that one of the independent variables was possibly the intervening link between the other two. When the results from multiple regressions did not significantly add to the predictive value of the independent variables, as was usually the case with these findings, we reported only the zero order correlations.

With regard to t tests and analyses of variance, again we only reported the findings as significant when they reached a level of $p \leqslant .05$, two-tailed.

Description of the Sample

The families for the study were recruited from private physicians and clinics. If a woman seeking early prenatal care expressed a willingness to participate, we described the study in some detail and asked if she and her husband would participate. If a woman said she was willing and her husband was not, we agreed to see her alone. In two private practices, the staff told patients about the study and 127 women agreed to be called by the research team. Of these, 96 women agreed to participate. Most women who attended the obstetrical clinics were not eligible for the study, either because they were not married or because English was not their native language. We called 17 women, and 11 initially agreed to participate. Thus, in all, 107 women initially agreed to participate, out of the 144 we asked.

A number of the original group were lost to the study at various stages of the project. Eleven women miscarried early in the project, several families moved away, nine withdrew for various personal reasons before they delivered, and two withdrew after the labor and delivery (these were included in the

Table 17. Demographic Characteristics of Initial Sample

	Mean Age	Range–Age	Mean Years Married	Socioeconomic Status[a]	Mean Number of Children	Range–Number of Children
Women						
All mothers	28.0	21–34	4.9	3.1		
First-time mothers	27.0	21–34	3.1	3.0		
Experienced mothers	28.9	21–33	6.6	3.3	1.4	1–4
Men						
All fathers	29.9	24–38		3.1		
First-time fathers	28.3	24–33		3.0		
Experienced fathers	31.6	24–38		3.3	1.4	1–4

[a] Socioeconomic status was rated on the Coleman and Neugarten (1971) seven-point scale, in which 1 represents upper social status, 3 and 4 middle social status, and 7 lower social status.

analyses). Of the final sample of ninety-three which provides the bases for the statistical analyses, eleven women participated without their husbands; slightly more than half the couples had had at least one child. Table 17 shows the demographic characteristics of the sample.

References

꙰꙰ ꙰꙰ ꙰꙰

Aberle, D. F., and Naegele, K. D. "Middle-Class Fathers' Occupational Role and Attitude Toward Children." *American Journal of Orthopsychiatry*, 1952, *22*, 366–378.

Ainsworth, M. D. S., and Bell, S. M. "Some Contemporary Patterns of Mother-Infant Interaction in the Feeding Situation." In A. Ambrose (Ed.), *Stimulation in Early Infancy*. New York: Academic Press, 1969.

Anzelone, M. K. "Postpartum Depression and Premenstrual Tension, Life Stress and Marital Adjustment." Unpublished doctoral dissertation, Boston University, 1976.

Apgar, V. A., and others. "Evaluation of the Newborn Infant." *Journal of the American Medical Association*, 1958, *168*, 15.

Bakow, H. A. "Individual Differences and Conditioning in the Human Newborn." Unpublished doctoral dissertation, University of Rochester, 1974.

Bakow, H. A., and others. "Relation Between Newborn Behavior and Mother-Child Interaction at Four Months." Paper presented at the meeting of the Society for Research and Child Development, Philadelphia, March 1973.

Ban, P., and Lewis, M. "Mothers and Fathers, Girls and Boys: Attachment Behavior in the One-Year-Old." *Merrill-Palmer Quarterly*, 1974, *20*, 195–204.

Bane, M. J. "Marital Disruption and the Lives of Children." *Journal of Social Issues*, 1976, *32* (1), 103–118.

Baxter, S. "Labor and Orgasm in Primiparae." *Journal of Psychosomatic Research*, 1974, *18*, 209–216.

Bayley, N. *Bayley Scales of Infant Development*. New York: Psychological Corporation, 1969.

Beckman, L. "The Relative Rewards and Costs of Parenthood and Employment for Employed Women." *Psychology of Women Quarterly*, 1978, *2*, 215–233.

Bell, R. Q., Weller, G., and Waldrop, M. F. "Newborn and Preschooler: Organization of Behavior and Relations Between Periods." *Monographs of the Society for Research in Child Development*, 1971, *36* (142).

Bell, S. M., and Ainsworth, M. D. S. "Infant Crying and Maternal Responsiveness." *Child Development*, 1972, *43*, 1171–1190.

Bem, S. L. "The Measurement of Psychological Androgyny." *Journal of Consulting and Clinical Psychology*, 1974, *42*, 155–162.

Bem, S. L. "Probing the Promise of Androgyny." In A. G. Kaplan and J. P. Bean (Eds.), *Beyond Sex-Role Stereotypes: Readings Toward a Psychology of Androgyny*. Boston: Little, Brown, 1976.

Bem, S. L., and Watson, C. "Scoring Packet: Bem Sex-Role Inventory." Unpublished manuscript, 1978.

Benedek, T. "The Organization of the Reproductive Drive." *International Journal of Psychoanalysis*, 1960, *61*, 1–15.

Benedek, T. "Fatherhood and Providing." In E. J. Anthony and T. Benedek (Eds.), *Parenthood: Its Psychology and Psychopathology*. Boston: Little, Brown, 1970a.

Benedek, T. "The Psychobiology of Pregnancy." In E. J. Anthony and T. Benedek (Eds.), *Parenthood: Its Psychology and Psychopathology*. Boston: Little, Brown, 1970b.

Bennett, S. L. "Infant-Caretaker Interactions." In E. N. Rexford, L. W. Sander, and T. Shapiro (Eds.), *Infant Psychiatry: A New Synthesis*. New Haven, Conn.: Yale University Press, 1976.

Benson, L. *Fatherhood: A Sociological Perspective*. New York: Random House, 1967.

Bergman, P., and Escalona, S. "Unusual Sensitivities in Very Young Children." *The Psychoanalytic Study of the Child*. 1947–1948, *3-4*, 333–352.

Bernard, J. *The Future of Marriage*. New York: World, 1972.

Bibring, G. S. "Some Considerations of the Psychological Processes in Pregnancy." *The Psychoanalytic Study of the Child*, 1959, *14*, 113–121.

Biller, H. B. *Paternal Deprivation*. Lexington, Mass.: Lexington Books, 1974.

Birns, B. "Individual Differences in Human Neonates' Response to Stimulation." *Child Development*, 1965, *36*, 249–256.

Birns, B., Barten, S., and Bridger, W. H. "Individual Differences in Temperamental Characteristics of Infants." *Transactions of the New York Academy of Sciences*, 1969, *31*, 1071–1082.

Birns, B., Blank, M., and Bridger, W. H. "The Effectiveness of Various Soothing Techniques on Human Neonates." *Psychosomatic Medicine*, 1966, *28*, 316–322.

Blalock, H. M. *Causal Inferences in Nonexperimental Research*. Chapel Hill: University of North Carolina Press, 1961.

Blank, M. "The Mother's Role in Infant Development." In E. N. Rexford, L. W. Sander, and T. Shapiro (Eds.), *Infant Psychiatry: A New Synthesis*. New Haven, Conn.: Yale University Press, 1976.

Blau, A., and others. "The Psychogenic Etiology of Premature Births." *Psychosomatic Medicine*, 1963, *25*, 201–211.

Blitzer, J. R., and Murray, J. M. "On the Transformation of Early Narcissism During Pregnancy." *International Journal of Psychoanalysis*, 1964, *45*, 89–97.

Blumberg, A., and Billig, O. "Hormonal Influence upon 'Puerperal Psychosis' and Neurotic Conditions." *Psychiatric Quarterly*, 1942, *16*, 454.

Bower, W. H., and Altschule, M. D. "Use of Progesterone in

Treatment of Postpartum Psychosis." *New England Journal of Medicine*, 1956, *254*, 157–160.

Bowlby, J. *Attachment and Loss*. Vol. 1. New York: Basic Books, 1969.

Bradley, R. "A Father's Presence in Delivery Rooms." *Psychosomatics*, 1962, *3*, 474–479.

Brazelton, T. B. "Psychophysiologic Reactions in the Neonate, I: The Value of Observation of the Neonate." *Journal of Pediatrics*, 1961, *58*, 508–512.

Brazelton, T. B. "Neonatal Behavior Assessment Scale." *Clinics in Developmental Medicine*, No. 50. London: Spastics International Medical Publications, 1973.

Brazelton, T. B., Koslowski, B., and Main, M. "The Origins of Reciprocity in Mother-Infant Interaction." In M. Lewis and L. Rosenblum (Eds.), *The Effect of the Infant on its Caregiver*. New York: Wiley, 1974.

Brazelton, T. B., and others. "Early Mother-Infant Reciprocity." In *Parent-Infant Interaction* (Symposium of the Parent-Infant Relationship, London, 1974). New York: American Elsevier, 1975.

Brody, S., and Axelrod, S. *Anxiety and Ego Formation in Infancy*. New York: International Universities Press, 1970.

Bronfenbrenner, U. "The Changing American Child: A Speculative Analysis." In F. Rebelsky and L. Dorman (Eds.), *Child Development and Behavior*. (2nd ed.) New York: Knopf, 1973.

Brown, L. B. "Social and Attitudinal Concomitants of Illness in Pregnancy." *British Journal of Medical Psychology*, 1962, *35*, 311–322.

Brown, L. B. "Anxiety in Pregnancy." *British Journal of Medical Psychology*, 1964, *37*, 45–57.

Brown, W. A., Manning, T., and Grodin, J. "The Relationship of Antenatal and Perinatal Psychological Variables to the Use of Drugs in Labor." *Psychosomatic Medicine*, 1972, *34*, 119–127.

Burgess, E., Locke, H. J., and Thomas, M. "The Companionship Family." In H. Rodman (Ed.), *Marriage, Family and Society: A Reader*. New York: Random House, 1965.

Burlingham, D. "The Pre-Oedipal Infant-Father Relationship." *The Psychoanalytic Study of the Child*, 1973, *28*, 23–48.

Byrne, D. "The R–S Scale, Rationale, Reliability, and Validity." *Journal of Personality*, 1961, *29*, 334–349.

Carey, W. B. "A Simplified Method for Measuring Infant Temperament." *Journal of Pediatrics*, 1970, *77*, 188–194.

Carey, W. B. "Clinical Applications of Infant Temperament Measurements." *Journal of Pediatrics*, 1972a, *81*, 823–828.

Carey, W. B. "Measuring Infant Temperament." *Journal of Pediatrics*, 1972b, *81*, 414.

Carey, W. B. "Measurement of Infant Temperament in Pediatrics." In J. Westman (Ed.), *Individual Differences in Children*. New York: Wiley, 1973.

Centers, R., and Blumberg, G. H. "Social and Psychological Factors in Human Procreation: A Survey Approach." *The Journal of Social Psychology*, 1954, *40*, 245–257.

Chertok, L. *Motherhood and Personality: Psychosomatic Aspects of Childbirth*. London: Tavistock Publications, 1969.

Chertok, L. "The Psychopathology of Vomiting of Pregnancy." In J. Howell (Ed.), *Modern Perspectives in Psycho-obstetrics*. New York: Brunner/Mazel, 1972.

Chess, S., Thomas, A., and Birch, H. "Characteristics of the Individual Child's Behavioral Responses to the Environment." *American Journal of Orthopsychiatry*, 1959, *29*, 791–802.

Christenson, H. T. "Children in the Family: Relationship of Number and Spacing to Marital Success." In J. S. Delora and J. R. Delora (Eds.), *Intimate Lifestyles: Marriage and Its Alternatives*. Pacific Palisades, Calif.: Goodyear, 1972.

Clarke-Stewart, A. *Child Care in the Family: A Review of Research and Some Propositions for Policy*. New York: Academic Press, 1977.

Cohen, M. B. "Personal Identity and Sexual Identity." *Psychiatry*, 1966, *29*, 1–14.

Cohen, R. "Some Maladaptive Syndromes of Pregnancy and the Puerperium." *Obstetrics and Gynecology*, 1966, *27*, 562–570.

Coleman, A., and Coleman, L. *Pregnancy: The Psychological Experience*. New York: Seabury Press, 1971.

Coleman, R. P., and Neugarten, B. L. *Social Status in the City*.

San Francisco: Jossey–Bass, 1971.

Cowan, C. P., and others. "Becoming a Family: The Impact of a First Child's Birth on the Couple's Relationship." In W. Miller and L. Newman (Eds.), *The First Child and Family Formation*. Chapel Hill, N.C.: Carolina Population Center, 1979.

Cox, R. D. *Youth into Maturity*. New York: Mental Health Materials Center, 1970.

Crammond, W. A. "Psychological Aspects of Uterine Dysfunction." *The Lancet*, 1954, *2*, 1241–1245.

Crowne, D. P., and Marlowe, D. A. "A New Scale of Social Desirability Independent of Pscyhopathology." *Journal of Consulting Psychology*, 1959, *24*, 349–354.

Dalby, J. T. "Environmental Effects on Prenatal Development." *Journal of Pediatric Psychology*, 1978, *3* (3), 105–109.

Davids, A., and DeVault, S. "Maternal Anxiety During Pregnancy and Childbirth Abnormalities." *Psychosomatic Medicine*, 1962, *24*, 464–470.

Davids, A., DeVault, S., and Talmadge, M. "Anxiety, Pregnancy and Childbirth Abnormalities." *Journal of Consulting Psychology*, 1961, *25*, 74–77.

Deutsch, H. *Psychology of Women*, Vol. 2. New York: Grune & Stratton, 1945.

Deutscher, M. "Brief Family Therapy in the Course of a First Pregnancy: A Clinical Note." *Contemporary Psychoanalysis*, 1970, *7* (1), 21–35.

Doering, S. G., Entwisle, D. R., and Quinlan, D. *The Birth Event: Couples' Preparation and Participation*. Unpublished manuscript, Baltimore: Johns Hopkins University, 1978.

Duvall, E. M. *Family Development*. (3rd ed.) Philadelphia: Lippincott, 1967.

Dyer, E. D. "Parenthood as Crisis: A Restudy." *Marriage and Family Living*, 1963, *25*, 196–201.

Earls, F. "The Fathers (Not the Mothers): Their Importance and Influence with Infants and Young Children." *Psychiatry*, 1976, *39* (3), 209–226.

Enkin, M., and others. "An Adequately Controlled Study of the Effectiveness of PPM Training." In M. N. Morris (Ed.), *Psy-*

chosomatic Medicine in Obstetrics and Gynecology. Basel: Steines, 1972.

Entwisle, D. R. "Socialization and the Young Family." Paper presented at the meeting of the American Sociological Association, Chicago, September 1977.

Epstein, C. F. "Reconciliation of Women's Roles." In R. L. Coser (Ed.), *The Family, Its Structures and Functions.* New York: St. Martin's, 1974.

Erickson, M. T. "Method for Frequent Assessment of Symptomatology During Pregnancy." *Psychological Reports*, 1967, *20*, 447–450.

Erikson, E. H. *Childhood and Society.* New York: Norton, 1963.

Fasteau, M. F. *The Male Machine.* New York: McGraw-Hill, 1974.

Fein, R. A. "Men's Experiences Before and After the Birth of a First Child: Dependence, Marital Sharing and Anxiety." Unpublished doctoral dissertation, Harvard University, 1974.

Ferreira, A. J. "The Pregnant Woman's Emotional Attitude and its Reflection in the Newborn." *American Journal of Orthopsychiatry*, 1960, *30*, 553–561.

Fisher, S. *The Female Orgasm.* New York: Basic Books, 1973.

Forssman, H., and Thuwe, I. "120 Children Born After Therapeutic Abortion Refused." *Acta Psychiatrica Scandinavia*, 1966, *42*, 71–78.

Fox, M. L. "Unmarried Adult Mothers: A Study of the Parenthood Transition from Late Pregnancy to Two Months Postpartum." Unpublished doctoral dissertation, Boston University, 1979.

Freeman, T. "Pregnancy as a Precipitant of Mental Illness in Men." *British Journal of Medical Psychology*, 1951, *24*, 49–54.

Freud, S. "Some Psychological Consequences of the Anatomical Distinction Between the Sexes." In J. Strachey (Ed.), *Collected Papers.* Vol. 5. New York: Basic Books, 1959. (Originally published 1925.)

Friedman, E., and Greenhill, J. *Biological Principles and Modern Practices of Obstetrics.* Philadelphia: Saunders, 1974.

Fries, M. E., and Woolf, P. J. "Some Hypotheses on the Role of the Congenital Activity Type in Personality Development." *The Psychoanalytic Study of the Child*, 1953, *8*, 48–62.

Gardner, L. P. "A Survey of the Attitudes and Activities of Fathers." *Journal of Genetic Psychology*, 1943, *63*, 15–55.

Gavron, H. *The Captive Wife: Conflicts of Housebound Mothers.* London: Routledge & Kegan Paul, 1966.

Gerson, E. F. "Dimensions of Infant Behavior in the First Half Year of Life." In P. M. Shereshefsky and L. J. Yarrow (Eds.), *Psychological Aspects of a First Pregnancy and Early Postnatal Adaptation.* New York: Raven Press, 1973.

Glick, I., Salerno, L., and Royce, J. "Psychophysiological Factors in the Etiology of Pre-Eclampsia." *Archives of General Psychiatry*, 1965, *12*, 260–266.

Gofseyeff, M. H. "Pregnancy and Maternal Adaptation in Women with Different Childbearing Motivations." Unpublished doctoral dissertation, Boston University, 1976.

Gordon, R. E., and Gordon, K. K. "Social Factors in the Prediction and Treatment of Emotional Disorders of Pregnancy." *American Journal of Obstetrics and Gynecology*, 1959, *77*, 1074–1083.

Gordon, R. E., and Gordon, K. K. "Factors in Postpartum Emotional Adjustment." *American Journal of Orthopsychiatry,* 1967, *37*, 359–360.

Gorsuch, R., and Key, M. "Abnormalities of Pregnancy as a Function of Anxiety and Life Stress." *Psychosomatic Medicine*, 1974, *36*, 352–362.

Goshen-Gottstein, E. R. *Marriage and the First Pregnancy: Cultural Influence on Attitudes of Israeli Women.* Philadelphia: Lippincott, 1966.

Green, M. *Fathering.* New York: McGraw-Hill, 1976.

Greenberg, M., and Morris, N. "Engrossment: The Newborn's Impact upon the Father." *American Journal of Orthopsychiatry*, 1974, *44* (4), 520–531.

Grimm, E. "Women's Attitudes: Reactions to Childbearing." In G. D. Goldman, and D. Milman (Eds.), *Modern Woman: Her Psychology and Sexuality.* Springfield, Ill.: Thomas, 1969.

Grimm, E., and Venet, W. "The Relationship of Emotional

Adjustment and Attitudes to Course and Outcome of Pregnancy." *Psychosomatic Medicine*, 1966, *28*, 34–49.

Group for the Advancement of Psychiatry. *Joys and Sorrows of Parenthood*. New York: Scribner's, 1973.

Hall, D. E., and Mohr, G. J. "Prenatal Attitudes of Primiparae, A Contribution to the Mental Hygiene of Pregnancy." *Mental Hygiene*, 1933, *17*, 226–231.

Hamburg, D. A., Moos, R. H., and Yalom, I. D. "Studies of Distress in the Menstrual Cycle and the Postpartum Period." In R. P. Michael (Ed.), *Endocrinology and Human Behavior*. London: Oxford University Press, 1968.

Hamilton, J. A. *Postpartum Psychiatric Problems*. St. Louis: Mosby, 1962.

Handel, G. "Sociological Aspects of Parenthood." In E. J. Anthony and T. Benedek (Eds.), *Parenthood: Its Psychology and Psychopathology*. Boston: Little, Brown, 1970.

Hetzel, B. S., Brewer, B., and Poidevin, L. "A Survey of the Relation Between Certain Common Antenatal Complications in Primiparae and Stressful Life Situations During Pregnancy." *Journal of Psychosomatic Research*, 1961, *5*, 175–182.

Hibbard, L. "Changing Trends in Caesarean Section." *American Journal of Obstetrics and Gynecology*, 1976, *125* (6), 798–804.

Hicks, M., and Platt, M. "Marital Happiness and Stability: A Review of the Research in the Sixties." *Journal of Marriage and the Family*, 1970, *32*, 553–574.

Hobbs, D. F. "Parenthood as Crisis: A Third Study." *Journal of Marriage and the Family*, 1963, *27*, 367–372.

Hobbs, D. F. "Transition to Parenthood: A Replication and an Extension." *Journal of Marriage and the Family*, 1968, *30*, 413–417.

Holmes, T., and Rahe, R. "The Social Readjustment Rating Scale." *Journal of Psychosomatic Research*, 1967, *11*, 213–218.

Horowitz, F. D., and others. "Newborn and Four-Week Retest on a Normative Population Using the Brazelton Assessment Procedure." Paper presented at the meeting of the Society for Research in Child Development, Minneapolis, April 1971.

Horsley, S. "Psychological Management of the Pre-Natal Period."
In J. G. Howells (Ed.), *Modern Perspectives in Psycho-obstetrics*. New York: Brunner/Mazel, 1972.

Illsley, R. "The Sociological Study of Reproduction and Its
Outcome." In S. A. Richardson and A. F. Guttmacher (Eds.),
Childbearing—Its Social and Psychological Aspects. Baltimore:
William & Wilkins, 1967.

Jessner, L., Weigert, E., and Foy, J. L. "The Development of
Parental Attitudes During Pregnancy." In E. S. Anthony and
T. Benedek (Eds.), *Psychology and Psychopathology of
Parenthood*. Boston: Little, Brown, 1970.

Johnston, L. D. "A Psychosocial Approach to the Experience of
Terminal Illness." Unpublished doctoral dissertation, Boston
University, 1971.

Jones, O. "Caesarean Section in Present-Day Obstetrics." *American Journal of Obstetrics and Gynecology*, 1976, *126* (5),
521–530.

Jordan, J. R. "Marital Adjustment and Satisfaction: The Role
of Companionship." Unpublished doctoral dissertation,
Boston University, 1976.

Kaij, L., and Nilsson, A. "Emotional and Psychotic Illness Following Childbirth." In J. Howells (Ed.), *Modern Perspectives
in Psycho-obstetrics*. New York: Brunner/Mazel, 1972.

Kapp, F. T., Hornstein, S., and Graham, V. T. "Some Psychologic Factors in Prolonged Labor Due to Inefficient Uterine
Action." *Comprehensive Psychiatry*, 1963, *4*, 9–18.

Karnosh, L. J., and Hope, J. M. "Puerperal Psychoses and Their
Sequellae." *American Journal of Psychiatry*, 1937, *94*, 537–
550.

Katz, J., and others. "Stress, Distress and Ego Defenses." *Archives of General Psychiatry*, 1970, *23*, 131–142.

Keniston, K., and Carnegie Council on Children. *All Our Children: The American Family Under Pressure*. New York: Harcourt Brace Jovanovich, 1977.

Kestenberg, J. S. "On the Development of Maternal Feelings in
Early Childhood." *The Psychoanalytic Study of the Child*,
1956a, *11*, 257–291.

Kestenberg, J. S. "Vicissitudes of Female Sexuality." *Journal of the American Psychoanalytic Association*, 1956b, *4*, 453.

Kestenberg, J. S. *Children and Parents: Psychoanalytic Studies in Development*. New York: Jason Aronson, 1975.

Kilpatrick, E., and Tiebout, H. "A Study of Psychoses Occurring in Relation to Childbirth." *American Journal of Psychiatry*, 1942, *6*, 145–159.

Kimmel, D., and Vanderveen, F. "Factors of Marital Adjustment in Locke's Marital Adjustment Test." *Journal of Marriage and the Family*, 1974, *36*, 57–63.

Klaus, M. H., and others. "Maternal Attachment: Importance of the First Postpartum Days." *New England Journal of Medicine*, 1972, *286*, 460–463.

Klein, H. R., Potter, H. W., and Dyke, R. B. *Anxiety in Pregnancy and Childbirth*. New York: Hoeber, 1950.

Klusman, L. "Reduction of Pain in Childbirth by the Alleviation of Anxiety During Pregnancy." *Journal of Consulting and Clinical Psychology*, 1975, *43*, 162–165.

Knox, W., and Kupferer, H. "A Discontinuity in the Socialization of Males in the United States." *Merrill-Palmer Quarterly*, 1971, *17* (3), 251–261.

Kohn, M. L. "Social Class and Parent-Child Relationships: An Interpretation." *American Journal of Sociology*, 1963, *68*, 471–480.

Korner, A. F. "Individual Differences at Birth: Implications for Early Experience and Later Development." *American Journal of Orthopsychiatry*, 1971, *41*, 608–619.

Kotelchuck, M. "The Infant's Relationship to the Father: Experimental Evidence." In M. E. Lamb (Ed.), *The Role of the Father in Child Development*. New York: Wiley, 1976.

Lacoursiere, R. "Fatherhood and Mental Illness: A Review and New Material." *Psychiatric Quarterly*, 1972, *46*, 105–124.

Lakin, M. "Assessment of Significant Role Attitudes in Primiparous Mothers by Means of Modification of the TAT." *Psychosomatic Medicine*, 1957, *19*, 50–60.

Lamb, M. E. (Ed.). *The Role of the Father in Child Development*. New York: Wiley, 1976.

Lamb, M. E. "The Development of Mother-Infant and Father-Infant Attachment in the Second Year of Life." *Developmental Psychology*, 1977a, *13*, 637–648.

Lamb, M. E. "The Development of Parental Preferences in the First Two Years of Life." *Sex Roles: A Journal of Research*, 1977b, *3* (5), 495–497.

Lamb, M. E. "Father-Infant and Mother-Infant Interaction in the First Year of Life." *Child Development*, 1977c, *48*, 167–181.

Laws, J. L. "A Feminist Review of Marital Adjustment Literature: The Rape of the Locke." *Journal of Marriage and the Family*, 1971, *33*, 483–516.

Leifer, M. "Psychological Changes Accompanying Pregnancy and Motherhood." *Genetic Psychology Monographs*, 1977, *95* (1), 55–96.

LeMasters, E. E. "Parenthood as Crisis." *Marriage and Family Living*, 1957, *19*, 352–355.

Levine, M. "Scientific Method and the Adversary Model." *American Psychologist*, 1974, *29* (9), 661–677.

Levinson, D. J. *Seasons of a Man's Life*. New York: Knopf, 1978.

Levy, D. M. *Maternal Overprotection*. New York: Columbia University Press, 1943.

Lewis, M., and Weinraub, M. "The Father's Role in the Child's Social Network." In M. E. Lamb (Ed.), *The Role of the Father in Child Development*. New York: Wiley, 1976.

Liebenberg, B. "Expectant Fathers." *Child and Family*, 1969, *8* (3), 265–277. Also in P. M. Shereshefsky and R. F. Yarrow (Eds.), *Psychological Aspects of a First Pregnancy and Early Postnatal Adaptation*. New York: Raven Press, 1973.

Locke, H. J., and Wallace, K. M. "Short Marital-Adjustment and Prediction Tests: Their Reliability and Validity." *Marriage and Family Living*, 1959, *21*, 251–255.

Lowenthal, M. F., and others. *Four Stages of Life: A Comparative Study of Women and Men Facing Transitions*. San Francisco: Jossey-Bass, 1975.

Luckey, E. B., and Bain, J. K. "Children: A Factor in Marital Satisfaction." *Journal of Marriage and the Family*, 1970, *32*, 43–44.

Lynn, D. B. *The Father: His Role in Child Development*. Monterey, Calif.: Brooks/Cole, 1974.

McDonald, R. L. "Personality Characteristics in Patients with

Three Obstetric Complications." *Psychosomatic Medicine*, 1965, *27*, 383–390.

McDonald, R. L. "The Role of Emotional Factors in Obstetric Complications: A Review." *Psychosomatic Medicine*, 1968, *30*, 222–237.

Mahler, M. S., Pine, F., and Bergman, A. *The Psychological Birth of the Human Infant: Symbiosis and Individuation.* New York: Basic Books, 1974.

Meares, R., Grimwade, J., and Wood, C. "A Possible Relationship Between Anxiety in Pregnancy and Puerperal Depression." *Journal of Psychosomatic Research*, 1976, *20* (6), 605–610.

Melges, F. T. "Postpartum Psychiatric Syndromes." *Psychosomatic Medicine*, 1968, *30*, 95–108.

Meyerowitz, J. H. "Satisfaction During Pregnancy." *Journal of Marriage and the Family*, 1970, *32* (1), 38–42.

Meyerowitz, J. H., and Feldman, H. "Transition to Parenthood." *Psychiatric Research Reports*, 1966, *20*, 78–94.

Miller, S. M. "The Making of a Confused Middle-Class Husband." *Social Policy*, 1971, *2* (2), 33–39.

Moss, H. A., and Robson, K. S. "Maternal Influences in Early Social-Visual Behavior." *Child Development*, 1968, *39*, 401–408.

Nash, J. "The Father in Contemporary Culture and Current Psychological Literature." *Child Development*, 1965, *36*, 261–297.

Nilsson, A. "Paranatal Emotional Adjustment: A Prospective Investigation of 165 Women—Part I." *Acta Psychiatrica Scandinavia*, Supplement 220, 1970, 9–61.

Nott, P. N., and others. "Hormonal Changes and Mood in the Puerperium." *British Journal of Psychiatry*, 1976, *128*, 379–383.

Nuckolls, K., Kasl, J., and Kaplan, B. "Psychosocial Assets, Life Crisis, and the Prognosis of Pregnancy." *American Journal of Epidemiology*, 1972, *95*, 431–441.

Osborne, D. "MMPI Changes Between the First and Third Trimester of Pregnancy." *Journal of Clinical Psychology*, 1978, *34*, 92–93.

Osofsky, J. D., and Danzger, B. "Relationships Between Neonatal Characteristics and Mother-Infant Interaction." *Developmental Psychology*, 1974, *10*, 124–130.

Papiernik, E., and Kaminski, M. "Multifactorial Study of the Rise of Prematurity at 32 weeks of Gestation, I: A Study of the Pregnancy of 30 Predictive Characteristics." *Journal of Perinatal Medicine*, 1974, *2*, 30–36.

Parke, R. D., and Sawin, S. E. "Perspectives on Father-Infant Interaction." *Family Coordinator*, 1976, *25* (4), 365–371.

Pedersen, F. A. "Mother, Father and Infant as an Interactive System." Paper presented at annual meeting of the American Psychological Association, Chicago, September 1975.

Pedersen, F. A., and Robson, K. S. "Father Participation in Infancy." *American Journal of Orthopsychiatry*, 1969, *39*, 466–472.

Pines, D. "Pregnancy and Motherhood: Interaction Between Fantasy and Reality." *British Journal of Medical Psychology*, 1972, *45*, 333–343.

Pitt, B. "'Atypical' Depression Following Childbirth." *British Journal of Psychiatry*, 1968, *114*, 1325–1335.

Pleshette, N., Asch, S. S., and Chase, J. "A Study of Anxieties During Pregnancy, Labor and the Early and Late Puerperium." *Bulletin of the New York Academy of Medicine*, 1956, *32*, 436–456.

Poffenberger, S., and Poffenberger, T. "Intent Toward Conception and the Pregnancy Experience." *American Sociological Review*, 1952, *17*, 616–620.

Pohlman, E. H. *The Psychology of Birth Planning*. Cambridge, Mass.: Schenkman, 1969.

Pressman, R. A. "Father Participation in Child Care: An Exploratory Study of Fathers with Young Children and Working Wives." Unpublished doctoral dissertation, Boston University, 1979.

Price, G. McC. "Influencing Maternal Care Through Discussion of Videotapes of Maternal-Infant Feeding Interaction." Unpublished doctoral dissertation, Boston University, 1975.

Radin, N. "The Role of the Father in Cognitive, Academic, and Intellectual Development." In M. E. Lamb (Ed.), *The Role of the Father in Child Development*. New York: Wiley, 1976.

Rainwater, L. *Family Design: Marital Sexuality, Family Size and Contraception.* Chicago: Aldine, 1965.

Rapoport, R., Rapoport, R. N., and Strelitz, Z. *Fathers, Mothers and Society.* New York: Basic Books, 1977.

Reitterstol, N. "Paranoid Psychosis Associated with Impending or Newly Established Fatherhood." *Acta Psychiatrica Scandinavia*, 1968, *44* (1), 51–61.

Rendina, I., and Dickerscheid, J. "Father Involvement with First-Born Infants." *Family Coordinator*, 1976, *25* (4), 373–378.

Rheingold, J. C. *The Fear of Being a Woman.* New York: Grune & Stratton, 1964.

Robson, K. S., Pedersen, F. A., and Moss, H. A. "Developmental Observations of Dyadic Gazing in Relation to the Fear of Strangers and Social Approach Behavior." *Child Development*, 1969, *40*, 619–627.

Rosen, S. "Emotional Factors in Nausea and Vomiting in Pregnancy." *Psychiatric Quarterly*, 1951, *29*, 621–633.

Rosengren, W. "Some Social Psychological Aspects of Delivery Room Difficulties." *Journal of Nervous and Mental Diseases*, 1961, *123*, 515–521.

Rossi, A. S. "Transition to Parenthood." *Journal of Marriage and the Family*, 1968, *30*, 26–39.

Rubin, J. Z., Provonzano, F. J., and Luria, Z. "The Eye of the Beholder: Parents' Views on Sex of Newborns." In A. G. Kaplan and J. P. Bean (Eds.), *Beyond Sex-Role Stereotypes: Readings Toward a Psychology of Androgyny.* Boston: Little, Brown, 1976.

Rubin, R. A. "Maternal Tasks in Pregnancy." *Maternal-Child Nursing Journal*, 1975, *4* (3), 143–153.

Rubin, R. A., and Balow, B. "Measures of Infant Development and Socioeconomic Status as Predictors of Later Intelligence and School Achievement." *Developmental Psychology*, 1979, *15* (2), 225–227.

Rutter, M. "Maternal Deprivation, 1972–1978: New Findings, New Concepts, New Approaches." *Child Development*, 1979, *50* (2), 283–305.

Sander, L. W. "Infant and Care-Taking Environment: Investigation and Conceptualization of Adaptive Behavior in a System of Increasing Complexity." In E. J. Anthony (Ed.), *Explorations in Child Psychiatry*. New York: Plenum Press, 1975.

Schachter, S. *The Psychology of Affiliation*. Stanford, Calif.: Stanford University Press, 1959.

Scott, D. H. "Follow-up Study from Birth of the Effects of Prenatal Stresses." *Developmental Medicine and Child Neurology*, 1973, *15*, 770–787.

Shader, R. I., DiMascio, A., and Harmatz, J. S. "Studies of Premenstrual Tension." Paper presented at annual meeting of the American Psychiatric Association, May 1972.

Shapiro, M. P. "Men's Experience of Childbirth." Unpublished doctoral dissertation, Boston University, 1980.

Shereshefsky, P. M., and Yarrow, L. J. *Psychological Aspects of a First Pregnancy and Early Postnatal Adaptation*. New York: Raven Press, 1973.

Sherman, J. *On the Psychology of Women*. Springfield, Ill.: Thomas, 1971.

Shirley, M. *The First Two Years: A Study of Twenty-Five Babies*. Vol. 3. Minneapolis: University of Minnesota Press, 1933.

Siegel, A. E., and Haas, M. B. "The Working Mother: A Review of Research." *Child Development*, 1963, *34*, 513–543.

Sontag, L. W. "The Significance of Fetal Environmental Differences." *American Journal of Obstetrics and Gynecology*, 1941, *42*, 996–1003.

Spanier, G. B. "Measuring Dyadic Adjustment: New Scale for Assessing the Quality of Marriage and Similar Dyads." *Journal of Marriage and the Family*, 1976, *38*, 15–28.

Spelke, E., and others. "Father Interaction and Separation Protest." *Developmental Psychology*, 1973, *9* (1), 83–90.

Spielberger, C., Gorsuch, R., and Lushene, R. *The State-Trait Anxiety Inventory*. Palo Alto, Calif.: Consulting Psychologists Press, 1968.

Spielberger, C., Gorsuch, R., and Lushene, R. *STAI Manual*. Palo Alto, Calif.: Consulting Psychologists Press, 1970.

Spitz, R. A. "Hospitalism: An Inquiry into the Genesis of Psychiatric Conditions in Early Childhood." *Psychoanalytic Study of the Child*, 1945, *1*, 53–74.

Spitz, R. A. *The First Year of Life*. New York: International Universities Press, 1965.

Stayton, D. J., and Ainsworth, M. D. S. "Individual Differences in Infant Responses to Brief, Everyday Separations as Related to Other Infant and Maternal Behaviors." *Developmental Psychology*, 1973, *9*, 226–235.

Stern, D. N. "A Micro-Analysis of Mother-Infant Interaction." *Journal of the American Academy of Child Psychiatry*, 1971, *10*, 501–577.

Stern, G. G., and others. "A Factor Analytic Study of the Mother-Infant Dyad." *Child Development*, 1969, *40*, 163–181.

Strassberg, S. "Paternal Involvement with First-Borns During Infancy." Unpublished doctoral dissertation, Boston University, 1978.

Strecher, E., and Ebaugh, F. "Psychosis Occurring During the Puerperium." *Archives of Neurology and Psychiatry*, 1926, *15*, 239–252.

Swain, M. D., and Kiser, C. B. "The Interrelation of Fertility, Fertility Planning, and Ego-Centered Interest in Children." In P. K. Whelpton and C. B. Kiser (Eds.), *Social and Psychological Factors Affecting Fertility*. Vol. 3. New York: Milbank Memorial Fund, 1953.

Tanzer, S. "The Psychology of Pregnancy and Childbirth: An Investigation of Natural Childbirth." Unpublished doctoral dissertation, Brandeis University, 1967.

Tasch, R. J. "The Role of the Father in the Family." *Journal of Experimental Education*, 1952, *20*, 319–361.

Tetlow, C. "Psychoses of Childbearing." *Journal of Mental Science*, 1955, *101*, 629–639.

Thomas, A., Chess, S., and Birch, H. G. *Temperament and Behavior Disorders in Children*, New York: New York University Press, 1968.

Thomas, A., and others. *Behavioral Individuality in Early Childhood*. New York: New York University Press, 1963.

Trehowan, W. H. "The Couvade Syndrome." *British Journal of Psychiatry*, 1965, *111*, 57–66.

Tylden, E. "Hyperemesis and Physiological Vomiting." *Journal of Psychosomatic Research*, 1968, *12*, 85–93.

Uddenberg, N. "Reproductive Adaptation in Mothers and Daughters." *Acta Psychiatrica Scandanavia*, Supplement 254, 1974.

Uddenberg, N., Fagerstrom, C. F., and Hakanson-Zaunders, M. "Reproductive Conflicts, Mental Symptoms During Pregnancy and Time in Labor." *Journal of Psychosomatic Research*, 1976, *20*(6), 575–582.

Uddenberg, N., Nilsson, A., and Almgren, P. E. "Nausea in Pregnancy." *Journal of Psychosomatic Research*, 1971, *15*, 269.

Wainwright, W. "Fatherhood as a Precipitant of Mental Illness." *American Journal of Psychiatry*, 1966, *123*, 40–44.

Wenner, N., and Cohen, M. B. (Eds.). *Emotional Aspects of Pregnancy*. First report of the Washington School of Psychiatry project. Washington, D.C.: Washington School of Psychiatry, 1968.

Wenner, N. K., and others. "Emotional Problems in Pregnancy." *Psychiatry*, 1969, *32* (4), 389–410.

Westley, W. A., and Epstein, N. B. *The Silent Majority: Families of Emotionally Healthy College Students*. San Francisco: Jossey-Bass, 1969.

Whelpton, P. K., Campbell, A. A., and Patterson, J. *Fertility and Family Planning in the United States*. Princeton, N.J.: Princeton University Press, 1966.

Will, J. A., Self, P. A., and Datan, N. "Maternal Behavior and Perceived Sex of Infant." *American Journal of Orthopsychiatry*, 1976, *46* (1), 134–139.

Williams, C. "Pregnancy and Life Change." *Journal of Psychosomatic Research*, 1975, *19*, 123–129.

Williams, J. H. *Psychology of Women: Behavior in a Biosocial Context*. New York: Norton, 1977.

Winget, C., and Kapp, F. T. "The Relation of the Manifest Content of Dreams to Duration of Childbirth in Primiparae." *Psychosomatic Medicine*, 1972, *34*, 313.

Winickoff, S. A. "Obstetrical Complications and Psychological

Defense Style." Unpublished doctoral dissertation, Boston University, 1976.

Winnicott, D. W. *The Ordinary Devoted Mother and Her Baby.* London: Tavistock, 1949.

Wise, S. J. "Pregnancy Adaptation and the Development of Attachment in Adolescent Mothers." Unpublished doctoral dissertation, Boston University, 1979.

Yalom, I. D., and others. "'Postpartum Blues' Syndrome." *Archives of General Psychiatry,* 1968, *18,* 16–27.

Yang, R. K., and Moss, H. A. "Neonatal Precursors of Infant Behavior." *Developmental Psychology,* 1978, *14* (6), 607–613.

Yang, R. K. and others. "Successive Relationships Between Maternal Attitudes During Pregnancy, Analgesic Medication During Labor and Delivery, and Newborn Behavior." *Developmental Psychology,* 1976, *12,* 6–14.

Yarrow, L. J., and Goodwin, M. S. "Some Conceptual Issues in the Study of Mother-Infant Interaction." *American Journal of Orthopsychiatry,* 1965, *35,* 473–481.

Young, M., and Willmott, P. *The Symmetrical Family.* New York: Pantheon, 1973.

Zemlick, M. J., and Watson, R. I. "Maternal Attitudes of Acceptance and Rejection During and After Pregnancy." *American Journal of Orthopsychiatry,* 1953, *23,* 570–584.

Zilboorg, G. "Depressive Reactions Related to Parenthood." *American Journal of Psychiatry,* 1931, *10,* 927–962.

Zuckerman, M., and others. "Psychological Correlates of Somatic Complaints in Pregnancy and Difficulty in Childbirth." *Journal of Consulting Psychology,* 1963, *27* (4), 324–329.

Index

❧❧ ❧❧ ❧❧

A

Aberle, D. F., 182, 204

Adaptation: concept of, for father, 171; conceptual framework and methodology for, 1-11; at eighth month, 31-35; by father, 5, 169-209; in first trimester, 20-22, 66; and infant, 6-7, 210-243; to labor and delivery, 70-76; measures of, 8-9, 256-272; of mothers, fathers, and infants, 3-7; and motivation, 49-51; at one year postpartum, 118, 126, 134, 135; philosophy of, 10-11; to pregnancy, 22-31; research methods and goals for, 7-10; sample for, 9-10, 275-277; at two months postpartum, 84, 85, 96